Leadership and
Academic Librarians

Leadership and Academic Librarians

EDITED BY
Terrence F. Mech
and Gerard B. McCabe

THE GREENWOOD LIBRARY MANAGEMENT COLLECTION

GREENWOOD PRESS
Westport, Connecticut • London

Library of Congress Cataloging-in-Publication Data

Leadership and academic librarians / edited by Terrence F. Mech and
Gerard B. McCabe.
        p.   cm.—(Greenwood library management collection, ISSN
0894–2986)
    Includes bibliographical references and index.
    ISBN 0–313–30271–5 (alk. paper)
    1. College librarians—United States.   2. Leadership.   3. Academic
libraries—United States.   I. Mech, Terrence.   II. McCabe, Gerard
B.   III. Series.
Z682.4.C63L4   1998
025.1'977—dc21   97–53106

British Library Cataloguing in Publication Data is available.

Library of Congress Catalog Card Number: 97–53106
ISBN: 0–313–30271–5
ISSN: 0894–2986

First published in 1998

Greenwood Press, 88 Post Road West, Westport, CT 06881
An imprint of Greenwood Publishing Group, Inc.

Printed in the United States of America

The paper used in this book complies with the
Permanent Paper Standard issued by the National
Information Standards Organization (Z39.48–1984).

10 9 8 7 6 5 4 3 2 1

Contents

Contents

Introduction

Terrence F. Mech

Professions are dynamic associations. They thrive or die depending on the vision, adaptability, and leadership of their members. The future of academic librarianship in the United States and Canada is being shaped by the willingness and ability of its 26,341 and 1,887 respective academic librarians to lead and be creative in our responses to the pressures facing academe and our profession. Our job and career satisfactions also depend on our abilities to renew ourselves by meeting the professional and personal challenges before us.

The idea for this book grew out of my own experiences as well as the similar experiences of my friends and colleagues. In 1994, after serving as Library Director at King's College for 12 years, I was asked by my employer to serve as Vice President for Information and Instructional Technologies and Director of the Library. Friends and colleagues were being named associate provosts and assistant vice presidents for academic affairs. Others were picking up various instructional and technology-related responsibilities. In the process of adapting to the changes in our responsibilities, my colleagues and I recognized we were part of the larger evolution of academic librarianship and higher education. On a personal level, our new responsibilities brought with them a satisfying, renewed sense of challenge and professional development.

In retrospect, the common elements in our situations, besides the "dumb luck" or "misfortune" to be in the right place at the right time, were various aspects of leadership. Some of my colleagues would argue that it is the way we define ourselves, the way we do our jobs, and our sensitivity to some of the larger contextual issues on our campuses that contributed to our assumption of new responsibilities. The changes in our personal situations reflect the growing number of new opportunities for academic librarians. As higher education adapts to the challenges of its changing environment, it is calling upon all of its members to think, act, and lead in new ways.

These new challenges and opportunities remind us that academic librarianship is changing, one individual at a time. Just as a forest is composed of individual trees whose growth and development contribute to the health and nature of the forest, so is our profession made up of individual librarians whose actions and careers shape the profession's future. Sometimes in the course of our work we lose sight of the fact that our individual efforts and careers are part of the larger professional picture. Our individual actions and careers are the strands that create the larger tapestry. For every librarian whose career reflects a predominant pattern, there are librarians whose careers are creating and weaving new patterns.

Although higher education and academic librarianship have deep roots and draw from a long tradition, the modern academic profession as we know it is fairly new (Finkelstein 1984). "Despite its deep roots, academic librarianship is still evolving and needs leaders of all types to shape its future" (Mech 1996, 346). Usually, we think of leaders as remote, removed, or larger than life. In reality, leaders, individuals who exercise leadership, are all around us. Frequently, this leadership is displayed in response to some new work-related or personal challenge or opportunity. Our responses to changes in our work environment and our career are areas where leadership is frequently, but quietly, exercised. Although leadership may be defined in many ways, we all tend to recognize it when we see it. Leadership may be more of a relationship between people than a personal characteristic. According to role theory, individuals behave according to what is expected of them and how they perceive their roles are defined. Leaders' (and followers') perceptions of their roles are affected by their organizational environment, their colleagues, their past experiences, and their personal needs and values (Bass 1990, 38–41). Leadership can come from anyone, depending on the expectations of individuals and their colleagues.

While we can all point to librarians in the limelight or in leadership positions, there are many more librarians quietly implementing instructional initiatives, seeking ways to integrate print and digital services, and bringing their expertise to bear on other organizational challenges. Their situational leadership is shaping how our profession is defined and practiced.

The purpose of this book is to show how individual librarians and their personal leadership are contributing to the changes in our profession and the expanding career opportunities available to academic librarians. Separate chapters by Beverly Lynch and Raven Fonfa use the light of history to examine how the practices we take for granted came to be and how they can be traced to the actions of various individuals. Lynch reviews the library's development within American higher education and the evolving role of librarians. Using the example of collection development, Fonfa demonstrates how a succession of individual librarians who, perhaps unbeknownst to themselves at the time, contributed to changes in the practice of our relatively young profession. The evolution of any profession, much less one in an academic environment, is a slow process that is often revealed only in hindsight. When we are close to our work, it is sometimes difficult to see the gradual changes or the opportunities unfolding, much less see our role in them.

Delmus Williams calls our attention to the changes that are forcing colleges and universities to rethink how they do business. In this environment, library directors have no choice but to accept the leadership challenge before them. Pointing out that now is an exciting time to be an academic librarian, Donald Riggs advocates visionary leadership as a means of creating and shaping the future of libraries and librarianship. Rosie Albritton uses her research to show us that leadership is not a mysterious process. Rather, there are identifiable leadership behaviors that individuals can use to provide effective transformational leadership.

Barbara Dewey, Janet Hurlbert, and George Newman provide examples to remind us that the need for leadership is not limited to those at the top of the organization. Indeed, if libraries and librarians are to be innovative and effective, then all librarians must exercise leadership and facilitate change. Kenneth Oberembt points out that although the need for leadership in libraries is universal, those exercising leadership must be mindful of the national culture and norms. Noting that leadership is often defined and critiqued differently depending where the reviewer is in the organizational structure, Brian Champion calls our attention to legitimate leadership roles for librarians outside management or inside organized labor.

David Dowell reviews the four stages of a professional career and the development of leadership behavior. He points out that individuals' contributions to the profession are related to how well they progress through the four stages. Introducing the concept of the "protean career," Dowell reminds us that we are responsible for our careers and the personal satisfaction we experience from them. George Newman examines some of the obstacles to career development for academic library directors and offers some suggestions. Newman also points out that a library director's job can be difficult and that careers can take an unexpected downturn or that directors may want a different kind of challenge that necessitates a career transition.

One way to study the changes or observe the evolution of a profession is to examine the career and leadership behavior of those librarians who are extending the profession's boundaries or expanding the career opportunities available to librarians. Dennis Robison, Elaine Adams, Edward Jennerich, Chuck Broadbent, and Christie Koontz have written chapters that examine their careers and the paths they have taken both inside and outside librarianship and higher education. Not that long ago, many librarians thought of, and saw, their careers as limited to the confines of their libraries' four walls. Although there are many career options available to librarians (Sellen 1997), the careers of these authors are representative of the growing range of opportunities for librarians to hold influential positions outside the library. Their stories reveal that careers can provide both the personal satisfaction and the renewed challenge that keeps life interesting. Reading their stories, it is easy to see that these individuals, through their personal leadership, have created satisfying careers and contributed to the success of their organizations and their professions.

The bibliographic essay on leadership by Rashelle Karp and Cindy Murdock is the book's final chapter. In their conclusion they write, "Leadership begins with people who know how to take the best of yesterday and carry it into tomorrow (Kanter 1983). It is enhanced by people who are flexible, open, decisive, able to tolerate uncertainty, loyal to their institution, and caring toward human beings (Veaner 1990). But it is complete only when a clear vision becomes the driving force for an individual's actions."

It is my hope that this book helps individuals to see the connections between how we lead, how we practice our profession, how we develop our careers, and how our profession is defined and evolves. In these times of challenge and opportunity, we all make a difference, both professionally and personally, depending on how we envision academic librarianship and exercise leadership.

REFERENCES

Bass, Bernard. 1990. *Bass Stodgill's Handbook of Leadership Theory, Research, and Managerial Applications.* New York: Free Press.

Finkelstein, Martin. 1984. *The American Academic Profession: A Synthesis of Social Scientific Inquiry since World War II.* Columbus: Ohio State University Press.

Kanter, R. 1983. *Change Masters.* New York: Simon & Schuster.

Mech, Terrence. 1996. "Leadership and the Evolution of Academic Librarianship." *Journal of Academic Librarianship* 22 (September): 345–353.

Sellen, Betty-Carol. 1997. *What Else You Can Do with a Library Degree: Career Options for the '90s and Beyond.* New York: Neal-Schuman.

Veaner, Allen B. 1990. *Academic Librarianship in a Transformational Age: Program, Politics, and Personnel.* Boston: G. K. Hall.

Part I

The History and Evolution of the Librarian in Higher Education

Chapter 1

The Development of the Academic Library in American Higher Education and the Role of the Academic Librarian

Beverly P. Lynch

INTRODUCTION

This chapter sketches the historical development of the academic library, placed in the context of the history of American higher education. Particular emphasis is given to the role of the librarian in that development.

Libraries have been an integral part of American higher education ever since 1636, when the Massachusetts Bay Colony's college at Cambridge was founded and then, two years later, took the name of John Harvard in recognition of the bequest of his library (326 titles in more than 400 volumes). Today the more than 3,500 colleges and universities in the United States have collections that total many millions of volumes. Over the intervening years, the libraries have functioned in varying ways depending on the changing and developing purposes and policies of the institutions they have served. During this time, the role of the librarian has changed from that of keeper of the books to one of broad responsibilities for sophisticated information services. The academic library director of today is a consummate professional, responsible for information services to faculty and students through the provision of information in all formats, using every available technology.

THE COLONIAL PERIOD, 1636–1789

The nine colleges established during the colonial period—Harvard (1636), William and Mary (1693), Yale (1701), Princeton (1746), the University of

Pennsylvania (1749), Columbia (1754), Brown (1764), Rutgers (1766), and Dartmouth (1769)—though different in details, embraced the same general purpose: to train the leadership of the church and of the colonies. Colleges were formed to provide leaders for particular denominations and, in the event, found themselves also supplying the leaders of the secular society. Though only a tiny fraction of the population attended college, one-half of the signers of the Declaration of Independence were college graduates.

The college curriculum was drawn from the Reformation and from the Renaissance, so the ideals of educating the learned clergy and the gentleman scholar were merged. Within a short time, the American colleges developed their own character. While educating the clergy was an important objective, by the end of the colonial period, only about 40 percent of the graduates were entering the clergy; the others followed the occupations of farming, law, medicine, teaching, and commerce. The numbers entering the clergy continued to decline (Cohen 1974, 101).

The American colleges were small. For example, in 1710, Harvard had 125 students; Yale had 36. In 1770, there were 413 students at Harvard, 338 at Yale. The faculty comprised the president and a small group of itinerant young men who wanted to be preachers and who took the post of tutor until they could find a permanent appointment to the clergy. The tutors were young men about 20 years old who had just received their B.A. degrees and were preparing for careers in the ministry. A tutor was assigned to the 24-hour care of a single class, guiding the moral and spiritual development of students as well as their intellectual development. Tutors rarely stayed long in their post, for they were seeking a position in the clergy and left as soon as one was found. In the early years, the faculty consisted of a president/professor and one or two tutors. Later, professors responsible for particular subjects were appointed.

The finances of the colleges were precarious. Most depended on donations and a little bit of public money. The president spent much of his time raising money as well as teaching and administering. In the early days, the president was also the librarian.

Each college president acknowledged the importance of building a library to serve the institution. Solicitations for books were made regularly, and the libraries grew as a result of donations. Funds occasionally were allocated for the purchase of books, but most colleges were strapped for money, and the demands for salary support and facilities development took most of the available moneys.

During the colonial period, while book collections were being established and were growing, the methods of instruction remained lecture and recitation. Libraries were not important to the life of the student; they sometimes were important, however, to the life of the tutors and the emerging faculties, and they were important to the development of the American college curriculum. Kraus' study of the printed catalogs of Harvard, Yale, Princeton, and Brown shows that the libraries were much more than theological collections; half of the books were on other subjects, largely history, literature, and science (Kraus 1973, 142–159).

Additional insight into the character of the collections is found in the gift to Yale of books sought out by Jeremiah Dummer, the Connecticut agent in England. Dummer was one of the most important donors to Yale Library in its early years, and largely through Dummer's efforts, Elihu Yale became a benefactor of the college. Included in the Dummer gift of some 800 volumes were all of the issues of the *Tatler* and *Spectator* published between 1710 and 1713; the entire collection of works of Robert Boyle; the second edition of the *Works of Samuel Johnson*, published in 1713; John Locke's "Essay on Human Understanding"; a complete collection of the works of John Milton; and the works of Isaac Newton (Pratt 1938, 7–44; Bryant and Patterson 1938, 423–492).

Even in the early years, the books in the library began to exert an influence toward additional subject matter beyond that of the traditional classical curriculum.

Yale's first two tutors, Samuel Johnson and Daniel Browne, both of the class of 1714, [were so carried away by the secular books in the Yale Library that] [t]heir lectures and conversations with their students soon made clear that the "New Learning," which had arrived in Dummer's parcels of books, could not be understood without more mathematics than the meager arithmetic with which students entered Yale. In 1718 algebra appeared in the Yale course of study, in 1720 astronomy was being studied in mathematical terms. . . . The growth of mathematical studies in the curriculum was unavoidable once Newtonian physics made its way into the course of natural philosophy. (Rudolph 1977, 33–34)

In 1739, Yale changed its curriculum to make way for science and mathematics. The growing library collections were of major importance to the development and change in the curriculum of the American colleges.

As the collections grew larger and more diverse, the responsibilities for managing the library also increased so that the presidents had to delegate the care of the library to one of the tutors. Thirty years after its founding, Harvard appointed its first librarian, Solomon Stoddard. A graduate of Harvard in 1662, he was made a Harvard tutor in 1666, and in 1667 he was appointed "library keeper," a position he held for about 3 years. His was one of the longer tenures in those years, when tutors left as soon as a permanent church position was found. With the appointment of James Winthrop as librarian of Harvard College in 1772, the post became more stable, Winthrop continuing for 15 years. He was responsible for dispersing the Harvard Library collections during the Revolutionary War and then reassembling it.

Many libraries, private as well as collegiate, were lost during the Revolution, but there were other reasons besides war that the collegiate collections remained small. Books were scarce; with little publishing in the colonies, they had to be acquired from abroad. There were problems of fire; by 1764, Harvard had a collection of over 5,000 books, but these were lost in the calamitous fire of that year. Still, by 1790, through donations and purchases, the Harvard College library had more than 12,000 volumes.

The library of William and Mary had 3,000 volumes after the Revolution, with an annual rate of accession of 30 volumes. Yale, also growing by an annual rate of 30 volumes per year, had 2,700 volumes in its collection (Shores 1966, 56)

EARLY NATIONAL PERIOD, 1789–1870

During the period following the Revolutionary War, the country expanded westward, bringing new colleges to frontier towns. The emphasis on the founding of a college remained denominational. Once established, however, the colleges were open to all students, for the colleges served more a geographical clientele than a religious community. The denominational interest often came from the financial backers, who would stipulate that the trustees were to be of a certain denomination. The colleges, desperate for tuition-paying students and seeking faculty to teach those students, prohibited religious tests for students and faculty; they were interested more in attracting students than in proselytizing.

College-founding in the nineteenth century was undertaken in the same spirit as canal-building, cotton-ginning, farming, and gold-mining. In none of these activities did completely rational procedures prevail. (Rudolph 1990, 48)

By 1860, about 250 colleges, enrolling about 25,000 students, had been founded; of these, 182 still survive (Rudolph 1990, 47).

The curriculum continued as it had been established in the colonial period. The subjects were primarily Latin, Greek, and mathematics. Rote recitation was standard practice. The purpose was to strengthen and discipline the mind. There was emerging, however, a discontent with the rigidity of the curriculum, reflecting the American interest in the practical and mechanical arts. The U.S. Military Academy, established in 1802 at West Point, and the Rensselaer Polytechnic Institute, established in 1824 at Troy, New York, were the first technical institutes in the United States. Their founding marked the beginning of a shift in the curriculum to science and engineering. Despite the attempts at reform of the curriculum by a few leaders, little change took place until after the Civil War. What did happen, the development of a thriving extracurricular activity, was led by students.

Undergraduates established debating clubs and literary societies and supported society libraries, strong in modern works, containing English literature and American fiction, current works of history, and current politics and science. These libraries not only were larger than those of the college but also reflected a wider range of content. Unlike the college libraries, which were opened perhaps only one or two hours a day and discouraged circulation, they were much more accessible. The literary societies introduced the concept of the student-centered college library. The undergraduate literary societies also introduced subjects not yet included in the college curriculum, exerting the influence that finally led to curricular changes (Rudolph 1990, 136–155; Harding 1959, 110–111).

In 1849, the society libraries of Yale had an estimated total of 27,700 volumes; the collection of the Yale College library at the time was 20,500. Amherst College's society libraries had 8,000 volumes; the college library had 5,700. By contrast, Harvard's library had 56,000 volumes, and the society libraries 12,000 (Brough 1953, 14–15).

During this period, productive scholarship was not associated with a career in college teaching. While professors did do some serious writing, it had little connection with the author's teaching responsibility. Scholars did not rely on the college library for their work, except for the transactions of learned societies, which the librarians did seek to acquire (Bestor 1953, 166). The college libraries were more the kind of library an educated man would expect to possess. To support their scholarship, professors sought to build their own personal collections, but while doing so, they also criticized the state of the college library. The often-quoted letter by George Ticknor, written in 1816 while in Germany, reflected the thinking of many:

One very important and principal cause of the difference between our University [Harvard] and the one here is the different value we affix to a good library, and the different ideas we have of what a good library is. . . . We found new professorships and build new colleges in abundance, but we buy no books; and yet it is to me the most obvious thing in the world that it would promote the cause of learning and the reputation of the University ten times more to give six thousand dollars a year to the Library than to found three professorships, and that it would have been wiser to have spent the whole sum that the new chapel had cost on books than on a fine suite of halls. (Morison 1936, 266)

There were exceptions, of course. Thomas Jefferson, instrumental in the founding of the University of Virginia in 1824, worked diligently to select a library suitable to the purposes of the university and one that would support the work of the faculty he was appointing and the curriculum he was designing. President Tappan at Michigan solicited library funds from the citizens of Ann Arbor in the 1850s, and the first book purchased at Michigan was Audubon's *Birds*. Francis Wayland, president of Brown in the 1830s, also worked to build the library. John Langdon Sibley, librarian at Harvard from 1856 to 1877, emphasized the building of collections to support scholarship. Primarily a collector, Sibley raised moneys and sought gifts that would be useful to the scholar. As a general rule, however, during this period, other newly established colleges were not as diligent in developing their libraries.

As the century progressed, the curriculum was changing, albeit more slowly than some would want. Professors with strong backgrounds in particular subjects were being appointed. While tutors remained, their roles began to change; a fledgling junior faculty was being established. Library collections were growing, even if the collections were not appropriate or did not serve well the students and faculty. The library, while not playing much of a role in the life of the college during this period, still was regarded as one of the institution's principal assets. Elaborate codes of rules were written to govern its activity. The story is told often of Sibley, who upon meeting Harvard's president, Charles Eliot, was asked where he was going, whereupon Sibley replied with enthusiasm that all the books were in the library but two, and he was on his way to get those. (The faculty member who had these books is reported to have been Louis Agassiz.) While people reciting this story use it as an example of the custodial nature of librarianship, the truth is that the librarian was responsible and was held accountable for every item in the collection. He was expected to pay for those items not accounted for.

Harvard's library remained the premier academic collection of the country. Most college libraries were much more feeble institutions. Charles Coffin Jewett, librarian of the Smithsonian Institution, in his famous report on the libraries of the 1850s, dismissed the college libraries as "frequently the chance aggregations of gifts of charity; too many of them discarded, as well-nigh worthless, from the shelves of the donors" (Jewett 1850, 39).

Although the quality of many of the collections may not have been high, libraries were continuing to grow. Those people in charge were becoming increasingly concerned about how to manage the organization of the collections and the attendant building conditions (Carlton 1907). The first steps were taken in the professionalization of the librarian.

The Rise of Leadership: Charles Coffin Jewett

The meeting of 1853 called by the publisher and bookseller Charles B. Norton was a milestone in the development of American librarianship. The meeting was led by Jewett, who was the premier librarian of the day. Of the 83 men attending the three-day meeting, 45 were librarians, and 12 of those were librarians of colleges and universities. In addition to his report on libraries published in 1850, Jewett had published in 1853 *On the Construction of a Catalogue for Libraries*, the first attempt in the United States to codify a standard cataloging practice. The issues addressed in the meeting ranged widely: cataloging practice at the Smithsonian, the formation of a national central library, the distribution of government documents, the problems of library classification, the international exchange of publications, and the indexing of American literature. Four major resolutions were adopted. One favored the establishment of public libraries in every town. The second approved the plan and execution of Poole's *Index*, just published in its second edition. The third proposed the compilation of a manual of standard library practice. The fourth called for the appointment of a committee to draft plans for the formation of a permanent association of librarians (Utley 1951).

For those college librarians attending the 1853 conference, there was little expectation that any special qualifications were needed to be a librarian, and the developing hierarchy in the college had no special place for the librarian. While it was obvious that care of the library was necessary, it was a minor task for a professor but one of the tasks necessary in the life of the college. During the period, appointment of a professor as librarian was the standard practice, but it was by no means universal. If it were convenient to place a student or someone else such as the janitor in charge of the library, that was done (Shiflett 1981, 45–48). Only at the end of the century, as the university movement developed, did librarianship as a profession emerge.

Before the committee to draft plans for a professional association of librarians could be established, the fortunes of the organizers changed, and the Civil War intervened. So it was not until 1876 that the next meeting of librarians was held. During the intervening period, though, librarians continued to reflect upon the issues relating to the growth and the development of libraries.

CIVIL WAR, INDUSTRIALIZATION, AND EXPANSION, 1860–1890

The Civil War and its aftermath produced a transformation of American society and its demands upon higher education. The colleges, though in many cases still denominational, began to serve the secular society directly. With western expansion and the passage of the Morrill Act, the states themselves began to take responsibility for higher education. The new curriculum no longer bowed to preparation of the clergy but sought to prepare the graduates for places in the new industrial society.

Following the Civil War, the country prospered. Men made fortunes, the North became industrialized, and many of the newly rich were beginning to think of philanthropy. The desire for practical, scientific knowledge as opposed to the classical education still emphasized in the colleges was bringing change, as was the demand to introduce scientific inquiry as found in the German universities.

In 1862, the Morrill Federal Land Grant Act was passed. This led to the formation of the land-grant colleges, ultimately one in every state, doing more to change the face of American higher education than any other event. It placed responsibility for college education in state government and emphasized the importance of vocational and technical education. Morrill, a senator from Vermont, was as early as 1848 seeking ways in which students could receive an education of more practical value. He placed in his legislation the reform notions sought by others regarding technical education. The purpose of the legislation was "to promote the liberal and practical education of the industrial classes in the several pursuits and professions of life" (Rudolph 1990, 249).

The founding in 1869 of Cornell University, which merged the land-grant idea along with a curriculum in science and technology and the spirit of scholarship of the time, was a major innovation. President Andrew White, at the time of opening, had one new building, 17 resident and 6 nonresident faculty, and a student body of 400 students. The university had the incredible luxury of turning away 50 applicants for admission. Clearly, the curriculum of Cornell in its equality of studies, its de-emphasis of the classics, and the introduction of freely elective courses appealed to the college student. Other colleges were watching.

Money remained an important concern. Many of the older colleges opposed the development of the land-grant colleges, fearing the loss of the state support that they had enjoyed and seeking federal support for their own institutions. Competition among institutions for resources characterized much of American higher education. By contrast to this competitive environment among institutions, librarians had begun to seek ways to work together and to cooperate on issues of importance to their emerging service mission.

THE EMERGENCE OF THE UNIVERSITY, 1890–1944

Strong leadership by presidents and Boards of Trustees enabled American higher education to transform itself from a college with a limited curriculum, a small, amateur faculty, precarious finances, and modest facilities, to the complex system it has become. Eliot at Harvard, White at Cornell, Daniel Coit Gilman at Johns Hopkins, William Rainey Harper at Chicago, Nicholas Murray Butler at Columbia, and James B. Angell at Michigan are among the presidents who led in the development of the research university. Except for Gilman, who decided to make use of the strong libraries already in place in Baltimore and allow the building of seminar libraries in the university rather than build a strong central library, these presidents gave high priority to the development of strong libraries containing collections useful to the scholarship of their faculties.

A Strong President: A Great Library Begins

Before the University of Chicago was opened, Harper, traveling in Germany, bought an entire bookshop, making Chicago, in 1892, the third or fourth largest university library in the United States overnight, and six years later it was the second largest library behind Harvard. By the end of the 1800s, faculties had become professionalized, and the competition among universities for outstanding faculty members was intense. The availability of a strong library was a decided asset in faculty recruitment. Harper recruited professors away from Yale, took the majority of the academic staff at Clark, including 15 professors, and hired eight former college presidents, succeeding in hiring in his first year 120 faculty members (having money to hire only 80). Harper offered the post of librarian to Melvil Dewey, but Dewey declined.

No librarian was appointed at Chicago until 1910, four years after Harper's death; the general library was managed by an assistant librarian. By the time Ernest Burton, a professor of New Testament theology, was appointed librarian, the dominance of the faculty over library acquisitions, administrative regulations, and departmental branch collections was secure. The pattern of library development at Chicago, after Harper's initial efforts, was dominated by strong academic departments less interested in a general library than in forming their own departmental libraries. While library directors debated the merits of centralized versus departmental collections at their conferences and in their publications, faculties at the University of Chicago were competing for money, resources, and recognition. Having one's own departmental collection was an indicator of success in a fiercely competitive academic environment. While Harper placed strong emphasis on building a major library at the university yet did not appoint a university librarian, the faculty worked to build specialized collections. The faculty played the central role in library development. Librarians, interested in efficiency and in the promotion of the rational argument that a centralized collection, serving the entire campus, would enable the purchase of more books and the parsimonious use of staff, could not convince the scholar who wanted materials as close to the workplace as possible and wanted to control directly the acquisition of those materials.

The role of the faculty in library development in this period was a critical factor in many institutions. The world of scholarship was changing rapidly. Institutional support for that scholarship had emerged as an important incentive to faculty recruitment. Strong faculty members had strong views as to what should be included in the collections they and their students were using. The university librarian had to manage well the relationships with the president and influential donors and also had to work, preferably as a faculty colleague, with the faculty being served. Some of the important library collections central to research today grew out of a single-minded purpose of a faculty member who was steadfast in his demands for collections to support his work.

The Melville J. Herskovits Library of African Studies at Northwestern University is an example of the impact the single-mindedness and strong interest of one faculty member have had upon university library development. The Herskovits collection now is the largest separate library for the study of Africa in existence. Neither the university's administration nor the library's administration planned or anticipated that the collection would develop into the extraordinary resource it now is. Herskovits, appointed to the faculty of sociology at Northwestern in 1927, immediately began to develop the collection. He sought out and found external money to buy materials. Not until 1942 did the institution provide support for the collection. Only in 1959 did the library appoint a curator of the collection.

The larger institutions had full-time librarians by the latter part of the 1800s, and Harvard and Yale had assistants, including several young ladies who carried out clerical tasks. But most college libraries still were one-person operations, and the librarians in these institutions had other duties and responsibilities; some were teaching several subjects.

Library Leaders Emerge

Some extraordinary library leaders emerged during this period, and they set the direction for academic librarianship. The model of the library director as faculty member became well established. As staffs grew in order to care for the growing collections and to maintain longer hours of service, formal programs of library training were established, first at Columbia in 1887. By the time of the famous Williamson report on library education published in 1923, 15 institutions were offering professional programs of training for library service. These were training programs in the techniques required to deal with the internal operations of libraries. There was no theoretical underpinning that would support scholarly inquiry.

University library collections continued to grow. By 1920, Harvard and Yale had collections over 1 million: Yale 1,250,000; Harvard, 2,971,000. By 1940, eight university libraries had collections over 1 million volumes: University of California, Berkeley, Chicago, Harvard, Illinois, Michigan, Minnesota, and Yale. But the college libraries were not faring as well. In an analysis of about 200 four-year liberal arts colleges in the United States published in 1932, only 33 institutions had libraries with more than 60,000 volumes (Randall 1932).

William Warner Bishop

Leaders of American librarianship during the late 1920s and 1930s, led by William Warner Bishop, librarian of the University of Michigan, with the support of the Carnegie Corporation, were seeking to improve the college libraries. Under a mandate of the college library program of the Carnegie Corporation, standards were proposed and then used in making decisions about which college libraries would receive Carnegie grants (Bishop 1938). Institutions were uneven in the support they provided to their libraries. Many colleges continued to work under constrained fiscal conditions, and most college libraries suffered from lack of support. Only in the 1960s, following the publication of the American Library Association's *Standards for College Libraries* in 1959, did college libraries improve. The standards specified that a college library budget should be a minimum of 5 percent of the total general and educational budget of the college, that three professional librarians constituted the minimum number of professional staff, and that the minimum size of the collection should be 50,000 volumes. The impetus for improvement came from the standards, from the application of the standards in collegiate accreditation reviews, and from the infusion of moneys for libraries from the federal government through the Higher Education Act of 1965. College libraries prospered.

College librarians worked diligently to provide library service to their students, and many sought ways to inform the college presidents of the important role the library played. But many presidents were preoccupied with other issues and so ignored the library. Bishop described the role of the college librarian:

The demands which a college makes on its librarian are really manifold and extremely difficult to fill with any success. The college requires its librarian to be a business man, an administrator, a scholar, and an effective instructor of students, and at the same time to oversee and guide reading in many fields. It is practically impossible to produce a paragon who will succeed in all these lines of activity. The most that can be expected is that we shall develop of necessity a type of scholarly administrator who will understand the problems of instruction and will be able to deal sympathetically with the problems of students and at the same time will be sufficiently versed both in the technique of his profession and in the management of financial affairs to administer a college library with a fair degree of success. (Bishop 1938, 47)

One sees in Bishop's characterization of the college librarian the antecedents in the early college president: the president had to do everything; so did the librarian. In mastering this role, the library director in many colleges emerged as an important and powerful member of the community. The library staff, as it grew and developed, however, did not share in the esteem, nor were they expected to be scholars or faculty members.

Justin Winsor

During this transformation period, American librarianship emerged as a profession, and academic librarianship developed. The American Library Association (ALA), founded in 1876, had as its first president, Harvard's Justin Winsor, who served as ALA's president from 1876 to 1885. Winsor was a founding member of the American Historical Association (1884) and during this period also edited the eight-volume *Narrative and Critical History of America.*

As a result of the Williamson report, the first advanced program in library science, including a program leading to the doctoral degree, was established at the University of Chicago in 1926 with the support of the Carnegie Corporation. In 1931, the Graduate Library School began publishing *The Library Quarterly,* the major research publication of the field. Many of those earning the Ph.D. at Chicago went on to direct major university libraries: Lewis Branscomb, Ohio State; John Dawson, Delaware; Andrew Eaton, Washington University; Ralph Ellsworth, Colorado; Herman Fussler, Chicago; Carl Hintz, Oregon; Richard Logsdon, Columbia; Arthur McAnally, Oklahoma; Archie McNeal, Miami; Stephen McCarthy, Cornell; Errett McDiarmid, Minnesota; Robert Miller, Indiana; Benjamin Powell, Duke.

In 1931, the Association of Research Libraries was founded as an organization separate from the American Library Association and as an organization of research libraries, not librarians. The founding group comprised library directors of institutions that held membership in the Association of American Universities, along with a few other institutions whose directors were prominent in university library circles. In 1938, the Association of College and Research Libraries (ACRL) was organized by the restructuring of the College and Reference Section in the American Library Association, and in 1939 ACRL began publication of *College & Research Libraries*. Finally, in 1947, the first executive secretary of ACRL was appointed, giving the American Library Association a full-time staff member expert in the affairs of college and university libraries.

As the staffs of the university libraries grew in size to accommodate the growing collections and the growing demands on use, the position of the library staff within the framework of the university was emerging as a concern. The position of the library director was secure, generally as a scholar/administrator and often as member of the faculty. Library staff members, however, generally fell into the classification of clerical workers, for the administrative classification of positions had not yet emerged, and the growing size of the professional staff had not been anticipated. In 1911, Columbia University trustees voted, "The Librarian shall have the rank of professor, the Assistant Librarian that of Associate Professor, and the Supervisors shall rank as Assistant Professors and Bibliographers as Instructor," and in 1944, the University of Illinois granted full faculty status and rank to all professional staff. Unlike Columbia, Illinois did not tie rank to position. The nature of the appointment and rank of library staff continued to vary from institution to institution. Even in those institutions with faculty rank for the professional staff, the librarians did not organize themselves as a faculty, did little teaching, and did less research and publication. The professional body of librarians was joined by a larger group of clerical workers, who in many of the state university libraries were organized under civil service regulations.

Much of the impetus for faculty rank at the University of Illinois was to remove librarians from the clerical/civil service categories and recognize them as professionals in the only way the university then had, the faculty rank.

MASS EDUCATION PERIOD, 1945–1990

The expansion of higher education after World War II was driven by three major events: the adoption in 1944 of the GI Bill (the Serviceman's Readjustment Act), the establishment of the National Science Foundation in 1945, and the Higher Education Act of 1965. Libraries also expanded.

The GI Bill marks the agreement on the policy that higher education should be available to all who qualified and desired it, a social policy that is firmly in place. The legislation, providing direct financial assistance to returning veterans, enabled 2.25 million veterans to go to college (Levine 1978, 510). The demand for places led to a great expansion in facilities and an expansion in faculties. By 1964, college enrollments nationwide equaled 40 percent of the 18–21-year-old population. By 1970, college enrollments equaled 48 percent of the 18–21-year-old population.

The goal of the National Science Foundation was to harness the scientific capabilities developed during wartime for peacetime uses. Universities increased their scientific capabilities, and the federal money supplied to universities for research vital to the interests of the nation helped fuel the expansion of higher education after the war. Anyone watching the development of American higher education could have predicted that the universities would expand greatly on the side of the natural sciences and engineering and in the applied social sciences such as business and public administration. Such expansion would come about not because society needed more people educated in the natural sciences and engineering but, rather, because strong and powerful social pressures would push universities that way, as they had been doing since the early years. The research dollars from the federal government were powerful persuaders.

The liberal arts colleges also shifted their curriculum to reflect student choice, adding professional programs in business, computer science, and other professional and vocational areas to match the interests of potential students. American colleges have been very resilient. Colleges that rely heavily on tuition as a source of revenue have been as likely to add professional programs as have colleges that rely on state funds for support.

Library budgets for collections began to shift toward the sciences, but the humanities and social sciences benefited as well from the great increases in the library budgets that came about in this period as a result of the Higher Education Act.

Universities, anxious to develop into major research institutions, appointed strong librarians who sought out collections, embarking upon a period of collection building that has been described as "imaginative and resourceful, often imprudent and risk-taking, and remarkably successful" (Vosper 1971, 89). University libraries bought private collections, entire bookshops, every item in the catalog of an antiquarian dealer. Institutional collecting was a major force in the support universities provided to their scholars. Competition for faculty during this period was as intense as it was during the late 1800s, and the library continued to be an asset in faculty recruitment. By 1990, all members of the Association of Research Libraries (107 universities) had collections over 1 million volumes (Association of Research Libraries 1992, 44).

The size of the library staffs grew during this period, for more professional librarians were added as the collections grew, and more nonprofessional staff were needed as well. But salaries remained low. In 1973, fewer than 10 percent of the professional librarians were in positions in which the average compensation exceeded that of assistant professors in similar institutions (Cameron and Heim 1974).

In the 1950s and 1960s there was a push for faculty status for librarians, led by Robert Downs at the University of Illinois and Arthur McAnally at the University of Oklahoma and culminating in the "Standards for Faculty Status" adopted by the Association of College and Research Libraries in 1972. Faculty rank and status were achieved by librarians in many of the midwestern land-grant universities, and librarians in the state universities and colleges in California, the State University of New York (SUNY), and the City University of New York (CUNY) also were appointed as faculty. In those institutions in which the faculty were organized as unions, the salaries of librarians were raised to match the salaries of the other faculty.

There was resistance by other universities ("What teaching and research does a librarian do?"), by librarians who did not relish the responsibilities of the faculty ("I don't want to publish; I just want to do my job"), and by library administrators ("I can't run a library like an academic department"). There also was an attack on the faculty status of academic librarians by those faculty members teaching in schools and departments of library science. As one put it: "[A]pplying publish-or-perish to academic librarians, devalues their role as librarians. The implication is that it is better to be pseudo-faculty, than genuine librarians with their own distinct expertise and unique contribution to the university community. This is damaging to the profession's image within the university and to its self-image as well" (Van House 1991, 96).

Although librarians might not have wanted the responsibilities of faculty, they did want a share in the governance of the library. Many libraries experienced discontent, particularly among newly hired library school graduates who were eager to participate in what they saw to be the central affairs of the library, not just the issues relating to their own work.

As collections continued to grow, librarians turned to the new developments in computing for help in managing the collections. During the 1980s, libraries introduced automated circulation systems and shared copy cataloging on a regional and national basis, bringing cost-savings and improvements in library efficiencies. On-line catalogs, and electronic access to databases through on-line services or CD-ROM technology were important additions to the improvements in quality library services. Academic libraries, by using existing staff to introduce and implement the new technologies, experimented early with the team-based approaches to library management. Library committees and task forces were formed to develop many of the automated programs in libraries. The successful adoption of new technologies lessened the tensions between the library administration and the professional staff, which might have continued had academic libraries not begun to change their methods of operations.

The absorption of computing technologies in libraries brought librarians early into the information age. For many faculty and students, the use of on-line catalogs was their first experience with computing technologies. Academic librarians at first applied computing technologies to internal operations; then extended the new technologies to all aspects of information service. Because of the scale of the libraries' internal operation, the library staff were important players in the development of automation on the campus. Because librarians were knowledgeable and well versed in the technology of the day, they were influential in much of the planning of the campus infrastructures.

The New Era: Technological Imperatives

Academic librarianship's successful adoption of information technology to improve library services, operations, and management emphasized the administrative aspects of the profession, not the scholarly aspects. The leadership of the university library for the last 20 years or so has concentrated on its relationships to the campus administration, where the decisions on resource allocations are made. The interactions with faculty members and students were left as the responsibility of the library's professional staff. College librarians, by contrast, continued to be more closely allied to the faculty and to the teaching programs of the college campus. The integration of the college library in the academic life of the college campus has been more immediate and direct than it has been for the university library.

Those librarians who work closely with faculty and students relate to the scholarly and instructional side. A difficulty academic librarianship has is that academic scholarship has become so specialized that it is difficult to keep up with what faculty members are doing or even in what direction a particular academic department is moving. Furthermore, the central role the library might have played in the work of a particular department or discipline has changed as the way the faculty member does his or her work also has changed. Big science has dominated the American university for the last 40 years and has dominated the acquisitions budgets of university libraries. Now, as the move to electronic publishing of journals grows, the use that faculty and students are making of collections of scientific publications is changing. Will libraries assess the information-seeking behaviors of their users and allocate budgets accordingly? Will the library still be seen as an asset in faculty recruitment, in institutional prestige, in donor support? What indicators besides print collections might be used in deciding whether or not the library is an asset? These questions confront academic librarianship today.

As the core functions of librarianship were automated, acquisitions, cataloging, and circulation became routine tasks assigned to lower-level staff. At the same time, librarians were looking for ways to measure performance of libraries beyond just the historical input measures of size of collection, size of staff, and size of budget. During the 1980s, greater attention was being given to the information services provided by reference units and to methods of instruction in the use of libraries, formally through library-based classes or more informally through cooperative arrangements with various faculty and academic departments. Now, librarians are being asked to address the issue of what value the library adds to the educational mission of the campus. So the role of the library in the instructional process has become an important issue and one to which librarians are responding, using their experience and knowledge with the new technologies to great advantage.

The faculty's influence in the administrative life of the campus, while significant, is not strong. Strong presidents and strong boards continue to dominate the important issues of organizational change, major programmatic shifts, and budget allocations. Faculty committees can and do propose change, but if resources are needed to implement proposals, the administration determines the implementation. While some would say that the faculties are impediments to change, the history of change in American higher education belies that. Change has been embraced from the beginning, with the college adapting to social pressures and the demands made upon it by students, but that change has come not quickly but more deliberately.

Significant changes in higher education are in the offing; on that everyone agrees. There are changes in student demographics, in the nature of public support for higher education, in the costs of higher education. There are changes in the scholarly disciplines that will lead to changes in teaching, research, and scholarly communication. There are changes in student expectations about higher education. The technological changes libraries made in the 1980s were guided by agreed-upon library priorities that emphasized the use of technology to improve library operations. The changes coming about in the next 10 years will be guided more by academic programs, institutional priorities, and economic concerns. As Clifford Lynch so aptly stated,

[L]ibraries will have increasingly less latitude in the coming years to pursue autonomously defined, technologically determined manifest destiny at a pace that is comfortable to the library administration and staff (and patrons), and hope that this future will conveniently and serendipitously converge with university programmatic needs. Instead, libraries will be expected to provide leadership in supporting institutional programmatic objectives and to move more rapidly than they have in the past. (Lynch 1995, 95)

The successful adaptation of the American academic library to the new technologies and the ability of library staff members, at every level, to use computer technologies in their work have been obvious to all users. Campus administrators, confronted with the budget requests from libraries for more wiring, for network improvements, for equipment upgrades, for materials in new formats, and for leasing arrangements instead of purchasing agreements, have recognized the knowledge and abilities of librarians to manage the technologies and the change. This recognition has led to a growing movement of adding responsibility for campus computing and telecommunications to the librarian's role. The director of libraries is emerging as the chief information officer in many colleges and universities.

Beginning in the early 1990s and accelerating rapidly as digital information resources become more pervasive, librarians and faculty members are assessing the impact of the networked environment on instruction and research. Resources formerly available only in print at a specific place now are accessed through the networked desktop. The role of the librarian and the nature of the library are being influenced profoundly.

FINAL COMMENT

Academic librarians have retooled themselves continuously. Upgrading their knowledge, skills, and abilities, librarians now are experts in the use of new technologies. They are developing new methods of providing support to users who do not use libraries and are adapting the digital technologies to the development of new resources and services. Librarians are being asked by faculty members and educational policy committees to help in the delivery of new information services, unfettered by time and place. Librarians are placing themselves in academic departments, being asked to assist directly in the provision of instruction using the new technologies. While the library director may have policy and program responsibilities for all forms of information, the professional staff, well educated and well trained, are implementing the programs.

Academic librarians do not have a monopoly on the provision of information services and the selection of resources. They never have. From the beginning, though, librarians have played a central and vital role in the development of scholarship and in the support of instruction. That role remains, and the profession has positioned itself to continue in it. Campus administrators and faculties rely on the librarians for support for the academic enterprise—as they always have.

NOTE

I am indebted to Arthur M. Cohen, William L. Williamson, and the editors for their help with this chapter.

REFERENCES

Association of College & Research Libraries. 1959. "Standards for College Libraries." *College & Research Libraries* 20: 274–280.

Association of Research Libraries. 1992. *ARL Statistics 1990–91*. Washington, DC: Author.

Bestor, Arthur E., Jr. 1953. "The Transformation of American Scholarship, 1875–1917." *The Library Quarterly* 23: 164–179.

Bishop, William Warner. 1938. *Carnegie Corporation and College Libraries 1929–1938*. New York: Carnegie Corporation of New York.

Brough, Kenneth J. 1953. *Scholar's Workshop: Evolving Conceptions of Library Service*. Urbana: University of Illinois Press.

Bryant, Louise May and Mary Patterson. 1938. "The List of Books Sent by Jeremiah

Dummer.'' Chapter 20 in *Papers in Honor of Andrew Keogh*. New Haven, CT: privately printed, pp. 423–492.

Cameron, Donald F. and Peggy Heim. 1974. *Librarians in Higher Education; Their Compensation Structures for the Academic Year 1972–73*. Washington, DC: Council on Library Resources:

Carlton, W. N. Chattin. 1907. ''College Libraries in the Mid-Nineteenth Century.'' *The Library Journal* 32: 479–486.

Cohen, Sheldon S. 1974. *A History of Colonial Education 1607–1776*. New York: Wiley.

Hamlin, Arthur T. 1981. *The University Library in the United States*. Philadelphia: University of Pennsylvania Press.

Harding, Thomas S. 1959. ''College Literary Societies: The Contribution to the Development of Academic Libraries, 1815–76.'' *The Library Quarterly* 29: 1–26, 94–112.

Jewett, C. C. 1850. ''Statistics of American Libraries.'' In Fourth *Annual Report . . . of the Smithsonian Institution . . . during the Year 1849*. Washington, DC: Smithsonian Institution.

———. 1853. *On the Construction of Catalogues of Libraries, and Their Publication by Means of Separate, Stereotyped Titles: With Rules and Examples*. Washington, DC: Smithsonian Institution.

Kraus, Joe W. 1973. ''The Book Collections of Early American College Libraries.'' *The Library Quarterly* 43: 142–159.

Levine, Arthur. 1978. *Handbook on Undergraduate Curriculum*. San Francisco: Jossey-Bass.

Lynch, Clifford A. 1995. ''The Technological Framework for Library Planning in the Next Decade.'' In Beverly P. Lynch, ed., *Information Technology and the Remaking of the University Library*. San Francisco: Jossey-Bass, pp. 93–105.

Morison, Samuel Eliot. 1936. *Three Centuries of Harvard, 1636–1936*. Cambridge, MA: Harvard University Press.

Pratt, Anne Stokeley. 1938. ''The Books Sent from England by Jeremiah Dummer to Yale College.'' Chapter 2 in *Papers in Honor of Andrew Keogh*. New Haven, CT: privately printed, pp. 423–492.

Randall, William M. 1932. *The College Library: A Descriptive Study of Libraries in the War-Year Liberal Arts Colleges in the United States*. Chicago: American Library Association.

Ray, Gordon N. 1988. ''Bibliographical Resources for the Study of Nineteenth Century English Fiction.'' In *Books as a Way of Life*. New York: The Grolier Club and the Pierpont Morgan Library, pp. 185–208.

———. 1990. *The American College and University, a History*. Athens: University of Georgia Press.

Rudolph, Frederick. 1977. *Curriculum; a History of the American Undergraduate Course of Study since 1636*. San Francisco: Jossey-Bass.

Shiflett, Orvin Lee. 1981. *Origins of American Academic Librarianship*. Norwood, NJ: Ablex.

Shores, Louis. 1966. *Origins of the American College Library*. Hamden, CT: Shoe String Press.

Utley, George Burwell. 1951. *The Librarians' Conference of 1853, a Chapter in American Library History*. Chicago: American Library Association.

Van House, Nancy A. 1991. ''Assessing the Quantity, Quality, and Impact of LIS Research.'' In Charles R. McClure and Peter Hernon, eds., *Library and Information Science Research: Perspectives and Strategies for Improvement*. Norwood, NJ: Ablex, pp. 85–100.

Vosper, Robert. 1971. ''Collection Building and Rare Books.'' In Jerrold Orne, ed., *Research Librarianship: Essays in Honor of Robert B. Downs*. New York: R. R. Bowker, p. 99.

Chapter 2

From Faculty to Librarian Materials Selection: An Element in the Professionalization of Librarianship

Raven Fonfa

INTRODUCTION

In the development of academic librarianship in the United States from the founding of the first colleges in the seventeenth century to the present, a series of critical events defines the evolution of the profession. Significant achievements in the history of librarianship include the advances in bibliographic control, which improved access to materials, the provision of specialized reference services to support research activities, and the design of library instruction programs for students. Another such achievement in the professionalization of librarianship is the shift from faculty to librarian control of selection of materials for acquisition in university research libraries. This chapter describes the history leading up to this shift, identifies factors in the environment and in the library profession that effected changes, presents the development of professional awareness of the centrality of selection in library operations, and explores the relationship between selection responsibility and the building of research-level collections.

The significance of the shift from faculty to librarian responsibility for selection is characterized by the critical role of selection in the achievement of an academic library's objectives, the multiple factors involved in the change of accepted practices, and the changed role of the academic librarian as an indicator of the increased professionalization of librarianship as a whole. As a direct result of the movement that created this shift, the concept of ''collection development'' was introduced as a professional activity and as a subject for investigation in librarianship theory.

The shift to librarian control of selection was initiated, developed rapidly, and completed during the mid-1960s; however, a gradual evolution from the early history of higher education to the 1960s shows the many contributing factors that led to this seemingly radical change. These factors include the progress of the library profession and its concepts and practices; the impact of external events in the evolving social, political, and economic conditions of higher education; and the efforts of practicing librarians and strong leaders who initiated development, made change, and created progress.

Overview: A Model of Historical Development

The cumulative developments that led to the transition from the faculty-selection system to a librarian-selection system reflect a pattern of historical change. Distinct stages of development can be defined that represent transformations of the conceptualization of the system of practice. Within these periods, the interaction between external and internal factors propels advancements.

In the first stage, the foundation for the original system is constructed. The early colonial period to 1876 established the *context* and spanned the evolution of higher education. The system of faculty-controlled selection is the product of this era. In the next stage, external changes create new demands for the system, and, in response, key individuals express criticism of the system, identify flaws, and offer and implement solutions but defend and preserve the existing system. The years 1876–1939 encompass a period of *criticism* of the faculty-selection system. The system's inability to meet new demands engenders a period of challenge. The years 1939–1963 constitute the *challenge* stage in which librarians investigate and attempt alternative methods to the faculty-selection system.

In the final stage, the old system breaks down, and the gradual practical changes and the growing theoretical developments meet in a widespread institutionalization of a new system. In the *transition* stage, 1963–1970, external and internal events bring the university library to a crisis position, culminating in the near-universal transition to the librarian-selection system. Acceptance of the new system creates an atmosphere in which a proliferation of activity is fostered. By the 1970s, the postcrisis phase of acceptance of the new system of librarian control of selection is recognizable, and both practice and research in collection development have since become productive areas of academic librarianship.

1636–1876: CONTEXT

The period from the founding of Harvard College in 1636 to the founding of Johns Hopkins University in 1876 is one of vital development for higher education and for academic libraries. The evolution of higher education in the

United States from classical colleges to modern research universities is the context in which the nature of academic libraries and librarianship was first defined.

Colonial Era

Institutions of higher education began as colonial versions of British colleges dedicated to providing a classical education for the sons of the upper classes and to training the future civil and religious leaders of society (Rudolph 1968, 13–19). The first nine schools started with small libraries modeled on the gentleman's private library. Due to tradition carried over from England and isolated conditions in the colonies, schools relied on donation of materials. Early efforts were made for providing funds for purchase, but this remained a secondary method (Kaser 1980, 34–37).

Both of these means of acquisition required practical methods by which the institutions could discover, "select," and acquire materials. Methods included solicitation of donations of materials, purchases of whole collections, and modern arrangements with publishers and booksellers (Kaser 1980, 42). Acquisition through purchase can be traced to the earliest records and show the beginnings of methods for ordering and for assignment of responsibility for selection. At this time, the purchasing agent could be anyone affiliated with the school, and selection was performed by all college personnel, including the president, trustees, and faculty members (Shores 1966, 53, 71, 102).

Independence to 1830

With independence, higher education gained a new mission: preparing the citizenry for building the new nation. The main objective was growth met by the expansion of existing institutions and the rapid creation of new ones (Rudolph 1968, 36–40). Libraries had developed slowly during the colonial era and were subject to the same pressure for growth (Kaser 1980, 43).

Selection of materials and control of funds were a critical issue, given the limited funds available and the great need for materials. In the earlier years, the trustees had retained strong control of funds and their expenditure. In the 1800s, separate faculty committees formed to oversee selection of materials (Hamlin 1981, 97) These early faculty committees laid the foundation for faculty control of selection and of fund allocation and expenditure. In this era the first roles and responsibilities of the librarian were defined. The "librarian" was, for a long period of time, a member of the professorial staff who was given the additional duty of managing the library. As this became a full-time position in the mid-1800s, the managerial role without authority for selection continued (Hamlin 1981, 27, 33, 34).

1830–1876

The primary focus of these years was modernizing the curriculum to meet the practical needs of the nation spurred by the Industrial Revolution and to assimilate changes in scholarship since the Enlightenment. Technological, scientific, and professional classes were taught alongside, and gradually replaced, the classical courses (Rudolph 1968, 110–115). The purpose of higher education was changing to mean not just the perpetuation of knowledge but its advancement. Scholarly and scientific societies were founded and fostered the division of scholarship into specialized disciplines. The first attempts at true disciplinary graduate programs were made in this time. The University of Michigan offered the first "earned master's degree" based on a specific program in 1853, and Yale University granted the first Ph.D. in 1861 (Levine 1978, 505).

For the library, this meant providing a new kind of service beyond the custodial preservation of books but offering true reference assistance in finding materials appropriate to a line of inquiry. Being able to provide these services was contingent on ownership of the relevant materials, and librarians were now placed in the crucial position to know what the library had and what was needed. When librarians began to criticize and, ultimately, challenge professors' control over selection, this behavior was based on the knowledge gained in this role.

Following the Civil War, both the standard of living and the student population grew, and the popular expectations for the role of higher education changed. The federal government increased its role in the creation and design of institutions with the passage of the Morrill Act in 1862 (Brubacher and Rudy 1976, 264). The Morrill Act legislated the land-grant university system and explicitly called for the construction of institutions with programs in the practical sciences (Brubacher and Rudy 1976, 228). The founding of the land-grant Cornell University in 1868 devoted to the scholarly study of pure science was a transitional step between the vocational land-grant schools and the new movement in higher education dedicated to original research and scholarship that would create the modern research university (Rudolph 1968, 265–266).

1876: Johns Hopkins University

The greatest influence on the design of universities in the United States was the seminar model of German universities with doctoral programs, a dedication to original research, divisions of departments by subject, and strong subject library collections controlled by the individual departments. Beginning in 1815, thousands of American students traveled to study in German universities (Brubacher and Rudy 1976, 175). These scholars returned to lead a reform movement that culminated in the founding of Johns Hopkins University in 1876, the first true research university in the United States. The success of Johns Hopkins inspired the larger colleges to adopt this model. The new academic environment in which faculty needed to disseminate the results of their research and use the research publications of others laid the foundation for the constant rate of increase of scholarly publications, which would have a critical impact on the practice of selection and acquisition.

The Faculty-Selection System

It became widely recognized by the faculty and administration of the new universities that the library served a crucial role in providing access to current materials to support the new curriculum and research. Acquisition through purchase rapidly increased, and formal administrative techniques were developed for selection, performed by faculty, and for acquisition, performed by librarians. The task of selection was distributed among the new subject departments. The faculty library committee became the official body for allocating funds to the departments, which could then be spent by professors with permission of the department head or faculty representative (Danton 1963, 62; Kaser 1980, 45). The system of faculty responsibility for selection was now codified and firmly in place.

1876–1939: CRITICISM

In the following era, the approach to the development of the library's collection was fixed fund allocation to departments, faculty responsibility for selection, and compensation by librarians for general materials, reference works, and insufficient coverage. While this system functioned sufficiently for the immediate needs of the time, its flaws soon became apparent to librarians as the implications of advanced scholarship and the new university structure unfolded.

Events in the political and economic environment added new demands to academic libraries that the existing system was unable to manage. The proposals for changes in the criticism period do not suggest taking selection responsibility from faculty but put the librarian in a new kind of managerial position to supervise faculty selection.

Certain aspects of the new structure facilitated criticism and subsequent change. The new reference librarian mediating between the university community and the collection held a unique perspective on how the collection was used, what was needed, and how the collection met, or failed to meet, those needs. The acquisitions librarian responsible for ordering all materials was in a position to oversee all selected purchases. Specialized librarians in the departmental libraries could contribute subject knowledge to selection review and would later provide a means by which the eventual transition from faculty to librarian responsibility for selection could be gradually and smoothly implemented.

At the same time that faculty were establishing a new scholarly community, librarians were establishing a professional community. The founding of the

American Library Association (ALA) in 1876 and of library periodicals and of library schools provided channels of communication through which librarians could share concerns and develop solutions. Advances in library education would provide justification for the acknowledgment of unique and valuable library skills and knowledge.

1897: Alfred C. Potter

A *Library Journal* article by Harvard librarian Alfred C. Potter marks the beginning of professional criticism of the faculty-selection system. The issues Potter describes are almost unchanged during the next 60 years of debate. The benefits of faculty's performing selection include that they are trained subject specialists, know the needs of the college, and know the literatures of their subject fields. The disadvantages include the dangers of the busy or "negligent professor" and the biased or "hobby-horsical professor," the risk that subjects not in the curriculum will not be represented in the collection, and the lack of organization and coordination (Potter 1897, 40–41).

Potter's suggestions as to the "librarian's duty" were to serve an advisory role with "veto power" over acquisition, advising the professor in suggesting works for purchase, monitoring faculty activity, and providing aid and assistance to ease the acquisition process (Potter 1897, 40–42). Potter acknowledges that a "more radical remedy would be to grant the professors only the right of suggestion instead of a practically absolute control over the appropriations" but rejects this solution, fearing the loss of professors' input of special subject knowledge (Potter 1897, 42). The criticism period focused on the relationship between faculty and librarians in the building of collections and on the importance of subject knowledge in the selection process. The critics consistently defended preserving the current system based on these arguments.

The 1930s: Society and Professional Research

Serious events in the economic and political conditions during this era impacted on every aspect of society and led to internal reflection and redefinition of the role and practices of the library. The effects of these events on the university library were communicated in professional articles analyzing the role the library served and how the library's operations fulfilled that role in an increasingly demanding environment.

Dramatic growth in funds and collections in the 1910s and 1920s was followed by an equally dramatic reduction in funds during the years of the Great Depression. Reflection and criticism of acquisition methods became more urgent. The increasing participation of the scholarly community in international and political concerns during the era between the two world wars changed the way libraries perceived their role and their responsibility to select relevant materials. This changing role of the academic library in the university, in scholarship, and in the broader society would contribute to a greater independence of the library and lead to a perception of the library as a unit unto itself responsible for, and in control of, its own decision making and operational functioning. This combination of a financial imperative and a shift in mission served to facilitate analysis and change.

During the 1930s, criticism was expressed in a series of articles describing surveys, research studies, and potential modifications to practice. These works represent the advent of research by librarians into the methods and results of library operations without which tangible changes in practice later on would not have been possible. The work of this phase serves as the inspiration for the activities of the challenge period.

1935: Flora Ludington

Ludington, reference librarian at Mills College, conducted one of the earliest surveys of selection policy and practice and discussed the need for library supervision of faculty selection based on its results. The questionnaire surveyed the existing state of book selection procedures, including library supervision over departmental selections (Ludington 1935, 9). Three respondents reported a "positive degree" and four reported no supervision; the remaining majority described serving in advisory roles (see Potter, earlier) by comparing faculty orders to "book reviews" and "best book" lists and offering suggestions but rarely challenging faculty selections. Ludington gleaned from her respondents that "in general, they show a perplexity as to the means of bettering our present policies, but an awareness that improvement is needed" (Ludington 1935, 10) This statement can serve to define the tone of the criticism period.

Ludington was inspired by *College Library Standards*, published in 1932 by the Advisory Group on College Libraries of the Carnegie Corporation (Ludington 1935, 8). The perceived need for standards was the direct result of advances in the curriculum that increasingly required students to use books and journal articles in their studies. Ludington suggested that librarians would need to take responsibility for supervision of selection in order for collections to meet these standards and proposed long-term planning with the librarian in a leadership role in order to achieve the improved collections (Ludington 1935, 8, 11). The specific programs must come from practicing staff librarians; Ludington observed that "the reference librarian is in the peculiarly strategic position of being the most intensive single user of the entire book collection and in close contact with the faculty and students," and in libraries with staff having "some degree of specialization, expert book selection assistance can be given" (Ludington 1935, 11). This work summarized the contemporary state of selection, the need for changes, and the various potential means by which changes could be implemented.

1935: J. Periam Danton

Danton later became a significant force in the challenge and transition periods advocating librarian control of selection. In this early work, Danton discussed his research showing that libraries with the best collections have librarians who had a better professional education, who have more direct responsibility for book selection and particular responsibility for the systematic growth of collections, and who give more time to book selection (Danton 1935, 446).

Danton strongly recommended that book selection be the responsibility of the librarian and that funds for acquisition be managed by the library (Danton 1935, 449). "This does not for a moment imply that the librarian should supplant the faculty member in the selection of books for course or other teaching needs . . . it does mean that the librarian should be the person chiefly responsible for the growth of the reference and general collections, and for the systematic development of the library's collections as a unified, correlated whole" (Danton 1935, 450–451). This work anticipated the arguments of the challenge period, which depended on increased education of librarians, and focused on acquisition policy for systematicness and on fund allocation as the root of control over selection.

1936: Waples and Lasswell

The important Waples and Lasswell study *National Libraries and Foreign Scholarship* became one of the most frequently cited studies of the later stages. Douglas Waples, professor at the Graduate Library School at the University of Chicago, conducted the study, evaluating the collections of international social science research publications in public and academic libraries in the United States and Europe. Harold D. Lasswell, associate professor of political science at the University of Chicago, wrote commentary on the political and scholarly implications of shared international research in a time of growing nationalism. That the academic library has a role to play in the great events of the world and that the functional operations of the library materially impact on its ability to fulfill that role are ideas that crystallized during this history.

Waples compared the holdings in all types of research-level libraries. Implicit within this study was a comparison of the selection results of public libraries with librarian selectors and university libraries with faculty selectors. Waples studied six research libraries in the United States: New York Public Library and the Library of Congress and the libraries at Harvard University, University of Chicago, University of California, and University of Michigan. (Waples and Lasswell 1936, 71). The data revealed "better" collections in the public libraries.

Across every parameter, New York Public Library ranked first, and the Library of Congress ranked second. Each had a higher number of international books and journals (Waples and Lasswell 1936, 71). Both held more titles "per dollar spent" (Waples and Lasswell 1936, 72). They showed significantly more balanced holdings for the languages represented and the years of publication and among the various subject disciplines within the social sciences (Waples and Lasswell 1936, 75, 76, 78). Finally, more of their holdings consisted of titles selected from standard bibliographies and by experts as the "best books" in the field (Waples and Lasswell 1936, 77). Waples and Lasswell comment that "the New York Public Library appears more attentive than the other five

American libraries to the future needs of American scholars in the social sciences. It pays greater deference to posterity'' (75). The Waples and Lasswell report provided the empirical evidence needed to justify challenging the faculty-selection system.

1939: Nathan Van Patten

Van Patten, director of libraries at Stanford University, bridges the criticism and challenge periods by presenting a compromise stance on selection control, while proposing an innovative role of the librarian in the university.

Van Patten suggests that selection of material for curricular needs should be performed cooperatively by faculty and librarians and that selection of material needed for research be conducted mainly by the faculty who use it but that librarians should be responsible for the purchase of general materials (Van Patten 1939, 65–66). In this context, Van Patten asserts that the librarian should have academic status with the same opportunities and responsibilities of a full professor (Van Patten 1939, 66). The discussion of librarian status indicates that the existing position is felt to be insufficient to assume the responsibility for selection. The position and status of the librarian in the university prove to be crucial for the eventual transfer of selection responsibility.

It is significant that Van Patten's article appeared in the first volume of the journal *College & Research Libraries*. The transition from the criticism to the challenge stage is facilitated by an increased professionalization of academic librarianship that is highlighted by the founding of the Association of College and Research Libraries (ACRL) Division of the ALA in 1939.

1939–1963: CHALLENGE

During this period, the effects of changes initiated in 1876 and new changes, including the growth of international studies and the growth and democratization of the student population due to the GI Bill of 1944, began to be felt more acutely and to impact directly on library operations.

The changes in the work and role of faculty in their increased commitment to teaching and research within a specialized discipline left little time for selection. Simultaneously, tremendous increases in the rate of publications by these faculty demanded that more attention be paid to selection. Observations and warnings by librarians on the decreasing faculty participation in what was historically a faculty responsibility are a primary element of the professional literature of the challenge period.

To compensate for the faculty inability to fulfill this responsibility, selection activity was gradually assumed by librarians. Lacking a system to smoothly integrate these changes into the library administration, inventive methods were developed on individual, case-by-case bases. Two innovations in library practice during and following World War II provided the impetus for acceptance of more responsible roles for the librarian: first, the success of cooperative collection development programs showed the professional community what could be achieved through strategic organized activity; and second, the introduction of area studies bibliographers to meet the increased need for international materials showed that librarians with specialized knowledge and education could fulfill the role of selector (Downs 1949; McNiff 1963).

In much of this history, practice preceded and inspired theory. The challenge period can be seen as a response to the need for an organizing theoretical model under which to enact comprehensive, effective change.

Leaders Emerge

1949: Herman Fussler and Felix Reichmann

In 1949, at a meeting of the University Libraries Section of ACRL, Herman Fussler, director of the University of Chicago Library, and Felix Reichmann, assistant director at Cornell University Library, presented models for librarian control of book selection with detailed descriptions and explanations of what a bibliographer is and does and why.

Fussler defined a bibliographer as "the principal coordinating officer of bibliographical activity" (Fussler 1949, 201). The bibliographer's characteristics include knowledge of the scholarly field; being a scholar; knowledge of books, book values, and dealers; sound bibliographic judgment; and knowledge of the faculty, what they are researching, and how individual members can aid selection (Fussler 1949, 201). Similar to Van Patten's proposal (see earlier), Fussler suggested the librarian be a practicing member of the faculty serving in a "critical liaison capacity" (Fussler 1949, 203). Fussler concludes that this model should be "the most effective way of achieving the necessary integration and coordination of acquisition policy in a large and complex university library" (Fussler 1949, 203).

Reichmann presented a model in which the acquisitions librarian with an academic perspective serves as coordinating agent for book selection. To support this model, he defined bibliography in relation to the role of the librarian. Bibliography is a discipline of scholarship "primarily interested in the material aspects of publication . . . the book as physical witness in the court of cultural history" (Reichmann 1949, 204). The correlation to librarianship lies in its tendency to "cut across subject departmental organization" and in its "service function . . . [to] not organize knowledge itself but groups records of knowledge for the use of the subject specialist" (Reichmann 1949, 204). Reichmann argued for the central administration of book selection in the library, asserting that while "subject departmentalization is a necessary administrative device, . . . book dealers rarely fit in academic subject departmentalization and only a central selecting agency can view the entire market" (Reichmann 1949, 204).

1953: Herman Fussler and Eileen Thornton

The growth and specialization of scholarship made the library indispensable to, and more responsible for, the success of the research and teaching activity in the university. At a Symposium on Acquisition Policy sponsored by the ACRL College and University Libraries Sections, Fussler argued that the necessary changes to meet this demand are best enacted through organized, systematic planning, which was lacking in the past. For this strategic planning to be accomplished, libraries require formal acquisition policies (Fussler 1953, 363). The rapid decrease in the number of faculty members who performed selection meant that it would fall to librarians to implement the acquisition policy. Fussler warned that effective methods to manage this transition must be in place; "[t]he transfer of this responsibility from the faculty or, to be more realistic, a very limited portion of the faculty, to members of the library staff imposes real hazards unless the library staff and the faculty both understand the required acquisition policies and are able to match the policies with adequate resources in money, space, and staff" (Fussler 1953, 365). To guarantee that selection responsibility be assigned to librarians, Fussler concluded that the responsibility for defining policy should be undertaken by librarians (Fussler 1953, 367).

Thornton, librarian of Vassar College, added this comment on the changing role of the librarian: "Newer views incline toward great freedom and encouragement of faculty participation but hold the librarian responsible for final judgment" (Thornton 1953, 371). Thornton's insight was that changes in librarianship theory and practice facilitate this development; "[t]here is increasing backing for policies which, while they urge full faculty participation in book selection do give the librarian final responsibility. It is easier now to point to reputable literature in librarianship or in educational administration which defines the faculty library committee as advisory rather than executive" (Thornton 1953, 372).

1957: Harry Bach and LeRoy C. Merrit's Survey

Bach, head of the Acquisitions Department at San Jose State College, reviewed and evaluated the responses to Professor LeRoy C. Merrit's 1955 survey on the policies and practices of acquisition. Bach showed the results as evidence of both the slow trend toward librarian control and the need for conscious effort to accelerate this trend. The respondent libraries are classified by the role of the librarian in selection: class 1, "self-effacing libraries . . . disclaim all responsibility for the development of the collection"; class 2, libraries that have the standard approach in which "materials are selected by the faculty with the aid and advice of librarians"; and class 3 libraries, "in which materials are selected by the library with the aid and advice of the faculty" (Bach 1957, 446). Of the 54 responses, fewer than six libraries fit in class 1, and exactly six fall in class 3, leaving the vast majority in class 2 (Bach 1957, 441, 446).

Bach cites practice at Columbia, Harvard, and his own institution as examples of the third model. At Columbia, librarians in supervisory positions and heads of subject libraries performed the "day-to-day" selecting, while faculty members made recommendations (Bach 1957, 446–447). At Harvard, Keyes Metcalf and Andrew Osborn developed the earliest model of selection by subject (versus area) specialist librarians. At San Jose, a Book Selection Department performed the majority of selection, supplemented by the divisional librarians and departmental library committees (Bach 1957, 447). It is seen here that the existence of department libraries with specialized librarians eased the transition from faculty to librarian control of selection. Bach concluded that while in "the majority of academic libraries . . . a small degree of library initiative and an increasing awareness of the need for planning" have taken place, "a small minority of libraries has gone one step farther" (Bach 1957, 451).

1963–1970: TRANSITION

The accumulated developments of the previous eras established the necessary foundation for the fundamental changes that occur in this period. In this final phase, events internally in librarianship and externally in higher education serve as catalysts for the "crisis" that led to the transition from the faculty-selection system to the librarian-selection system. J. Periam Danton's landmark study of 1963 comparing book selection methods in German and American university libraries provided the theoretical impetus, while the Higher Education Act of 1965 provided the practical mandate. Joining these events, a series of descriptive and prescriptive articles appears containing sophisticated and practical explication of the role of the librarian in the position of selector and giving examples of its implementation.

J. Periam Danton

In an in-depth historical study, Danton presents a detailed comparison of practices in Germany and the United States and points out serious flaws in the American system. Soon after American colleges adopted the German model of a university with faculty departments in charge of selection, the German universities underwent their own transition to a system of librarian subject specialists with exclusive responsibility for building collections (Danton 1963, 25–27, 35). Danton's description of the German model gives legitimacy to the claims of American academic librarians that they can and should control selection.

Danton's primary argument against the faculty system is its product, "the largely uncoordinated nature of selection and the resulting collections" (Danton 1963, 74). His primary argument for adopting the librarian selection system is that librarians have been held responsible, "de facto," for the resulting collections in their libraries but have been afforded no authority, "de jure," to ensure their quality (Danton 1963, 64, 70–72). With this influential work, Danton offered inspiration to academic librarians to take both responsibility and authority for what he proclaims their natural domain and provided a clear example of a successful librarian-selection system in their German counterparts.

The Higher Education Act of 1965

When the Soviet Union became the first nation to launch a satellite into space with Sputnik in 1957, the U.S. government, prodded by Cold War competition, responded by summoning higher education institutions to increase research and improve education. The Higher Education Act of 1965 provided the necessary funds for research, facilities, student aid, and more. Title II, Part C of the act created the National Program for Acquisitions and Cataloging (NPAC), allocating significant funds to materials acquisition (Danton 1967, 53). The influx of federal funds made management of selection a truly impossible task for faculty occupied with increased research and teaching responsibilities. Thus, the collection development "crisis" was created. The previous years of internal professional discussion and practical development had prepared academic librarians to face this crisis. Necessity joined with philosophy to bring a change that can, without qualification, be called revolutionary.

1966–1968: Exemplars

In 1966, Cecil K. Byrd, university librarian at Indiana University (responsible for bibliographic development of the collection), described the success of their program establishing 10 subject specialists in the social sciences, humanities, and area studies. Byrd explained that "the appointment of subject librarians for these disciplines . . . would both insure more comprehensive book selection and upgrade and personalize services" (Byrd 1966, 191). He described the relationship with, and response of, the faculty; "faculty members served by a subject librarian are encouraged to continue their traditional participation in book selection. Members of some departments continue to make recommendations, others feel released from a burdensome task which had been performed only spasmodically" (Byrd 1966, 192).

Danton described an early program at the University of California at Los Angeles under the leadership of Robert Vosper in which "nine specialists, called bibliographers . . . have been appointed *full-time* for book selection. . . . [and] contrary to the fears and, indeed, the experience at many university libraries in the United States, the faculty, far from opposing the scheme, has enthusiastically supported the Library's assumption of a responsibility from which they, the faculty, appear happy to be relieved" (Danton 1967, 50).

Robert P. Haro, social sciences bibliographer at the University of California at Davis, surveyed 70 academic libraries explicitly "to discover whether the library in question had librarians responsible for book selection" (Haro 1967, 104). Of the 67 responding libraries, 62 engaged in book selection: 8 libraries had subject bibliographers in reference departments, 13 in acquisitions, 11 had full-time bibliographers responsible only to the director or assistant director, 15 used the heads of divisional reading rooms, 5 used other department heads, and 2 had separate book departments (Haro 1967, 105–106). The results of Haro's study are dramatic compared to the findings of Bach's study, already described, conducted only 10 years earlier.

By 1968, the work in this area of librarianship had become extensive. David O. Lane, assistant university librarian of the University of California, San Diego, summarized the developments of the previous years through a survey of the professional literature. "The literature of book selection in academic libraries indicates that there has been for more than a half-century a continuing shift from faculty-dominated selection to library-dominated selection," and "it appears this trend will continue, because of the increased use of subject specialists on library staff, the growth of the publication industry, the articulation of more selection policy statements, as well increasingly widespread recognition of selection as part of the librarian's professional responsibility" (Lane 1968, 364).

CONCLUSION

By the 1970s, while the transition was not complete, the shift in thinking was. Publications following 1970 show a proliferation of research under this model focusing not on whether or not librarians should control selection but on how. The transfer of selection responsibility from faculty to librarians led libraries and the library profession to address progressively complex issues about how to fulfill this new responsibility. The concept of collection development as a discipline within academic librarianship was thus born, and librarians now directed their attention to designing methods to best accomplish this vital function of librarianship. The conceptualization of "collection development" in librarianship theory has since led to highly specialized work concerning its definition, organization, and implementation.

This event in the history of the profession did not occur suddenly or without struggle; rather, it came out of a gradual evolution of external changes and internal developments combined with the efforts of library leaders, practitioners, and researchers. The complexity and significance of the shift of the locus of decision making from the teaching staff to the library staff should not be underestimated. Over a span of many years, the growth of institutions and their funds and collections, the change in the nature of scholarship and faculty roles, the progress in library operations, and the emergence of a strong leadership for the library profession all converged to fundamentally change the nature and activities of academic librarianship. This shift both signified and impelled the professionalization of librarianship.

REFERENCES

Bach, Harry. 1957. "Acquisition Policy in the American Academic Library." *College & Research Libraries* 18 (November): 441–451.

Brubacher, John S. and Willis Rudy. 1976. *Higher Education in Transition: A History of American Colleges and Universities, 1636–1976.* New York: Harper and Row.

Byrd, Cecil K. 1966. "Subject Specialists in a University Library." *College & Research Libraries* 27(3) (May): 191–193.

Danton, J. Periam. 1935. "The Selection of Books for College Libraries: An Examination of Certain Factors Which Affect Excellence of Selection." *The Library Quarterly* 5: 419–456.

———. 1963. *Book Selection and Collections: A Comparison of German and American University Libraries.* New York: Columbia University Press.

———. 1967. "The Subject Specialist in National and University Libraries, with Special Reference to Book Selection." *Libri* 17(1): 42–58.

Downs, Robert B. 1949. "Wartime Co-operative Acquisitions." *The Library Quarterly* 19(3) (July): 157–165.

Fussler, Herman H. 1949. "The Bibliographer Working in a Broad Area of Knowledge." *College & Research Libraries* 10 (July): 199–202.

———. 1953. "The Larger University Library." *College & Research Libraries* 14 (October): 363–367.

Hamlin, Arthur T. 1981. *The University Library in the United States: Its Origins and Development.* Philadelphia: University of Pennsylvania Press.

Haro, Robert P. 1967. "Book Selection in Academic Libraries." *College & Research Libraries* 28 (March): 104–106.

Kaser, David. 1980. "Collection Building in American Universities." In James Thompson, ed., *University Library History: An International Review.* New York: Clive Bingley Ltd, K. G. Saur International Publishing Group, pp. 33–55.

Lane, David O. 1968. "The Selection of Academic Library Materials, A Literature Survey." *College & Research Libraries* 29 (September): 364–372.

Levine, Arthur. 1978. *Handbook on Undergraduate Curriculum.* San Francisco: Jossey-Bass.

Ludington, Flora B. 1935. "College Library Book Selection." *Library Journal* 60 (January): 8–12.

McNiff, Phillip J. 1963. "Foreign Area Studies and Their Effect on Library Development." *College & Research Libraries* 24 (July): 291–296, 304–305.

Potter, Alfred C. 1897. "The Selection of Books for College Libraries." *Library Journal* 22: 39–44.

Reichmann, Felix. 1949. "The Acquisition Librarian as Bibliographer." *College & Research Libraries* 10 (July): 203–207.

Rudolph, Frederick. 1968. *The American College and University: A History.* New York: Alfred A. Knopf.

Shores, Louis. 1966. *Origins of the American College Library 1636–1800.* Hamden, CT: Shoe String Press.

Thornton, Eileen. 1953. "The Small College Library." *College & Research Libraries* 14 (October): 370–372.

Van Patten, Nathan. 1939. "Buying Policies of College and University Libraries." *College & Research Libraries* 1 (December): 64–70.

Waples, Douglas and Harold D. Lasswell. 1936. *National Libraries and Foreign Scholarship.* Chicago: University of Chicago Press.

Part II

The Future, the
Responsibility of Leaders

Chapter 3

The Library Director as a Campus Leader

Delmus E. Williams

Academic libraries are traditional organizations that must now operate within a context that is changing. Society's expectations for higher education are very different than they were a half century or even a decade ago. But, at their hearts, American colleges and universities and especially the libraries that support them are still, or are still perceived to be, medieval institutions more adept at passing along traditional values than at fostering innovation. But the technology of teaching and learning and the pace at which technology is making itself felt in all phases of campus life are forcing campuses to rethink how they do business. This, in turn, is changing the roles assigned to campus leaders and producing challenges for the heads of libraries and other campus units. As a result, library directors are being asked by their constituents to reconsider their roles as leaders and administrators.

The impetus for this change is coming from the recognition that society requires people who are comfortable in an informated environment if it is to prosper. Higher education is being pressured to provide leaders for a society that is constantly being challenged to absorb and interpret critical, sophisticated data that are being transmitted to it through a dizzying array of technologies. To meet this objective, new programs and services are finding their ways onto the campus, programs and services that could not have been anticipated when traditional university structures were developed. As a result, missions assigned to campus units are being redefined, combined, and eliminated to adapt these structures to modern realities so that resources can be used to best advantage.

THE UNIVERSITY LIBRARY AND INFORMATION MANAGEMENT

It is not surprising that the library is finding itself in the middle of this mael-strom, given its traditional role as the main source of information upon which teaching and research are based. But this position is now being contested by other campus agencies like the computer center or instructional media offices, and, in this time of transition, it is critically important for the library director to step forward. Directors must develop their influence both within and outside their domain if they are to ensure that the capabilities of the library are exploited to best advantage and that the capabilities of this, the most traditional of campus services, are fully appreciated. Only in this way can the library be assured it will remain a vital part of the institution.

The challenge faced by the university community is very real. Academics must deal with dangerous levels of fragmentation of knowledge dictated by the advances made in science, learning, and scholarship over the past century. The exponential growth of information has changed the university from a pastoral, nineteenth-century haven of learning to a multiversity within which loosely linked communities of scholars and students pursue very different objectives. The result has been the creation of a vibrant community that is developing information about ever more discrete fields of inquiry at a rate that is far faster than can be processed (Mech 1996).

But the dawning of the information age and the scientific progress accom-panying it have come at a price. The orderly system we have used to pass information along from generation to generation through the printed word has been expanded to include an ever-increasing array of technologies, none of which have had the time to mature into predictable formats. No one will argue that the Internet, CD-ROMs, or audiovisual materials do not represent a signif-icant step forward for researchers. But each individual title provided in any of these formats is likely to have been organized in a unique way that reflects the individual producer's philosophy rather than any agreed-upon standard. As a result, the proliferation of materials published in these formats has presented challenges as we try to fit new tools into old structures.

The results achieved from the efforts to bring new technologies into the library and the university have been very positive, but the fit has not always been comfortable. Different scholars adopt technology at different rates, and deter-mining who will be an ''early adopter'' is not always easy. At the same time, tailoring services to bring those who accept change less well up to speed can be difficult and time-consuming. But the effort expended to change the way we do business is important, and that importance is increasing. Technology has enabled the university to support an exponential growth in the rate at which the amount of information available is expanding. Adapting organizational struc-tures to make sure that the available information can be used to support new initiatives is a challenge. At the same time, preparing the next generation of scholars to use both older and newer information technologies in their teaching and research and preparing them to use new tools as they emerge present an additional challenge. The question for colleges and universities posed by Vartan Gregorian, Brian Hawkins, and Merrily Taylor (1992) has become, How do we "separate the confusions and self-deceptions from the truths and insights—and effect the real information technology revolution, adjusting our organizational structures to discern, accommodate, assimilate, and exploit what is lasting and valuable in these technological developments?" (p. 7).

LEADERSHIP IN INFORMATION MANAGEMENT

Answering this question requires a leadership team on campus that clearly understands and focuses on the values, identity, and mission of the campus and encourages those working there to take risks as they come to understand how information is created, processed, and used by campus constituents. The impact of the development of information technology on campus is revolutionary, but as Gregorian, Hawkins, and Taylor point out, "The focus is not technology, but information. . . . The real revolution in information technology is about communication, not computation" (p. 8). Where do the library and the library director fit into this team? The fact is, no one really knows. For librarians, the bad news is that there is no consensus to support the idea that the library is the key to understanding and using information technology on campus. The good news is that no consensus has developed at all as to who should provide leadership in this arena. As a result, leadership in information services is being assigned to individuals based more on their specific skill levels than either their credentials or their standing in the hierarchy of the university.

There are librarians who have been thrust into leadership as campuses cope with new technologies, and for good reason. Barbara Moran (1989) noted that libraries have traditionally served as a gateway between users and information, and this role has been quietly transformed from the purveyors of services largely based on print resources to other technologies over the last 20 years. The emergence of optical and electronic storage tools, on-line and Web-based information resources, and the interdependence of libraries that has given rise to resource sharing on many levels have prepared libraries well for the new information environment in which they find themselves. But it is not entirely clear that the library's capacity to contribute in a time of technological innovation is fully appreciated on most campuses. Most users understand that libraries now include a variety of technologies. However, as often as not, the library has not been effective in redefining itself to the satisfaction of other campus constituents in such a way that there is an understanding that its expertise goes beyond providing traditional services at fixed locations.

Too often libraries have separated themselves from the teaching process. While they have worked hard to build sophisticated information systems within their buildings, their place in the university's organizational structure may actually retard their capacity to work with faculty to redefine both the teaching/ learning process and the role of the library in the larger academic community. Librarians have worked hard to establish the library as a free-standing college within the university. This is in keeping with the strong tradition of autonomy and specialization among academics, a tradition that separates them into departments and still further within departments into tight areas of specialized interest and research. The main positive result of this effort has been that librarians have established themselves as professionals and as faculty colleagues on campus. But, at the same time, this segmentation has meant that librarians and the library tend to be isolated in their own box, a box that is often defined very traditionally by other academics. As a result, the role assigned to the librarians is too often confined to that traditionally occupied by the library, the role of shepherding books and booklike things. This is especially problematic in a time when the prosperity of the library depends on the degree to which it involves itself in the development of the university's mission, values, and standards. In the future, the capacity of the library to command resources will depend on the ability of library leaders to reposition it within the university and redefine its role within both the university's formal and informal cultures (Engle 1990).

There is no doubt that the library has a place in the university of the future, but it is less clear what that place will be. More to the point, it is not at all clear who will have the opportunity to define that place. Most campuses value the library as a bridge to the past that is important as a symbol of learning, but the view that the library can also be a bridge to an informated future is less widely held. For the latter role to be assigned, the library director must be both an active and an effective advocate for the library on campus and a full participant in the life of the academic community. Librarians must participate in planning for the use of electronic technologies on campus, work collaboratively with computer professionals and others on campus, retrain staff, secure funding for both infrastructure development and operations, understand intellectual property issues, and learn to work in an environment in which change is a constant (Moran 1989). "Librarians should be attempting now to define the roles they want libraries and librarians to play, because if they do not, others will define those roles for them" (p. 39).

THE ROLE OF THE LIBRARY DIRECTOR

The library director is responsible for making the case for this level of participation on campus in the face of administrators who believe that others more effectively represent the future. Too often, libraries and librarians are seen as committed to old, stodgy scholarship, and less frequently (but often enough to cause problems) that reputation is deserved. But even when it is not true, library directors tend to operate as if they should be a part of the planning process at the most intimate levels simply because of the position they hold. In theory, this may be so, but, more often than not, people on campus will not yet have come to understand that involving the library is important or that the library will bring anything of value to the table. Altering this impression requires a combination of dues-paying, thick-skinned advocacy and general tenacity designed to portray the library organization as a savvy participant in campus decision making that understands the campus, the traditions of scholarship it pursues, and the technologies required to sustain and advance it. But, above all, librarians must assert their right to play in the arena. "If librarians are not advocates for themselves, they will not be perceived as advocates for the broader campus" (Mech 1996, 5).

This kind of reorientation requires a different view of leadership within the library. In addition to competence in administering the library, Keith Cottam (1989) contends that librarianship needs more entrepreneurial managers, that is, managers who introduce entrepreneurial ideas within bureaucracies. These leaders must be people who will break with tradition and act to develop new roles and responsibilities, secure risk capital, co-opt emerging information technologies for the library and develop new ones, and figure out new ways to make libraries essential in an information-based society. Entrepreneurial leaders must see possibilities in their program and act on their ideas. They must want to get things done and must be secure enough with their knowledge, skills, and abilities as library practitioners to accomplish the tasks at hand. But they must also be people who have established themselves as competent professionals who are trusted by their colleagues for their common sense, for their commitment to the university and its program, and for their understanding of both technical and policy issues relating to evolving technologies. This kind of leadership can (and should) develop at all levels of the library. It is the responsibility of the library director to lead by example, to develop an atmosphere that will encourage entrepreneurial spirit, and then to showcase developing leaders on campus in such a way that the breadth and depth of expertise within the library are appreciated.

But, at the same time, library directors must become campus leaders if they expect to have influence in discussions about new technologies and new services. They must function as part of a team consisting of college deans, faculty leaders, technical professionals, and members of the central administration to bridge the gap between traditional values and advancing technology. In the confederacy that is a university, this represents a serious challenge. Most good library directors have been prepared by training and experience to fulfill the internal roles assigned to them. They are good librarians who have learned to think strategically about library operations; they are technically competent professionals; they are committed to service; they understand and empathize with those they supervise; and they can communicate in the jargon of their profession. As they rise through the ranks, directors learn what it means to lead the library, to disseminate information within it, to handle conflict among the people who work there, and to efficiently allocate resources in such a way that work in the library gets done (Mech 1990).

THE LIBRARY DIRECTOR AS A POLITICAL OPERATIVE

However, directors are far less often prepared by experience and training to fulfill the duties assigned them within the larger academic community. Too frequently, good librarians fail as directors because they fail to understand that their technical skills are necessary for success in a leadership position but not sufficient to ensure that success. The library director is a campus leader who must learn to exercise the kind of political skills on campus that Allan Lau and Cynthia Pavett (1980) say are equally critical to long-term success. David Teather (1982) quite correctly describes universities as miniature political systems in which interest groups come together in temporary coalitions to influence policy within the organization. Universities are like small cities with decentralized decision making and networks of influence that often rely more on reputation than on position or even competence. To be effective in this context, the library director must learn to develop strategic alliances with other campus leaders by developing a reputation as a full partner on the campus leadership team (Wilcox and Ebbs 1992). When many diverse groups are trying to exercise their influence, those who are not invited to participate in the policy-making process or who are not perceived to be effective in this forum are at a disadvantage.

Too often this disadvantage becomes readily apparent when resources are distributed and when policies for the campus are developed (Teather 1982). Directors cannot assume universities are willing to pay for traditional library services, even though their leaders speak often of the library's centrality (Birdsall 1995). As D. J. Smith (1989, 144) said somberly, "Most academic librarians must be quite accustomed to the idea that they are not a major factor in the planning of higher education." He contends that libraries are too often considered relics. Their buildings and their collections and their machines are viewed as necessary equipment, somewhat shabby and neglected, perhaps, but worth an occasional infusion of new money to see if they can be made to function as the heart of the college or university. As painful as this situation might be, it may well become even more painful as organizations on campus jockey for control of newer information technologies.

Library services are almost universally viewed as important, but paying for them is not always given the same priority as newer, more glamorous information technologies, even within the library itself. When libraries are finding it increasingly difficult to pay for good collections, the idea that technology is making those collections obsolete can be very attractive to both administrators trying to assure the reputation of the institution on a budget and librarians trying to shake their laded reputation. The failure of the library to be perceived as instrumental in balancing the need to develop alternative technologies with the need for traditional library service can be damning. The result can easily be that money and influence will be diverted to places on campus where it is perceived that they can make a difference (Birdsall 1995).

LIBRARIES AS A BRIDGE BETWEEN THE OLD AND THE NEW

But this does not have to be. Michael Engle (1990) points out that librarians are not without advantages as campus leaders move to establish who should be the primary information provider to students and faculty. He notes that librarians bring to the university a sense of the past and an interdisciplinary perspective that is well established in a tradition that allows them to move easily between traditional views of what higher education is about and the technological future. Frequently viewed as faculty colleagues, even when they are not considered to be faculty, as people who have always met the information needs of campus constituencies, librarians are uniquely suited to interpret changes in the way information is being delivered for even the most traditional members of the academic community. This positioning is no small advantage in gaining acceptance among people who would prefer not to see things change.

Information technologies are fundamentally technologies for communications, and their employment in the university is, as often as not, an exploration of new connections among the traditional disciplines that help identify new possibilities for explanation and understanding and new ways of finding significance and meaning (Gregorian et al. 1992). The integration of technology into teaching and research programs requires a substantial investment in mechanisms to be used for their delivery, substantial expertise developing software to deliver messages via sound, video, animation, images, and the like, and a sound marketing program designed to gain acceptance among teachers and students. But information technologies are, at once, both fragmenting and integrative. They allow scholars to process far more information and integrate the results more effectively, and they allow scholars to cross disciplinary lines in their explorations. But taking this advantage means investing money where change can be effected, and that may mean funding those disciplines and individuals that embrace technology at a higher level than those that lag behind in implementation. These decisions are likely to challenge the political traditions on campus that give preference to senior faculty, and their fairness may be challenged, but risks must be taken in the allocation of these funds if change is to happen.

Convincing faculties that include very traditional people to buy into the investment and to use the new technologies can be facilitated if the message is associated with an agency with which they identify. Speculations about radical changes in education are always interesting, but arguments based on these paradigms are not always helpful. Viewing new technology as a variant of older technologies makes them appear more reasonable. If technological innovation can be sold as a better, easier way to do what is already being done or to extend established programs, it is relatively easy to sell. If change is portrayed as a logical progression that makes research easier or instructional delivery more effective rather than as a revolutionary change in the way scholars do business, then more people will accept it. Radical ideals draw big crowds at conferences, but they do not help assuage the fears of people who have difficulty with change.

This view of change as an incremental process can be accommodated within the mission of the library perhaps better than anywhere else on campus. As Gregorian, Hawkins, and Taylor (1992) conclude, "[A]ll of the dreams to achieve a greater integration of knowledge ultimately revolve around the core of information, not the technologies of information processing. Thus, logically, we are looking at integrating information resources. We must look to the unit which has historically been charged with this mission, namely the library" (p. 10). If the campus views the library as keeper of the books, and even this conservative crew is advocating change, then who is to argue?

But the role assigned to librarians and the library within the culture of many universities often limits the part they will be asked to play in this process. Even though the level of technological sophistication of most academic librarians has risen sharply in recent years, librarians are perceived too often as technophobic and associated with an outworn culture designed to protect books rather than to serve people. The library is associated only with those who want to preserve the past (Gregorian et al. 1992). But this perception is changing. While "neither the publishing industry nor the universities have fully embraced a significant change in the ways libraries could do business, the pace and acceptance of change have been picking up" (Sherron 1989, 203). To accelerate the rate at which this change of image takes place, those who lead libraries and those who work within them must integrate their organizations into the institutions they serve.

LIBRARY DIRECTORS AS CAMPUS LEADERS

Those who lead libraries must establish themselves as academic leaders on campus, leaders who understand campus culture, understand and appreciate the mission and program of the university, and are always willing to contribute their energy, expertise, and ideas to the general well-being of the campus. "With the growing complexity of today's interconnected higher education environment, academic librarians can no longer afford to confine their leadership to the library" (Mech 1996, 345). Effective leadership in this context is distinguished by a vision that considers the "big picture," that focuses the energy and human possibilities of the library, those who work within it, and its other resources on areas that concern the larger university. To accomplish this, the university librarian must gain the trust of those who make decisions for the campus in order for the library to contribute to the process and must work with others in the library to constantly renew, modify, and/or redefine the values and goals in the libraries so that they stay within the changing priorities of the institution (Wilcox and Ebbs 1992, 27–28).

One of the key elements of this effort is the need to integrate the library program into the teaching and research efforts of the university. Anne Wood-sworth and her associates (1989) surmised that "the administration of the university will assume a corporate decision-making approach or attitude, expecting more accountability from divisions and units in the institution" (p. 135). If this is so, it is reasonable to expect that the success of agencies like the library that are charged with supporting teaching and research will be called upon to relate to these activities. To accomplish this, the library director must be prepared to function in a campus political environment that has been developed to support the efforts of teaching faculty and that is dominated by them. A director's leadership must constantly emphasize the need to support their efforts and to ensure that they understand what is required to continue that support (Carrigan 1993). Universities as institutions are controlled by a dominant profession, the teacher/researcher, and success requires that librarians understand that the faculty will set the rules for the campus.

The library director will have to assume new roles that may not be entirely comfortable. In some cases, they will be formalized by changing the formal structure of the library. But, as often as not, the changes that take place will begin as informal moves designed to redefine the place of the librarian in the decision-making process. To be successful, the library director must learn to operate under rules that discount hierarchy and move beyond the librarians' technical expertise (Engle 1990). Universities must give first preference to the teaching faculty's activities, because they do the things upon which the reputation of the institution rests and that generate income for the university. Their activities generate student credit hours, retain students, provide quality instruction, and produce research. While the university also assigns value to other activities on campus like the quality of student life, parking, the physical plant, the personal safety of students and faculty, the use of technology, accreditation, and, of course, the library—things that give it standing within the academic community and contribute to the environment—the first preference for funding will be assigned to these things if they are related to the capacity of the university to teach and do research (Birdsall 1995).

The implication of this for library leaders is clear. "If librarians feel their job is doing traditional library work and nothing else, they may not define themselves as campus leaders. If librarians ignore the fact that they are educators too, they will not take advantage of their options for wider participation" (Mech 1996, 351). The ultimate success of the library depends on the library director's capacity to associate it with these and other things that are valued by the institution. Those who lead libraries must do whatever is required to reduce the level to which the library is isolated from the classroom and the laboratory, using both formal channels of communication like dean's council and informal conversations with colleagues on campus to understand the needs of its constituents. Guy Lyle (1963) noted 35 years ago, "There seems to be a reasonable amount of evidence . . . that when the faculty speaks administrators hear and heed. The librarian's first tasks, therefore, are to identify the library with the faculty, library aims with teaching, and to transform latent faculty interest in the library into active resolve'' (p. 60).

THE LIBRARY DIRECTOR AS CHANGE AGENT

To make this association, the library director must assume the role of change agent within the university and must transform the library into an organization that facilitates institutional change while maintaining its bridges to the traditions of the academy. That person must learn to read the campus and to continually develop the role of the library as a place that will try interesting things and accomplish what is possible. Working in tandem with others on campus, the library director must be prepared to "evangelize the staff, the administration, and the campus at large in promotion of the dream" (Sherron 1989, 203). Directors must present the library as a place that is both facile at dealing with the politics of the campus and above the kind of divisions that take place between colleges and departments. The "players" on campus will always be the colleges and teaching departments, and the success of the library, working as a supporter of the teaching and research missions, will always be based on its capacity to develop campus coalitions in support of its activity. Library leaders must be scrupulously apolitical. They must understand the political climate and be able to project the idea that the library is a vital part of the information infrastructure of the campus without being perceived as an active participant. They will never have the power to dictate campus policy but must develop the kind of influence required to shape the program.

Moskowitz (1986) contends that the library director must fulfill a number of roles when working with the campus if the library is to have a vital role in the university. She contends that this person must, first, be viewed as an appropriate figurehead for the library program. This person must present a face for the library that inspires confidence in both the service posture of the library and the capacity of the library to get things done and must also serve as a liaison with other elements of the campus, bringing ideas to the library from its constituencies, making sure that those served by the library understand what it is trying to do and why, and vigilantly acting to ensure that its program meets their needs. The library director is also the person charged with monitoring the library program to see that it is using its resources well and the spokesperson who makes sure that the community appreciates library programs while, at the same time, making the library understand how their efforts support the academic community. Finally, the library director is the negotiator for the library program, the person responsible for ensuring that resources are available for the program at the appropriate time, that the goals and expectations for library programs are clearly defined, and that the programs that emerge meet user needs and expectations (Mech 1990).

REDEFINING THE LIBRARY DIRECTOR'S ROLE

These things are important, but they may not be sufficient to ensure the place of the library in a modern university. To accomplish this, those who lead the library will have to take on new and unfamiliar roles that may not be entirely comfortable. They must look to the future and carefully develop the role they will, or will want to be asked to, play in defining new information delivery systems designed to ensure that everyone on campus has appropriate access to both the information resources and the tools required to do their work (Gregorian et al. 1992). The library director must also actively seek out opportunities for collaboration with others on campus, filling holes in the university's service program, and inserting the library's influence and expertise in places where they can be used to advantage. "Computer specialists, librarians and faculty will need to forge and strengthen partnerships to permit the best use of emerging technologies" (Moran 1994, 67). The challenge is to identify opportunities for collaboration and develop an atmosphere of trust between their organizations and those with whom they are cooperating (Sherron 1989). Roles in cooperating organizations where services overlap must be defined clearly enough to provide some comfort level, because tension between these units is likely to develop. The library director and the library staff and faculty must come to understand who the key leaders for change will be on the campus and place themselves among that group. But, at the same time, they must understand that the implementation of new programs cannot, and should not, wait until a structure can be developed to support the new program. Dynamic organizations use program initiatives to define structure, not the other way around. As a result, leadership based on mutual trust will be required as organizations, like libraries, computer centers, instructional media, and other services, seek to work collaboratively with classroom faculty (Widner and Lawlor 1994). To accomplish this kind of relationship, library directors will be required to operate ethically, respecting the autonomy of their collaborators, committing to do no harm either to colleagues or the program of the university, working to benefit others in the academy, being just, and remaining faithful to commitments and confidences of colleagues (Wilcox and Ebbs 1992).

PREPARING THE LIBRARY DIRECTOR TO LEAD

To be successful in the universities that are emerging, library directors must move beyond the library to appreciate how the campus works, what the important elements of the campus culture are, and how they can participate within that culture. This is not always easy. Dale Schrag (1990) described the term "academic librarian" as an oxymoron and noted that librarians are often ill at ease in the academy with its emphasis on degrees and the academic credibility that comes with them, on specialization, and on the value placed on rigid research. He also noted that librarians exhibited little understanding of the history, development, and politics of higher education (pp. 120–135). This puts them at a disadvantage. As Helen Gater (1989) puts it, "[W]e have learned that the more individual librarians know about 'the Academy' and our local version of it, the more capable we are of an institutional perspective. The more we reflect that institutional perspective, the more credibility and value we earn as individuals and as an organization. The more credible we are, the more we are invited to participate. The more we contribute, the greater the support we receive" (p. 47). Librarians do not have to be scholars to take their place as partners to the faculty, but they do have to be scholarly people who appreciate scholarship and stand ready to support it. According to Ed Holley (1985), the best academic librarians come to the profession because they enjoy academic life, want to be a part of the learning process, have some interest in the research, and value the place of the library in learning and scholarship. Holley goes further to say that, for academic librarians to succeed, they must have:

1. A background in the history and development of higher education.
2. An appreciation for the history of scholarship and learning.
3. An understanding of how knowledge is obtained in various disciplines.
4. An ability to evaluate research findings.

Holley reinforces his point by contending that a "lack of knowledge about how our own institutions operate and what is their function in society must surely be included among guilty ignorance" (p. 464). He contends that librarians also need to know how the organizational structure works. Ignorance of the specific ways in which an institution makes decisions serves neither the administrator nor the library well, and a strong, but naive, sense of what should be done is no substitute for a reasonable idea of what will happen in a given circumstance.

Another thing that puts library leaders at a disadvantage on campus is the preoccupation of many librarians with "status." "On most campuses little thought is given to the status of librarians by anyone except the librarians" (Hoadley 1990, 35). Faculty in teaching departments tend to see themselves as engineers or English faculty or philosophers, and they tend to rank faculty by their accomplishments rather than by their academic rank. Some are more willing than others to view librarians as faculty colleagues, but, generally speaking, their judgments of individuals working in the library relate more to the service given than to the status afforded librarians within the administrative structure. There is no doubt that there are times when being a member of the faculty and having a dean for the library matter, but, in general, a continuing reemphasis of this issue is of no help. It is important for the library director to fight for salaries, benefits, entreé into the governing process, and respectful treatment for librarians, but continuing discussions of status per se can serve to trivialize other discussions of personnel matters or deflect attention from the library's mission.

"Staff members should apply their time, energy, and initiative in ways which earn them status as a by-product" (Lyle 1963, 30–31). On most campuses, meaningful status is based on accomplishments, not personnel classification.

Those who lead libraries are also limited by their lack of academic credentials. While the debate continues as to what credentials a library director should have, there is no doubt at this point that the credential of choice on a college campus is the doctorate, and anyone in a leadership position on campus who does not hold a Ph.D. is at a disadvantage. Academics understand what a doctorate stands for and relate to that. They do not necessarily know how to interpret the M.L.S. Ed Holley (1985) said some years ago, "We should note that our insistence the M.L.S. is the 'terminal degree' for librarians has not achieved wide acceptance on most campuses and, in my opinion, is likely to be even less persuasive in the future" (p. 467). This is no less true today. While one might differ about whether or not the subject content of most doctorates applies to the work of the head of a library, there can be little doubt that the degree gives a different kind of standing on campus than can be achieved in any other way.

THE LIBRARY DIRECTOR AND THE BULLY PULPIT

Tactically, the library director must use the position of head of the library as a bully pulpit and as a vantage point from which opportunities can be found for the development of the library program. A seat on the dean's council will be useful, in part because it allows the librarian to defend the interests of the library but perhaps more because it offers an opportunity to discern how the leadership of the campus works and to develop a reputation for the library. This can provide an excellent opportunity for library directors to get to know their colleagues among the deans and seek out opportunities for collaboration; make them more aware of changes in the library and more sensitive to its nuances; develop for the library a position in the university governance structure; and participate in mission-setting activities for the campus (Hoadley 1990, 31–35). It is also an excellent vehicle for gaining the confidence of the academic deans and developing within them a trust in the capacity of the library to get things done. The idea is not that the librarian must constantly dwell on the needs and programs of the library but that the person leading the library can establish a reputation as a reasonable person who can be expected to make reasonable arguments that should be considered by the campus leadership. It can also help the library director understand the values of those who make decisions on campus. In the final analysis, investments made in building relationships among the deans and vice presidents on campus are critical to the success of the library program. In fact, on some campuses, attending football games, graduation ceremonies, social events, faculty senate meetings, and the like may have more bearing on the library's capacity to influence policy and garner resources than will the generation of lengthy policy documents or lengthy discussions of library problems or programs.

THE LIBRARY PROGRAM AND LEADERSHIP

But, above all, the leadership role of the library director must be buttressed by a program that is interesting, dynamic, innovative, and especially responsive to the needs of the library's clientele. "If libraries and librarians wish to be active participants as information providers, they must continually reach out and seize opportunities to create new services, to apply new technologies, and to offer new services to clients" (Mason 1989, 169). Librarians must develop programs that will take risks rather than avoiding them. They must be constantly on the lookout for new ideas for developing their program and enhancing services. They must constantly criticize themselves in ways that will help them develop. When the information environment is moving quickly, libraries must have a bias for action, developing action plans that can be adjusted quickly to eventualities, experimenting, incorporating successful results and discarding failures as soon as it is clear they are not working, and encouraging almost a chaotic search for ways to adjust the library program to changing circumstances.

Good leaders understand the value of having creative people in the organization; recruit creative people; create an environment that encourages people to take risks and encourages staff to dream; and sets the example for those who work for them (Cluff 1989). Creative people can be difficult to manage, and, in many cases, their desire to change things can cause friction with colleagues inside and outside the library who would prefer that things remain as they are. They tend to be impatient, and sometimes this can cause anxiety. But the ideas they bring to the table can help make the library consider its future in a different way and can be invaluable as the library tries to develop new programs and forge new relationships.

All of this requires that the manager take calculated risks, and, unfortunately, this requires behaviors that are out of character for many librarians. Librarians are, as a class, conservative people who are inclined to minimize or eliminate risk whenever possible (Mason 1989, 169–170). Often they rely on lengthy processes to develop decisions that are as safe as possible. As Joanne Euster (1989) noted, librarians are, more often than not, intellectual and introspective people. They are naturally good at careful planning, thorough research, good attention to detail, and the ability to get along with other people—all qualities needed to run libraries well in a stable environment. But the environment we live in calls for a high level of tolerance for ambiguity and change, the ability to continually reassess circumstances and adjust programs and goals in a timely fashion as needed, and, above all, the ability to anticipate and plan for the future even in times of uncertainty. Developing this kind of program requires a new kind of leadership that encourages decision making at all levels of the organization, that emphasizes flexibility in program planning, and that is designed to build a program that can respond quickly to emerging needs within the university community.

CONCLUSION

The day when the campus library was a quiet haven for scholarship unchanged by time is gone forever, and the libraries that are emerging are very different from those that came before them. While they still serve, as they always have, as a bridge between information and users, the nature of that bridge continues to change. Those who lead libraries can keep up with what is happening to their organizations only if they are active in the university community. They can influence policies relating to the introduction of new information technologies onto the campus only if they are willing to insert themselves as both servants and leaders into all facets of campus life. The challenge that has been issued to the people in these positions is more uncertain and more difficult than it has ever been, forcing them to balance their allegiance to the library faculty and staff with their allegiance to the campus community, their commitment to the printed word with a new commitment to technology. But those who lead libraries have no choice but to accept the challenge. What was will soon be gone, and the library director's success in influencing what is to be will be mirrored in the strength of the library program on campus.

REFERENCES

Birdsall, D. G. 1995. "The Micro Politics of Budgeting in Universities: Lessons for Library Administrators." *Journal of Academic Librarianship* 21 (November): 427–437.

Carrigan, D. P. 1993. "The Director as Entrepreneur: Increasing Patron Benefits at a Time of Austerity." *Public Libraries* 32 (July–August): 200–203.

Cluff, E. D. 1989. "Developing the Entrepreneurial Spirit: The Director's Role." *Journal of Library Administration* 10(2–3): 185–195.

Cottam, K. M. 1989. "The Impact of the Library 'Intrapreneur' on Technology." *Library Trends* 37 (Spring): 521–531.

Engle, M. O. 1990. "Moving beyond the Library Sphere: Academic Librarians in the Larger Institution." In H. Palmer Hall and C. Byrd, eds., *The Librarian in the University: Essays on Membership in the Academic Community.* Metuchen, NJ: Scarecrow Press, pp. 9–18.

Euster, J. R. 1989. "Creativity and Leadership." *Journal of Library Administration* 10(2–3): 27–38.

Gater, H. 1989. "Creation of an Academic Library: Lessons from an Empty Slate." *Journal of Library Administration* 10(2–3): 39–48.

Gregorian, V., B. Hawkins and M. Taylor. 1992. "Integrating Information Technologies: A Research University Perspective." *Cause/Effect* 15 (Winter): 5–12.

Hoadley, I. B. 1990. "Among Friends: Involvement in Academic Collegiality." In H. Palmer Hall and C. Byrd, eds., *The Librarian in the University: Essays on Membership in the Academic Community.* Metuchen, NJ: Scarecrow Press, pp. 30–38.

Holley, E. G. 1985. "Defining the Academic Librarian." *College & Research Libraries* 46 (November): 462–468.

Lau, A. W. and C. M. Pavett. 1980. "The Nature of Managerial Work: A Comparison of Public and Private Sector Managers." *Group and Organizational Studies* 5 (December): 513–520.

Lyle, G. R. 1963. *The President, the Professor and the College Library.* New York: Wilson.

Mason, F. M. 1989. "Libraries, Entrepreneurship, and Risk." *Journal of Library Administration* 10(2–3): 169–183.

Mech, T. 1990. "Academic Library Directors: A Managerial Profile." *College & Research Libraries* 51 (September): 415–428.

———. 1996. "Leadership and the Evolution of Academic Librarianship." *Journal of Academic Librarianship* 22 (September): 345–354.

Moran, B. 1989. "The Unintended Revolution in Academic Libraries: 1939 to 1989 and Beyond." *College & Research Libraries* 50 (January): 25–41.

———. 1994. What Lies Ahead for Academic Libraries? Steps on the Way to the Virtual Library." In Delmus E. Williams et al., eds., *For the Good of the Order: Essays in Honor of Edward G. Holley.* Greenwich, CT: JAI Press, pp. 55–72.

Moskowitz, M. A. 1986. "The Managerial Roles of Academic Library Directors: The Mintzberg Model." *College & Research Libraries* 47 (September): 452–459.

Schrag, D. R. 1990. "Deflating the Oxymoron; or, Searching for a Shoe beneath the Leather and Lasts." In H. Palmer Hall and C. Byrd, eds., *The Librarian in the University: Essays on Membership in the Academic Community.* Metuchen, NJ: Scarecrow Press, pp. 123–137.

Sherron, G. T. 1989. "Encouraging the Dreamers." *Journal of Academic Librarianship* 15 (September): 202–203.

Smith, D. J. 1989. "An Examination of Higher Education: A View from the College Library." *Journal of Academic Librarianship* 15 (July): 140–146.

Teather, D. C. B. 1982. "Contemporary Universities: Characteristics and Challenges." In David C. B. Teather, ed., *Towards the Community University: Case Studies of Innovation and Community Service.* London: Kogan, pp. 15–30.

Widner, J. and A. Lawlor. 1994. "Library/Computer Center Relations: A Comprehensive State University View." *Cause/Effect* 17 (Fall): 45–46.

Wilcox, J. R. and S. L. Ebbs. 1992. *The Leadership Compass: Values and Ethics in Higher Education.* Washington, DC: ASHE.

Woodsworth, A. et al. 1989. "The Model Research Library: Planning for the Future." *Journal of Academic Librarianship* 15 (July): 132–138.

Chapter 4

Visionary Leadership

Donald E. Riggs

Why is there a dearth of articles and books on the topic of leadership in libraries? This reality was one of the reasons I assembled the first book on the topic (*Library Leadership: Visualizing the Future*, 1982). Fifteen years later we continue to find very few pieces in the literature on library leadership. Schools of library and information science continue to place more emphasis on management; very few schools offer leadership courses.

Is library leadership not important? Of course, it is important and becoming more important! Academic libraries are undergoing unprecedented changes; they are becoming more complex and continually reshaping themselves. Technology is driving most of the changes. Library staff are hungry for new direction, new values, inspiration, and articulation on what the future holds.

WHAT CONSTITUTES LEADERSHIP?

There are many definitions of "leadership." Due to the large number of characteristics constituting leadership, it cannot be easily described empirically or operationally studied. Leadership can be represented by an emotional or unconscious attitude rather than an intellectual or rational approach. This is possibly the one reason the attempt to study leadership scientifically has not provided a widely accepted body of knowledge as to what leadership is and does.

Dictionaries provide different definitions of leadership. Various verbs are used to describe leadership; they include to act, to begin, to continue, to achieve, to finish, and to lead. Taking the lead could be interpreted as assuming the point, and point could mean the end or death; thus, one can ascertain the multitude of words used to characterize "leadership." In recent years, the word "vision" has become more closely associated with leaders and leadership. "Vision," in essence, is what a library "wants to become."

MANAGERS AND LEADERS

Managers and leaders are different types of people in many ways. Both types are necessary in the effective and efficient library. Warren Bennis offers the following distinctions between managers and leaders: the manager administers, the leader innovates; the manager is a copy, the leader is an original; the manager focuses on systems and structure, the leader focuses on people; the manager relies on control, the leader inspires trust; the manager has a short-range view, the leader has a long-range perspective; the manager asks how and when, the leader asks what and why; the manager imitates, the leader originates; the manager accepts the status quo, the leader challenges it; and the manager does things right, the leader does the right things (Bennis 1989, 45).

Managers who also provide some day-to-day leadership are known as transactional managers, while the leaders who provide a compelling vision of the library's future are called transformational leaders. One should not undervalue the importance of both types of leadership. Leadership is certainly an art and has only a few characteristics of a science. Transactional leaders' roles are more determined by formal processes or expectations, while transformational leadership brings them into the picture. Another way of describing this difference is to say that transactional leadership is more evolutionary, while transformational leadership is more revolutionary.

WHY VISIONARY LEADERSHIP?

Aforementioned, there are different types of leadership, and it follows that there are different types of leaders. Leaders who get great results are those who have a vision. Burt Nanus, in his classic *Visionary Leadership: Creating a Compelling Sense of Direction for Your Organization* (1992, 7), defines "vision" as a realistic, credible, attractive future for an organization. Vision deals with the future; it is where tomorrow begins. A vision expresses what a group that shares the vision will be creating. The right vision for a library energizes the staff to jump-start the future by calling forth the skills, talents, and resources necessary to make it happen. The right vision for the future of the library moves the staff to action. Because of their action, the library evolves and makes progress in a strategic direction. The right vision bridges the library's present with its future, it establishes a standard of excellence, and it can serve as a beacon in empowering the staff. Moreover, the right vision transcends the library's status quo.

For effective library leadership to exist, there must be a vision. For leadership to succeed, it needs form and function, process and purpose, and that all begins with a clearly articulated vision of the future of the library. This is the essence of visionary leadership.

Academic libraries must do better in setting the proper direction for the future. However, setting this important direction cannot be treated as "business as usual." The new direction must be strategic, and, just as importantly, it must be compelling. There has to be a commitment on the part of the library's leadership to find the resources to make the strategic and compelling direction happen. Foresight and insight are both required to move the library into the new century. Visionary leadership will bring clarity to the library's purpose, a renewed spirit of excitement to the staff's daily work, pride in the quality of service delivered, an environment fostering risk taking, and a shared sense of progress.

CONDITIONAL LEADERSHIP AND VISION

The well-worn phrase that expresses that someone was the right person at the right time to provide leadership for the library is as true today as it was yesterday. Specific human leadership characteristics and certain strategic visions that were judged important for the library five years ago may be quite inappropriate for the library today or tomorrow. In short, an excellent leader for the library today may not be such a good leader tomorrow.

It can be argued that academic libraries require certain basic leadership skills (e.g., creativity, entrepreneurship) regardless of changing conditions. However, academic libraries are no different from other organizations; the right person at the right time is necessary to provide the right vision for the given library. Unfortunately, library leadership is situational. The success of a library leader is contingent on many factors, including skills that match the library's needs at a particular time. A leader perceived as successful in one library environment may not be successful in another library setting. However, one should not jump to the conclusion that a visionary leader cannot grow, realize shared goals and values, and transform the library regardless of the given environment.

VALUES AND VISION

Values are those things we believe in, work and live for, and entrust to others. Dignity, trust, respect, and honesty are examples of straightforward values. In libraries and the evolving information environment, we also value protection of intellectual property, privacy of information and users, interoperability standards, security of information, and universal access to information. Values may be described as abstract ideas that influence thinking, planning, action, and, finally, vision in the library. Values are known for providing the context within which library issues are identified, and alternative actions are assessed.

While developing the library's long-term vision, library leaders must understand and appreciate the library's current values. Furthermore, as the information environment transforms, greater attention must be paid to the changing values of the library. Examples of issues that must be resolved with values in mind include charging for value-added services (e.g., information provided to users on a shorter than normal time cycle), access to additional resources for a fee, and the information-rich (the "haves") and the information-poor (the "have-nots"). Values in academic libraries are deeply rooted and could be perceived as obstacles in the path of the new vision. The ideal environment would include retaining those values that the library honors and infusing new values into the library that will cradle better service for students, faculty, and staff.

STRATEGIC PLANNING AND VISION

Not only is it important to create the vision for library leadership, but the vision must be followed and stabilized by a systematic and thoughtful planning process. Management of profit and not-for-profit organizations has found one of the best planning techniques to be strategic planning. Unlike traditional planning, which normally results in a neatly bound document collecting dust on a shelf, strategic planning is more dynamic with annual updates and primary emphasis on strategies (courses of action designed to achieve goals and objectives). Strategic planning is never completed; it is evolving, is flexible enough to include new ideas or approaches, and requires much work to keep it current and effective. It is complex, time-consuming, intellectually driven, based on assumptions and environmental factors (internally and externally), creative, and ongoing.

The library director is the chief strategist of the library, and this responsibility must not be delegated to a planning committee. The library's visionary leadership will become reality only if the library director makes a commitment to follow strategic planning principles. The time involved in the planning process should not be taken lightly. Even though strategic planning is not designed to emphasize budgetary matters, new strategic planning initiatives will require new or intellectual resources. Library leadership has to take the fiscal responsibility in strategic planning seriously and vigorously seek out the resources necessary to implement the priorities of the strategic plan. If new funds cannot be obtained, or if it is impossible to redeploy resources, then it may be better for the library not to engage in strategic planning. A consultant may be helpful in getting the planning process off the ground, but the library staff should do most of the planning activities. Since strategic planning forces the library to look continually at its strengths, weaknesses, opportunities, and the threats to its mission, some libraries may find the planning process more useful than the products and services realized from the plan.

A strategic plan of any significance will contain, at least, the following components: vision statement, mission statement, goals, objectives, strategies, timelines, responsibility delineation, resources required, and annual assessments.

Vision is the first component of strategic planning. The vision statement describes what the library wants to become in the future. The vision statement of the strategic plan is broad and general and should not project beyond 10 years into the future. Twenty-year vision statements are essentially worthless since the information environment is changing so rapidly. Owing to the speed of change, even 10-year projections are questionable. Anyone can predict anything as long as one does not have to make the prediction happen. One of the better ways to make the library's future happen is through effective strategic planning. However, it should be kept in mind that poor planning is worse than no planning at all.

The mission statement explains briefly what business the library is in; in other words, what are the library's aims and purposes? Naturally, to support the institution's curriculum, instruction and research are common elements found in an academic library's mission. The mission statement is more specific than the vision statement, but it still serves as an umbrella statement focusing on broad intentions.

Following the mission statement are the goals, objectives, and strategies. Goals bring more focus than the mission statement; they also bring a sense of order and priority to visionary leadership. They specify declarations of the library's purpose, give the library direction, and set forth long-range library priorities. Goals must be capable of being converted into specific, measurable objectives. Unlike goals, objectives are short-term, precise, measurable, and verifiable and are usually stated in terms of a particular result that will be accomplished by a specific date. Objectives could be described as the landmarks and milestones that mark the path toward the library's goal(s). A library's strategy formulation process is not complete until the objectives have been verified with the strategies. Strategy is the primary component of strategic planning that plays a significant role in the realization of visionary leadership. A strategy entails an explanation of what means (courses of action) will be used to achieve goals and objectives. Strategy is the cat's meow of strategic planning. The visionary library leader works with strategies, while the library manager focuses more on tactics (short-range operational activities).

Formulation and implementation of the right strategies are a major key to the library's success. Dynamic leadership is necessary to ensure that the library's strategies possess a magnetic and adhesive quality. The process of strategy formulation is never-ending. The director's role is to set the stage for understanding strategy formation, involving the appropriate staff in the process, providing motivation, mediating conflicts, fostering a healthy environment whereby strategies can be challenged and eventually refined, and ensuring an orderly integration of change. An example of a visionary leader doing the "right things" is selecting the correct strategy from several alternative strategies. A leader must generate alternative strategies for each goal and objective. Creating novel strategies and envisioning how they can be realized are a good example of how visionary leadership can be executed.

A specific timetable should be established for each strategy. The timeline should be reasonable and doable. It is quite common to discover that the staff wants to achieve most of the strategies within the first three years. The chief strategist (the director) has to make sure the staff does not overcommit itself in trying to accomplish too many strategies in a short time span. It is recommended that a responsibility chart be established to depict who is responsible for specific tasks necessary for achieving strategies. Also, resources must be identified (e.g., new resources or reallocation of existing resources). It is foolish to think that an effective strategic planning process will evolve without a commitment of resources. Targeting resources for new initiatives is a good opportunity to exercise visionary leadership. Perhaps the vision will call for "innovation by substitution" of funds for existing programs for new programs.

Another key component of the strategic plan is the annual assessment. During the review of the plan and the planning process, one needs to ask, What went right, and what went wrong? Strategies achieved should be rolled off the strategic plan, and new strategies should be added. The process of reviewing and removing completed strategies and adding new strategies for each respective objective should be done at least annually. Some strategies may need to be merged with other strategies. Managers, rather than leaders, can conduct the annual assessment and articulate its results to the library leaders responsible for envisioning and making the library's future happen.

DREAMS, IDEOLOGY, AND VISION

Library leaders should engage more in dreaming and fantasizing about the future. Too often, leaders of academic libraries view the future as being rather bleak, one that will be determined primarily by the availability of new financial resources. Rather than being pessimistic about the days that are yet to come, library leaders should create a construct, a mental image, of what their respective libraries should become. Leaders should learn to "live their visions." Martin Luther King, Jr., was an example of a leader who lived his vision ("I have a dream") and provided a model for others in the civil rights movement. We should discover and practice new ways of seeing our libraries. Thus, the challenge is to become skilled in the "art of seeing" and in the "art of reading" the future of libraries. Dreams, ideas, and even metaphors may be helpful in developing the mental model of the twenty-first-century library.

Over the years, the meaning of "ideology" has become somewhat ambiguous and debased. In the 1790s, French leaders advocated that "ideology" should advance the new "science of ideas." Ideology represents a significant strategy of thinking and of leadership, and it needs to be salvaged. The crucial quality of ideology is that it combines both *what* one believes and *how* one came to hold certain beliefs. It provides the lenses through which one sees the world, and it brings a semblance of order to the process of sorting out the stream of phenomena that one perceives (Burns 1978, 249).

Is there a need for a revised ideology in academic libraries? Perhaps there is. Considering the unprecedented rate of change in academic libraries, now is a good time for a metamorphosis in their ideology. The big challenge facing us is how much of the traditional practices of academic libraries can be discontinued in order to bring forth a new way of doing things. This concept is brought to reality when library leaders ask themselves one basic question, How much of what we are currently doing can be discontinued? For several reasons (e.g., faculty expectations), academic libraries are not known for discontinuing "old, traditional things" in order to redeploy funds for "new, value-added things." Visionary leadership is necessary to explain the difference between those who cling to the older view and those striving for new perspectives. Transformational, visionary library leaders are faced with the full congruence of the key elements of ideology: cognition, conflict, consciousness, value, and purpose.

THE PSYCHOLOGIST AND THE SELF-DIRECTED

The visionary library leader has many of the characteristics of a practical psychologist and a self-directed person. Working with the various library constituents, the leader has to build consensus in order to consolidate the interrelated goals in the strategic plan. There has to be a certain degree of appeal to the psychological conditions of the library's staff, faculty, administrators, users, and external supporters. In this context, the leader has to be the primary initiator of new ventures and the executor of the people's wishes. The leader also must possess the ability to feel the character and direction of the various constituents and to make them more conscious of the consensus, thereby generating a sense of concerted power.

Today, for several reasons, there appears to be a fever for impersonalizing leadership. Is there a vitriolic reaction to the "great librarian" theory? Is there a feeling of antiheroic when we think of leadership? These questions do not have easy answers; perhaps we can say that "the answers are blowing in the wind." However, today, there is a growing emphasis on having a multitude of leaders in the library, not "one library leader." Is this the better approach for moving an academic library forward in a revolutionary manner, or is it better to expect "group leadership" to provide an evolutionary transformation of the library?

Be it in group leadership or in an individual leader, there has to be a degree of self-direction. Leaders must have a high level of confidence, an unalterable belief in the vision of the library, and a "bulldog" determination. Self-discipline has to be in abundance. Self-direction will require "walking the talk" in specific areas (e.g., cultural diversity among the library staff). Leaders must have a rare and singular measure of the library's values and should reflect a sensitivity in spheres where others in the library are indifferent. Self-directed leaders must establish and maintain the highest standards and be the library's norms and values creator. Indeed, this is a high calling!

MORE THAN AN ORATOR

It is a given that leaders are expected to be good communicators. The vision of the library can be communicated in a variety of ways (e.g., at the state of the library address, press releases, annual reports, videotape presentations). It is very important that the entire library staff and various constituents receive the library's vision in some form of communiqué.

In the communication process, leaders have the responsibility to share their vision of the library's future in as honest, direct, enthusiastic, and exciting a way as possible. The library staff deserves to feel positive, optimistic, supported, encouraged, and even inspired about the future. Thus, the importance of excellent communication should never be de-emphasized.

Communication takes place through various avenues. One does not have to be a great orator to be an effective communicator. It is well known that some library leaders can present the vision in colorful spoken words. However, one or two effective speeches per year about the vision of the library will not suffice. The leader has to "walk and talk the vision" throughout the year. Meeting with library departments, regular meetings with the staff, and talking with ad hoc groups and individuals in informal settings are examples of ways to communicate. There has to be an insistence on a fair amount of informality in the library's communication process. However, the intensity of communication is unmistakable in the transforming library.

CREDIBILITY, RESULTS ORIENTATION, AND VISION

Somewhat like our expectation of leadership being much more than electrifying oration, we want leadership to be credible, and we expect results. These expectations are reasonable and honorable. On the contrary, we do not expect leaders to get sucked into spending all of their time on the important, but stifling and mundane, tasks of organizational maintenance. Leadership involves looking forward and inward. In addition to having an effective vision in place, leaders must insist on the highest quality of performance and the employment and retention of the best staff.

Funding sources for libraries are insisting on more accountability and improved results. Notwithstanding the difficulty to measure the effectiveness of some library work, library leaders must give high priority to the development of means for assessing the performance of services. Accountability and credibility tend to go hand in hand toward realizing the library's vision. The library leader must seek out the truth and learn how to filter the unwieldy flow of information into coherent patterns. One of the biggest challenges of the leader is getting the truth. What works best for the users being served now and in the future?

One of the important roles of the leader is to perpetuate a measure of creativity in the library staff. Through creativity, one would hope that new value-added services and products will result. Better results should also be a by-product of an environment that encourages calculated risk taking. All too often the library staff function as "servants of what is" rather than "shapers of what might be." If visionary leadership does not exist in a library, one should hope for no more than the staff's becoming trained prisoners of the system (i.e., doing the day-to-day, routine functions). Productivity will likely remain stable; consequently, without that uplifting and credible vision, the annual results from the staff will not change dramatically.

FOLLOWERSHIP AND INTERDEPENDENCE

Why is it that so many of the books and articles written on leadership in general do not mention the followers? Can there be leadership without followership? Authors of pieces on leadership should ask themselves these types of questions. Followership of some nature has to exist before there is leadership. Leadership over human beings is normally exercised when persons with certain motives and purposes mobilize, in competition or conflict with others, institutional, political, psychological, and other resources to arouse, engage, and satisfy the motives of followers (Burns 1978, 1).

In reaching the stated vision, the library leader has to be a social architect who studies and shapes what is called the "culture of work"—those intangibles that are so difficult to discern but are very important in governing the way the library staff act, the values and norms that are subtly transmitted to individuals and groups and that tend to create bonding. The loyalty and support of subordinates must be obtained before the effective leader attempts to implement the vision of the future. Pride and sense of accomplishment that come from striving for, and achieving, the library's vision and concerted goals are the fuel that runs successful libraries. Library staff members want to be part of a winning team. Well-led followers feel useful, important, and part of a worthwhile endeavor. The library staff will not be motivated by failure; people are motivated by achievement and recognition.

The relationship between leaders and followers has to be one of strong, effective interdependence. It is easy to fall into thinking that leaders belong to one category and followers in quite a different category. Library leaders are almost never in charge as they are perceived to be, and followers (the library staff) are almost never as submissive as one might imagine. Influence flows both ways. There is probably more evidence of this type of democracy at work in academic libraries than other types of libraries. Academic freedom and faculty status are the primary factors determining this difference. The shared governance and interdependence between leaders and followers in academic libraries are a commendable situation. The two-way relationship in the interdependent environment encourages support ("buy in") of concerted goals and the envisioned future. Trust will be surely be an invaluable gain in a close leader–follower relationship. Trust is the glue that holds the entire library together, but if it dissolves, the capacity of the library to function effectively is seriously impaired.

When there is an effective interdependence between leaders and followers, the shared vision, norms, values, expectations, and purposes result in an empowerment that is critically needed in today's and tomorrow's library. However, in a visionary leadership capacity, leaders cannot abdicate their responsibility of calling the final shots on how power is to be used in bringing forth the library of the future. If there is too much dispersion of power (e.g., breaking it up, spreading it around), there could be the serious consequence of not getting anything done. Power has to lodge somewhere in the library. In a library without a vision, where should power lodge?

THE LIBRARY AS A LEARNING ORGANIZATION

The rapidly accelerating use of technology in academic libraries has had a profound impact on how these libraries do their business. Greater changes are in store, and these changes, resulting from technological advancements, will continue to influence the library staff's work. Within the near future, there will be dramatic changes in how users get the information they need, and this transformation will have a direct bearing on the library staff. Creativity, innovation, and entrepreneurship will become more common practices in the daily work of the academic librarian.

Considering all of these projected modifications, what can library leadership do to prepare libraries for this significant transformation? First, greater emphasis has to be given to the library's vision. What does the library really want to become? Second, the library has to be conceptualized as a learning organization. The learning organization construct would provide the means for the library staff to keep current with advancements in technology and new service delivery models, engage in creative approaches for performing work, and embrace change as an opportunity to offer improved service. In a library professing to be a learning organization, change simply cannot be managed; it must be led. Investment in the learning activities of the library staff will pay many dividends. Tomorrow's library staff will require an environment where they can think, exchange ideas, modify their work behavior, extend their knowledge and insights, reflect, and act. Visionary leadership should go hand in glove with the concepts and practices of the learning organization.

CONCLUSION

What an exciting time to work in academic libraries! The future looks extremely bright for academic librarianship. The value of librarians to the academic enterprise is higher now than ever before in the history of higher education.

However, we must place the development of the theme of ''visionary leadership'' in high gear. The twenty-first-century library demands visionary leadership. It cannot function without it. Without a sense of urgency for action, a realistic and credible long-term plan, and the actual development of a compelling vision for the library's future, the academic library is a viable candidate for self-destruction. In sum, visionary leadership has become indispensable for renewing and saving academic libraries.

> Where there is no vision, the people perish.
>
> —Proverbs 29:18

REFERENCES

Bennis, Warren. 1989. *On Becoming a Leader.* Reading, MA: Addison-Wesley.

Burns, James MacGregor. 1978. *Leadership.* New York: Harper & Row.

Nanus, Burt. 1992. *Visionary Leadership: Creating a Compelling Sense of Direction for Your Organization.* San Francisco: Jossey-Bass.

Riggs, Donald E. 1982. ''Library Leadership: Visualizing the Future.'' In Edward Shaw, ed., *The Courage to Fail.* Phoenix, AZ: Oryx, pp. 53–65.

Chapter 5

A New Paradigm of Leader Effectiveness for Academic Libraries: An Empirical Study of the Bass (1985) Model of Transformational Leadership

Rosie L. Albritton

INTRODUCTION

Transformational leaders are needed in academic libraries to help encourage librarians and other staff to move toward individual renewal and organizational revitalization. As technological and societal changes continue to affect librarianship, higher education, and the nature of library services in academic libraries, there is a corresponding need for leaders with vision and energy to foster the development of new paradigms for libraries. To develop leadership potential in future library administrators and to promote the success of incumbents, it is necessary to determine leadership effectiveness and its relationship to organizational outcomes in academic libraries. Very little research has been done on leadership in librarianship.

Transformational leadership, as defined by Burns (1978) and Bass (1985a), represents an important addition to previous conceptualizations of leadership. The purpose of this study was to determine whether or not perceptions of transformational leadership were present in medium-sized university libraries.

In 1985, Bernard Bass proposed a new model of leadership, based on the work of James M. Burns (1978), in which he described leaders as transformational or transactional. Bass theorized that a certain kind of leader is capable of inspiring subordinates to heights they never intended to achieve. He referred to these leaders as transformational. The transactional leader, on the other hand, is

Figure 5.1
Transformational versus Transactional Leadership

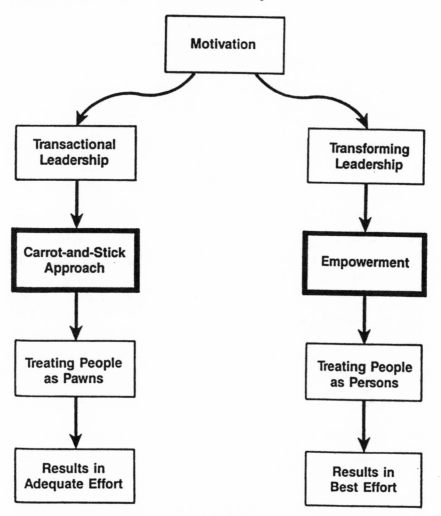

rooted in two-way influence: a social exchange in which the leader gives something and gets something in return, as illustrated in Figure 5.1.

Bass (1985a) stated that transactional leaders recognize what subordinates want to derive from their work and provide appropriate rewards for expected performance, that is, respond to subordinates' immediate self-interest (p. 11). He described transformational leaders as (1) motivating subordinates to do more than they ever expected to do by raising their level of awareness and consciousness about the importance and value of reaching designated outcomes; (2) en-

Figure 5.2
Transformational versus Transactional Leadership Model: Seven Factors as
Measured by the Bass MLQ

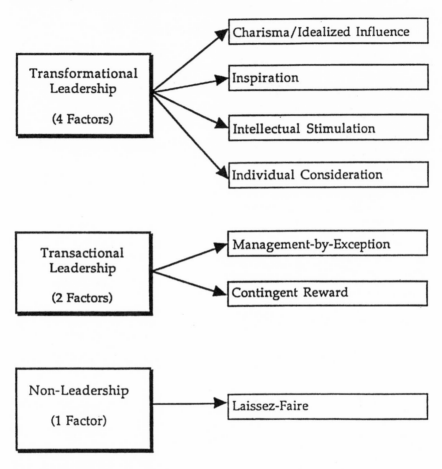

couraging subordinates to transcend their own self-interest for the sake of the organization; and (3) altering subordinates' need levels on Maslow's hierarchy or expanding their portfolio on needs and wants (p. 20). "The transactional leader works within the organizational culture as it exists; the transformational leader changes the organizational culture." (Bass 1985a, 24).

Burns (1978) identified these two types in the field of political leadership, and Bass applied the concepts to organizational management. He identified four factors of transformational leadership (charisma, inspiration, individualized consideration, and intellectual stimulation), two factors of transactional leadership (contingent reward and management-by-exception), and one factor of nonleadership (laissez-faire), as shown in Figure 5.2, and defined them as follows:

Transformational Leadership Factors:

Idealized Influence (Charisma)—Leader has a vision and a sense of mission. Gains respect, trust, and confidence. Acquires a strong individual identification from followers.

Inspirational—Leader gives pep talks, increases optimism and enthusiasm, and communicates his or her vision with fluency and confidence.

Intellectual Stimulation—Leader actively encourages a new look at old methods, fosters creativity, and stresses the use of intelligence. Provokes rethinking and reexamination of assumptions and contexts on which previous assessments of possibilities, capabilities, strategies, and goals were based.

Individualized Consideration—Leader gives personal attention to all members, making each individual feel valued and each individual's contribution important. Coaches, advises, and provides feedback in ways easiest for each group member to accept, understand, and use for personal development.

Transactional Leadership Factors:

Contingent Reward—Contracts exchange of rewards for effort and agreed-upon levels of performance. Gives individuals a clear understanding of what is expected of them.

Management-by-Exception—Intervenes only if standards are not met or if something goes wrong.

Laissez-Faire (Nonleadership Factor):

Indicates the absence of leadership, the avoidance of intervention, or both. There are generally neither transactions nor agreements with followers. Decisions are often delayed; feedback, rewards, and involvement are absent; and there is not an attempt to motivate the followers or to recognize and satisfy their needs. Leader is uninvolved, withdraws when needed, reluctant to take a responsible stand; believes the best leadership is the least leadership (Bass and Avolio 1990b).

Statement of Problem

The theoretical constructs presented by Bass and his colleagues (Bass and Avolio 1990a) provide a model of organizational leadership that explains differences in outstanding and ordinary leadership. These earlier research findings indicate that transformational and transactional leadership are related to organizational outcomes such as effectiveness, satisfaction, and extra effort of subordinates. However, transformational factors seem to have incremental effects on these outcomes, above and beyond those of transactional factors, suggesting that differences in transactional and transformational leadership may also differentiate between outstanding and ordinary leaders.

Although the transformational model has not been tested in libraries, it has potential for academic library management. The model provides a systematic approach for exploring leadership behavior as a means of enhancing the management of libraries and a conceptual link for the further explanation and development of approaches to the study of organizational effectiveness.

Exactly how and to what degree a leader influences the organization have been the subject of some research and much speculation. Even though the problem is yet to be resolved, leadership is a key element in understanding the functioning of organizations.

Purpose of Study

The purpose of this research was to increase our knowledge of leadership development and leadership processes in university libraries. The outcomes of this study could ultimately influence how library administrators and managers facilitate the improvement of library organizational effectiveness. Toward that end, this study tested the transformational versus transactional model to determine whether or not perceptions of transformational leadership were present in medium-sized university libraries and if these perceptions were related to leadership outcomes. Transformational leadership was tested for any incremental effect in satisfaction, effectiveness, and extra effort of subordinates beyond that of transactional leadership. The study also examined the influence of selected demographics on respondents' perceptions of leadership behavior and effectiveness outcomes.

While the primary intention was to test the transformational and transactional leadership model, there are secondary benefits to be gained from this research. These benefits include (1) an interdisciplinary approach to studying leadership and management in libraries and (2) the further validation of the Multifactor Leadership Questionnaire (MLQ) instrument and its usefulness for assessing leader and follower behavior in nonprofit/public sector organizations, most specifically in academic libraries.

Research Questions and Hypotheses

The research questions addressed in this study were:

1. Will the transformational versus transactional leadership model of organizational leadership appear in university libraries in configurations similar to those found in other formal organizations?
2. Will perceptions of transformational leadership be more highly correlated than transactional leadership with perceptions of subordinates' extra effort, satisfaction with leader, and perceived leadership effectiveness?

Based on the cited research of the Bass transformational leadership model and the research questions stated before, the following hypotheses were derived and tested.

Hypothesis 1

The transformational versus transactional model of leadership will appear in university libraries in configurations similar to those found in other formal organizations as follows: four transformational factors (charisma, inspiration, intellectual stimulation, and individual consideration) and two transactional factors (contingent reward and management-by-exception).

Hypothesis 2

Transformational leadership factors as perceived by the library sample will be more highly correlated than transactional leadership factors with the three "outcome" measures: extra effort of subordinates, satisfaction with leader, and leadership effectiveness.

SCOPE AND LIMITATIONS OF THE STUDY

The primary theoretical limitation of the study was the restriction of the concept of leadership to that found in formal organizations. A possible limitation is the fact the philosophical and historical positions of the libraries studied were not examined. These positions may influence leadership styles and perceptions of effectiveness. It must be noted that the results of other, similar studies weighed heavily in confirming the study's findings. The data represent conditions as they existed in the libraries only at the time of the survey.

Assumptions Underlying the Study

1. Transformational and transactional leadership are defined as distinct; therefore, since they are conceptually different, they have the potential for having different impacts on perceived leader behavior and effectiveness.

2. Since change is an implicit goal of transformational leadership, the assumption that organizational change is desirable is implicit.

3. Perceptions of the respondents are useful measures of both leadership behavior and the presumed outcomes.

4. Samples will be assumed to be reflective of their constituencies in university libraries at large.

5. The respondents will respond truthfully and accurately to the questions and items presented in the measurement instrument.

6. Members of the internal dominant coalition and their subordinates in each library will have sufficient knowledge to make meaningful judgments regarding leadership behavior of the directors and the corresponding effectiveness outcomes.

METHODOLOGY

The research was designed as a correlational (ex post facto) field study, and the data were collected within the existing organizations by using survey research methodology. In correlational research, the intent is to determine the degree to which various measures are related to one another.

Survey Instrument

The instrument used to assess perceptions of transformational and transactional leadership behavior was the Multifactor Leadership Questionnaire—5R (MLQ) (Bass and Avolio 1990b). The MLQ was developed by Bass to quantitatively assess the six constructs of the transformational versus transactional model. Exhaustive research since the early 1980s has proven the MLQ to be a reliable and valid instrument. There is substantial support for the construct validity of the theoretically and empirically based factors that constitute the MLQ. The scales are internally consistent with good test–retest reliability over six-month intervals (Bass and Avolio 1990b).

The questionnaire contains 80 items, 70 of which require a rating-scale response. Individuals completing the MLQ Rater Form evaluate how frequently, or to what degree, they have observed their leader engage in a specific behavior. Leaders completing the MLQ Self-Rating Form similarly evaluate how frequently, or to what degree, they believe they engage in the same types of leadership behavior toward their supervisees.

A five-point, ratio-based rating scale for rating the frequency of observed leader behaviors is used for both the leader and the follower forms of the questionnaire. The five response choices ranged from "frequently, if not always" to "not at all." Embedded in the questionnaire are items for each of the seven factor subscales. Four of these factor subscales (charisma, individualized consideration, intellectual stimulation, and inspiration) are measures of transformational leadership. Two of the factor subscales (contingent reward and management-by-exception) measure transactional leadership. A seventh factor (laissez-faire) is considered to measure nonleadership.

Respondents were asked also to give biographical and demographic information.

Sample

Subjects

University library directors, members of their management teams, and other library staff were randomly selected from medium-sized U.S. libraries holding membership in the Association of College and Research Libraries (ACRL) and the Association of Research Libraries (ARL). The choice of medium-sized university library settings was the researchers' preference, due to extensive experience and educational background in these libraries as an administrator, management intern, and research investigator. The *ACRL University Library Statistics: 1987–88* (ACRL 1989) and the *ARL Statistics: 1989–90* (ARL 1990) were used to develop a list of 104 medium-sized U.S. university libraries with a total staff size of 80 to 300 and a full-time appointed library director. Medium-sized libraries were identified by combining rank order tables for staff size from the ARL and the ACRL statistics and selecting those libraries from the bottom 50 percent of the ARL list and the top 50 percent of the ACRL table.

Sample Size and Data Collection

The sample size, the number of respondents (cases) available for this study for generating results from the application of statistical procedures (i.e., descriptive correlations, multiple regressions, and factor analyses), was considered acceptable. Pilot data and the literature review on the MLQ and the transformational leadership model were used to estimate the range of correlations (r), multiple correlations (R), and coefficients of determination (Rsq).

Pilot study data indicated a volunteer acceptance rate of approximately 35 percent. Applying proportional stratified random sampling to the sampling frame of 104 medium-sized libraries, letters and consent forms inviting participation in the study were sent to 90 library directors. Ninety letters of invitation were mailed to obtain as close to 30 directors as possible. The characteristics of these libraries are shown in Table 5.1.

Twenty-three directors agreed to have their libraries participate. From each of the 23 lists of library staff, 6 were randomly selected to evaluate leadership behavior and organizational effectiveness. The questionnaires were mailed along with a cover letter to the 23 directors and 138 library staff reporting to them (a total of 161 potential cases). Of the 161 questionnaires distributed, 146 (91 percent) were returned. The 23 libraries in the sample provided responses from 146 individuals, well within the acceptable sample size range required for the quantitative data analysis needed for testing the study's hypotheses. Table 5.2 indicates the characteristics of the 23 libraries in the sample. Since library directors were volunteers, there is a potential for bias in that part of the sample; furthermore, the possibility of reluctance to answer questions on the part of the subordinates about one's superior might have inhibited certain portions of the potential subordinate sample from participation.

Analysis of Data

The Multifactor Leadership Questionnaire was computer-scored by the Consulting Psychologists Press, Palo Alto, California. Summary reports, leadership profiles, descriptive data for each library site, and a floppy diskette containing all responses were returned to the researcher. Multiple regression models were used to determine the incremental contribution of transformational leadership above that of transactional leadership, to predict extra effort, satisfaction, and effectiveness in university library settings. Selected "background" or "status" variables (type of respondent-self or rater; respondents' institutional support—private or state-funded; respondents' library governance style—faculty status or

Table 5.1
Profile of 90 University Libraries Invited to Participate in the Study*

Campus Data:

Enrollment:
Total Full-Time**	3,300 - 22,800
Total FTE (Part-Time)**	360 - 18,000
Graduate Full-Time	300 - 5,500
Graduate FTE (Part-Time)	20 - 7,400

Faculty:	300 - 1,600
Ph.D. Fields:	5 - 90
Ph.D.'s Awarded:	10 - 280

Library Statistics:

Volumes in Library:	470,000 - 3,100,000
Current Serials (Total):	4,000 - 26,000
Professional Staff (FTE):	20 - 90
Non-Professional Staff (FTE):	30 - 150
Total Staff:	80 - 300

*All data reported in this profile are estimates, as a result of rounding statistics reported to ACRL or ARL.
**Includes both undergraduate and graduate students.

other; respondents' library type—research or college) were added to the analyses as control variables. Descriptive statistics were calculated for questionnaire items and demographic data from the instrument. Factor analysis and principal component analysis were applied to the MLQ to confirm the presence of the leadership model. The data were entered into SPSS-X mainframe computer statistical analysis programs to determine associations between variables, that is, correlations, multiple regressions, means tables, and ANOVA (Norusis 1990).

RESULTS

Both hypotheses concerning the perceptions of transformational and transactional leadership by library directors and their staff in medium-sized university libraries were supported.

Hypothesis 1

The university libraries in this study displayed perceptions of transformational and transactional leadership behaviors similar to those of the Bass model and

Table 5.2
Profile of 23 Participating University Libraries*

<u>Campus Data:</u>

Enrollment:	
Total Full-Time**	3,300 - 22,100
Total FTE (Part-Time)**	450 - 14,000
Graduate Full-Time	700 - 4,800
Graduate FTE (Part-Time)	150 - 5,600
Faculty:	300 - 1,600
Ph.D. Fields:	10 - 80
Ph.D.'s Awarded:	20 - 250

<u>Library Statistics:</u>

Volumes in Library:	504,000 - 2,300,000
Current Serials (Total):	4,000 - 22,800
Professional Staff (FTE):	20 - 80
Non-Professional Staff (FTE):	40 - 150
Total Staff (FTE):	100 - 300

*All data reported in this profile are estimates, as a result of rounding statistics reported to ACRL or ARL.
**Includes both undergraduate and graduate students.

other previous research. The factor analyses of the MLQ were compared with other factor analyses of the MLQ to discover whether or not similar factors could be accounted for in the library sample. Transformational and transactional leadership characteristics were confirmed and measured by six factors: idealized influence (charisma), inspiration, individualized consideration, and intellectual stimulation representing perceptions of transformational behaviors; and contingent reward and management-by-exception, representing perceptions of transactional behaviors. Factor analyses accounted for 67 percent of the common variance measuring the initial six factors extracted and represented all of the Bass transformational and transactional leadership factors, as indicated in Table 5.3. Some factor-groupings revealed slight deviations from the original Bass findings but were almost identical to results obtained by other researchers in settings similar to libraries, that is, colleges, universities, private and public secondary educational institutions.

Cronbach alphas were computed for each of the six subscales of the University Library Model that was derived from the factor analysis, to test reliability and internal consistency of the measures. With the exception of the management-by-exception scale, reliability coefficients are well within the range of .70 and

Table 5.3
MLQ Factor Analysis: 6 Factors—Initial Statistics

Principal-Components Analysis(pc)

6 Factors Extracted with Varimax Rotation:

Initial Statistics: (Factors with eigenvalues above 1.00)

Factor	Eigenvalue	% of Common Variance	Cumulative %
1	25.56	44.8	44.8
2	4.00	7.0	51.8
3	2.96	5.2	57.0
4	2.32	4.1	61.1
5	1.97	3.4	64.5
6	1.53	2.7	67.2
7	1.35	2.4	69.6
8	1.27	2.2	71.8
9	1.09	1.9	73.8
10	1.04	1.8	75.6

above (see Table 5.4). This suggests the MLQ factors, as derived from this sample, are composed of items with high internal consistency.

The factor analysis of the MLQ and the reliability coefficients of the scales derived from the factor loadings confirmed the suitability of the model and indicated perceptions of transformational as well as transactional leadership behaviors within university libraries.

Hypothesis 2

Transformational leadership behaviors (satisfaction with the leader, effectiveness of the leader, and extra effort of followers) were perceived as having more effect on leadership outcomes than did transactional leadership. Hypothesis 2 was tested by computing correlations between the leadership factors and the outcome measures and then applying hierarchical multiple regression analyses to the variables representing transformational and transactional leadership, satisfaction with leader, effectiveness of leader, and extra effort of followers. Independent variables were the transformational and transactional leadership variables; the dependent variables were the three "outcome" scales of extra

Table 5.4

Internal Consistency Reliabilities of the Scales Forming the University Library Transformational Leadership Model (Derived from the Multifactor Leadership Questionnaire)

Scale	Number of Items	Cronbach Alpha
Charisma	11	0.954
Inspiration	8	0.899
Individualized Consideration	9	0.924
Intellectual Stimulation	9	0.894
Contingent Reward	10	0.885
Management-by-Exception	10	0.474
Laissez-faire	10	0.709
Effectiveness	3	0.872
Extra-Effort	3	0.740
Satisfaction	2	0.925

(N=140)

effort, satisfaction, and effectiveness and two control variables—position of the respondent and support of institution.

The correlations of the transformational factors with the outcome measures, as indicated in Table 5.5, were strong (.634 to .869, $p > .01$), while the transactional factors are much lower. Contingent reward was .502 to .576, $p < .01$, and management-by-exception was only .023 to $-.137$, $p < .01$.

The results of the regression analysis of the MLQ leadership factors on the outcome measures are shown in Table 5.6, and indicate that transformational leadership behavior was perceived by the library sample as having more effect on the three outcome measures than did transactional leadership behavior. The transformational factors and significant incremental effects (from 28.7 percent to 43.2 percent more variance) on the predictability of extra effort, satisfaction, and effectiveness are above the effect of transactional factors. These findings suggest that perceptions of transformational leadership were associated with higher levels of performance by followers (extra effort), satisfaction with leader (satisfaction), and leadership effectiveness (effectiveness) in the university libraries.

CONCLUSIONS

The results of this study suggest that perceptions of leadership behavior (both transactional and transformational) are associated with perceptions of satisfaction with the leader, effectiveness of the leader, and amount of extra effort by

Table 5.5
Correlations of MLQ Factors with Outcome Measures

	Extra-Effort	Satisfaction	Effectiveness
Idealized Influence (Charisma)	.869**	.755**	.848**
Individual Consideration	.790**	.635**	.718**
Intellectual Stimulation	.856**	.634**	.686**
Inspirational Leadership	.838**	.709**	.829**
Contingent Reward	.576**	.516**	.502**
Management by Exception	-.032	.023	-.137

N=140   **p < .001

followers. As expected, "transformational" leadership was perceived as augmenting, or having more effect on, leadership outcomes and dimensions of organizational effectiveness than did "transactional" leadership. While these findings agree with the conclusions of Bass (1985a,b 1990) and his associates (Bass and Avolio 1990a; Hater and Bass 1988; Seltzer and Bass 1990; Waldman, Bass, and Yammarino 1990), they have further substantiated that the model may have meaning and applicability to settings other than industrial and military settings investigated by earlier studies and particularly to the academic library.

Based on the results of this study, the following conclusions may be drawn:

1. The university libraries in this study displayed perceptions of transformational and transactional leadership behaviors that are similar to the Bass (1985a) model and previous research on transformational and transactional leadership.
2. Transformational leadership behaviors (satisfaction with the leader, effectiveness of the leader, and extra effort of followers) are perceived as having more effect on leadership outcomes than did transactional leadership.
3. The background, status, and other demographic characteristics of the respondents had a strong influence on the perceived effect of transformational and transactional leadership behaviors on leadership outcomes. The background characteristics of leader versus follower affiliation with privately or state-supported institution faculty status or other governance structure for librarians at the university, and affiliation with a research or college-level library were found to have influence in this study. Group differences were significant for all four control variables in most cases.

Table 5.6
Summary of Hierarchical Multiple Regression of MLQ Factors Predictors of MLQ Outcome Measures (No Controls)

	MultR	Rsq	F(Eqn)	SigFch*
Extra-Effort				
Transactional	.597	.356	37.906	.000
Transformational	.913	.834	111.438	.000
Satisfaction				
Transactional	.516	.266	24.876	.000
Transformational	.758	.575	29.976	.000
Effectiveness				
Transactional	.573	.328	33.468	.000
Transformational	.868	.753	67.470	.000

N=140   **p <.01

Transformational Factors:
Intellectual Stimulation
Individual Consideration
Inspirational Leadership
Idealized Influence (Charisma)

Transactional Factors:
Management by Exception
Contingent Reward

This study of transformational leadership and leadership effectiveness is clearly only a beginning of research on these models in libraries, in general, and in university libraries, in particular. Recommendations and suggestions for further research:

1. Research should be conducted to further test, affirm, or expand the theoretical framework of transformational leadership in academic libraries.
2. Research should be conducted to examine possible gender differences in leadership behavior among library administrators.
3. This study could be replicated by studying different types of libraries and information centers.
4. The design of longitudinal studies should be encouraged to determine transformational

leadership and effectiveness changes in libraries in general, particularly university libraries, over time.

5. Case studies and other forms of in-depth, qualitative data collection and research methodologies should be conducted in libraries to determine similarities and differences in perceptions of transformational leadership and effectiveness and develop profiles from perspectives other than quantitative data and analyses.

The conclusions of this study are limited to the population of university libraries participating in the study and limited by the use of perceptual self-report instruments rather than direct measures. Despite these limitations, the results of the study suggest some implications for the practice of library administration and management, library education, and library human resource development. This study provides some evidence that certain factors of the transformational/transactional leadership model can, indeed, be used to enhance performance:

1. Charisma appears to be powerful in predicting satisfaction and effectiveness. This scale reflects the expression of enthusiasm, optimism, and confidence. Library leaders can be trained to develop these qualities and can be evaluated on their success in these areas.

2. Personal attention and intellectual stimulation can be taught as elements of leadership to library administrators. Since these concepts are important to the satisfaction and effectiveness of followers, individualized consideration and intellectual stimulation should be expected of library managers and encouraged by library administration. The Bass MLQ may be suitable for evaluating the extent to which library managers and administrators employ transformational leadership skills and behaviors.

3. Library administrators and leaders should be aware that rewards and contingent reinforcement may be transformational as well as transactional. They should be trained in using rewards to develop enhanced performance rather than using rewards that they control for meeting only the status quo or ordinary expectations. Academic libraries are labor-intensive organizations whose most important resource is its staff.

Efforts to develop transformational leadership require that we do more than just increase specific skills. As this study and other related research indicate, transformational leadership is not a mysterious process but a measurable construct of identifiable behaviors such as the articulation of transcendent goals, demonstration of strong self-confidence and confidence in others, setting a personal example for followers, showing high expectations for followers' performance, and the ability to communicate one's faith in one's goals. Therefore, what is needed are training and education that promote self-understanding, awareness, and appreciation of the range of potential leadership behaviors used by effective transformational and transactional leaders.

The study also suggests guidelines to library educators who seek to improve the preparation of students for managerial and administrative library positions. Better understanding of theoretical foundations of leadership and management should improve the education given to new and potential leaders. This should also be of great importance for continuing professional development.

The theoretical framework of this study focuses on the effective leadership and management of libraries. The results of this study do not necessarily mean that university libraries have the same kind of leadership as industrial or corporate organizations or that one kind of leadership is better or worse than another. Although leadership may consist of more than transformational and transactional factors, the study was designed to investigate one specific model of leadership. The study did not attempt to find one definitive strategy of leadership or of organizational effectiveness that could be universally applied to all libraries. The model investigated was theoretical and represented a conceptual framework that attempted to describe relationships between organizational constructs that were operationalized as leadership factors, leadership outcomes, and effectiveness measures. However, since the study was guided by theory and tested under real conditions, the research should be helpful in bridging the gap between practice and theory. The patterns revealed are similar to those in previous research. This suggests that libraries and other formal organizations are similar in their perceptions of leadership behaviors and descriptions of effectiveness and outcomes. The findings of this research help to increase awareness of the need to investigate leadership behaviors and their influence on organizational and leadership effectiveness.

ACKNOWLEDGMENTS

This chapter is based on the author's award-winning dissertation (ALISE Doctoral Dissertation Competition Award): "Transformational vs. Transactional Leadership in University Libraries: A Test of the Model and Its Relationship to Perceived Library Organizational Effectiveness," May 1993, Graduate School of Library and Information Science, University of Illinois, Urbana–Champaign.

This research was funded in part by the following: ACRL/ISI Doctoral Dissertation Fellowship, a University of Illinois Graduate College Dissertation Research Grant, and a University of Illinois Graduate School of Library and Information Science Reece Grant.

REFERENCES

Association of College & Research Libraries. 1989. *ACRL University Library Statistics: 1987–88*. Chicago: ALA.

Association of Research Libraries. 1990. *ARL Statistics: 1989–90*. Washington, DC: ARL.

Bass, Bernard. 1985a. *Leadership and Performance beyond Expectations*. New York: Free Press.

———. 1985b. "Leadership: Good, Better, Best." *Organizational Dynamics* 13: 26–41.

———. 1990. "From Transactional to Transformational Leadership: Learning to Share the Vision." *Organizational Dynamics* 18: 19–36.

Bass, Bernard and Bruce Avolio. 1990a. "The Implications of Transactional and Trans-
    formational Leadership for Individual, Team and Organizational Development."
    In William A. Pasmore and Richard W. Woodman, eds., *Research in Organiza-
    tional Change and Development*. Greenwich, CT: JAI Press, pp. 231–272.
————. 1990b. *Manual for the Multifactor Leadership Questionnaire*. Palo Alto, CA:
    Consulting Psychologists Press.
Burns, James M. 1978. *Leadership*. New York: Harper & Row.
Hater, James and Bernard Bass. 1988. "Superiors' Evaluations and Subordinates' Per-
    ceptions of Transformational and Transactional Leadership." *Journal of Applied
    Psychology* 73: 695–702.
Norusis, Marija. 1990. *SPSS-X Introductory Statistics Student Guide*. Chicago: SPSS.
Seltzer, Jerome and Bernard Bass. 1990. "Transformational Leadership: Beyond Initia-
    tion and Consideration." *Journal of Management* 16: 693–703.
Waldman, Edward, Bernard Bass, and Frank Yammarino. 1990. "Adding to Contingency
    Reward Behavior: The Augmenting Effect of Charismatic Leadership." *Group
    and Organizational Studies* 15: 381–394.

Part III

Leadership Roles in Nonmanagerial Settings

Chapter 6

Public Services Librarians in the Academic Community: The Imperative for Leadership

Barbara I. Dewey

INTRODUCTION

Public services librarians play critical roles in the advancement of academic library services and programs. This chapter reviews these roles and the knowledge and skills required to successfully move through what is likely to be a wide and varied career at different levels in our changing organizations. A focus on key qualities for the successful public services career reveals what is described in this chapter as "the imperative for leadership." The significance and place of leadership within the public services arena and how librarians can refine and improve their own leadership qualities are discussed within the context of previous research, practical knowledge, and current requirements articulated by the profession in recruitment efforts. Suggestions for further research and writing on the topic are addressed.

LEADERSHIP AND PUBLIC SERVICES

"Leadership" in *The New American Roget's College Thesaurus* is accompanied by the following synonyms: "guide, bellwether; director, conductor; head, commander, chief." The verb "to lead" follows with "conduct, direct; precede; open, start" (1962, 205). Which, if any, of these stately words describes the hardworking, front-line academic librarian? Most are certainly not heads of large departments supervising legions of staff. Many work in small academic communities with few librarian colleagues sharing their day-to-day activities. Others work in large research library settings serving thousands of students and faculty, along with many other librarians in the same department or work area. All, however, are challenged to carry out work activities in new learning environments comprising the intersecting worlds of print and electronic resources. Additionally, public services librarians are entering new or newly emphasized primary activities such as teaching, guiding, and providing direction in navigational and critical thinking. Increasingly, they are engaged in newly defined collaborative activities within and beyond the home institution. Essentially, public services librarians at all levels must internalize the imperative of leadership, a combination of key qualities, in order to be successful, productive, and effective workers as well as to build a truly meaningful and professional career.

In the recent past, librarians seeking careers in public services, working directly with the public, might follow specific course requirements in library school highlighting such areas as reference, information referral, bibliography, academic libraries, and collection management. In some cases, a management course was required. However, these "traditional" approaches to educating new public services librarians are being reevaluated (along with educational approaches for all types of librarians) based largely on the revolution in technological innovation, both in service delivery and in changes in the information resources themselves. The fundamental knowledge, skills, and abilities required of librarians in the academic community are changing dramatically and rapidly.

Leadership qualities and responsibilities required in what Sweeney refers to as "the post-hierarchical library" (1994, 62) include adopting a user-satisfaction approach, defining strategies, supporting a technology infrastructure, and fostering relationships and teams. He is referring to the trend of library organizations to flatten hierarchy and advance work in cross-functional teams. These qualities and responsibilities are important for all team members to exhibit. The library organization in which one works need not be flat. Libraries with more traditional organizational structures also contain many kinds of work groups and teams engaging in user-based service programs.

Leadership is also being redefined from the transactional, where expectations are specific and task-oriented, and motivation is typically related to the carrot/stick approach, to the transformational, where individuals are empowered to accomplish their best efforts. Albritton (1996) studied the relationship between perceptions of transformational leadership and perceived organizational effectiveness in academic library settings. She found that there was a perceived difference in outcomes. More importantly, her study also looks at the causal relationships between leader and others in the organization. More research needs to be accomplished examining the effect of leadership from "nonsupervisory" or "management" personnel. I believe the results of this kind of research will point to the strong influence that staff in lower to midlevels of the organization have in achieving goals, advancing programs, and improving overall quality of the work.

Changing roles of public services librarians, especially department heads, are addressed in an essay by Nofsinger and Bosch. Regarding the role of the head of the reference department, they review the importance of becoming a technology facilitator. The application of new technologies requires that "changes in reference service are taking place as librarians utilize new technologies to redefine their relationship with users while continuing to meet demands for personalized, direct service (1994, 92)." The theme or concept of operating successfully in dual environments now exists in all public service positions. Addressing the theme successfully requires hard work and willingness to step forward with ideas and strategies no matter where one's position falls in the hierarchy.

CLASH OF CULTURES IN HIGHER EDUCATION AND THE IMPERATIVE FOR LEADERSHIP

The culture of higher education provides the context and the catalyst for the leadership imperative. In fact, a clash of cultures and modern forces is in full bloom at most colleges and universities throughout the United States. What constitutes this clash, and what effect does it have on public services library work? The clash is described quite succinctly in Raelin's *The Clash of Cultures: Managers and Professionals* (Raelin 1986) as the conflict between one's allegiance to technical expertise learned as a member of a profession and expertise focused on managerial aspects of an organization. In the academy, the reverence bestowed on faculty as researchers and teachers in specialty areas was and, in some situations, still is traditionally strong and unquestioned. Today the academy exists within the increasingly sharp focus of accountability. Specifically, this accountability is focused on the ability to demonstrate institutional effectiveness and benefit to primary audiences—the student, the state (in the case of public institutions), and, to a lesser extent, the scholarly community as a whole. Participants in the higher education process are now expected to understand and apply management skills such as program planning and implementation, assessment and evaluation, and cost/benefit analysis within a more user-centered ("user" defined most often as "student") environment.

Librarians in all areas of the academic library setting are in the midst of reexamining their goals and priorities within this clash of cultures. The effective translation of goals into effective quality programs of demonstrable benefit to the academic community requires a comprehensive toolbox of leadership skills and abilities. Additionally, academic librarians at all levels must be able to integrate the cultures of the professional or academic specialist and the manager in an action-oriented fashion. Application of this integrated knowledge base "will enable new librarians to participate in the research enterprise with more acute skills and perceptions of effect" (de la Pena McCook and Gonsalves 1993, 200).

COMPETENCIES IN PUBLIC SERVICES
LIBRARIANSHIP: A BRIEF LITERATURE REVIEW

The library science literature has included, over the years, a number of articles on competencies, knowledge, skills, and abilities librarians need to acquire for a successful and productive career. One research essay notes four major core competencies needed for librarians to "focus on those value-added services that require our special expertise" and allow us "to eliminate redundant and extraneous activities." The areas include:

- ability to conceptualize information
- knowledge of internal and external information resources
- understanding of information resource management
- ability to synthesize and tailor information (Nichols et al. 1996, 11–12)

Shonrock and Mulder (1993, 145–146), in a research study focused on instruction librarians, identified the 25 most important proficiencies based on a survey of skills. Fourteen of the proficiencies were in the three areas of communication, instruction ability, and planning. The top three proficiencies were in the area of communication—the ability to organize and structure ideas logically, the ability to give clear and logical instructions, and the ability to present information effectively. Respondents indicated three preferred methods for obtaining these skills—library school courses, on-the-job training, and other formal means such as workshops. This study is important in that it reveals what the front-line public services librarian, in this case, the instruction librarian, perceives as important proficiencies. How does this compare to qualities articulated by employers?

A study from the employers' point of view conducted by Avery and Ketchner (1996, 253) found that 60 percent of a group of employers posting job announcements at a 1994 library conference ranked the importance of instruction as high. A catalyst for this study was the paucity of library instruction-based courses in library schools, and the authors concluded that a dialogue between schools and employers on this issue is needed. The study highlights, in a focused way, the debate about who should prepare librarians and how, so that they have the skills and proficiencies required or desired by employers.

QUALIFICATIONS RELATED TO LEADERSHIP: AN
EMPLOYER'S VIEW

The literature does not examine qualifications specifically related to, or implying, leadership. An examination of job advertisements from the leadership perspective was completed for the purposes of this chapter. Job advertisements listed in *College & Research Libraries News* were examined from January to June 1996. Approximately 106 descriptions representing positions with public services duties were reviewed. Included were positions in reference, electronic reference, access services, collection management, special collections, archives, and departmental or subject-based libraries. An examination of the qualifications implying leadership reveals the challenging and changing role of the public services librarian today and implies some major shifts in how we think about education, training, and continuing professional development for the future.

Position advertisements reveal a wide range of qualifications fundamental to a successful leader. The qualifications noted in this chapter represent the hopes and desires of employers seeking excellent candidates for openings. Primarily written by administrators or perhaps department heads, they do not necessarily reflect actual qualities held by the vast majority of public services librarians holding academic library positions. In fact, the importance of some of these qualities might be disputed by some in the profession. However, the existence of so many fundamentally important qualities found in the advertisements underscores the premise that leadership is a basic aspect of public services work at all levels. The data imply that persons with the desire to perform routine, similar duties day after day over a long period of time simply need not apply.

Communication Skills

Without a doubt, qualifications specifying the need for solid communication skills were the most prevalent in this particular survey. The need for proficiency in oral and written communication is expressed in many different and creative ways. Adjectives used to describe the level of skill sought included excellent, exceptional, effective, strong, good, accomplished, and demonstrated. One ad indicated that the successful applicant should be a listener, a communicator. Another indicated the need to be articulate. Excellence in interpersonal, oral, and written communication was widespread as a requirement. Certainly, high proficiency in all aspects of communication is fundamental to the leadership imperative.

Research related to public services in academic libraries backs up the need for a deeper understanding of the importance of effective communication. For example, Radford (1996, 123–137) used critical incidents recalled by library users and librarians to identify dimensions of interpersonal communication related to success or failure in academic reference interactions. She found that library users reported more incidents centering on relational aspects, and librarians reported those focusing on message content. Her conclusions point to the need for more emphasis on interpersonal dynamics incorporating the user's point of view. Librarians as service providers must be equally concerned with how they present themselves as with the accuracy of the message they are presenting. How the presentation affects the user is critical for current and future effectiveness.

Skill in articulating a program or goal, either verbally or in written form, to colleagues and other constituencies is also an important leadership quality. Often innovation comes from clear and specific proposals developed by a motivated staff who might be located deep within the organization. Contributions to the development of effective budget proposals, grants, and other tools for communicating directions and goals of the library require the talents of many staff.

It is assumed, perhaps incorrectly, that excellent communication skills include being an adept listener. Highly articulate people are not always good listeners and, indeed, may be quite poor at this critical activity. For example, a true service leader should be skilled at listening carefully and well to the user in order to present an articulate answer or perform a service sensitive to the user's particular needs and situation. The ability to apply excellent communication skills as consistently as possible is of paramount importance.

Service Orientation

Not surprisingly, an individual's commitment to service was a commonly stated requirement expressed in many different ways. A number of employers noted the general service commitment requirement such as commitment to service and information literacy; innovative, service-oriented, user-centered philosophy; and strong service orientation. The ability to translate service commitment to others was expressed as having the ability to champion and maintain service orientation in the department. The commitment is also reflected in content-related, action-oriented terms—strong commitment to developing patron-focused services, experience in planning and implementing outreach programs, and demonstrated effectiveness in working with library patrons.

Librarians seeking public services careers must be able to demonstrate and articulate a strong philosophical commitment to service provision. Providing leadership in translating the philosophy to concrete action is a central characteristic for the successful practitioner, whether or not the librarian is the head of a department or a front-line professional. Of equal importance is the ability to motivate colleagues in advancing quality service on a daily basis.

Another aspect of service commitment is a willingness to critically evaluate individual, departmental, and library-wide service. Though programs such as total quality management, needs assessment programs, and performance-based measures are more common in libraries, there exists a discomfort or even dislike among some librarians regarding evaluation and assessment activities. A leader, in this regard, constitutes a librarian who clearly understands positive benefits for users and staff of carefully analyzing programs and activities. The ability to critically examine practices and procedures in an open-minded way in order to enhance service is an equally important quality. A fundamental dedication to service should be inherent in the successful public services librarian.

Building Campus Relationships

The service provider, by definition, works within the larger academic community of students, faculty, and staff. The ability to interact effectively with all sectors of the academy is mentioned prominently in many public services job ads. Employers express this need by asking for librarians who can maintain effective relationships with administrators, faculty, staff, students, and the university's extended community; work well with undergraduate and graduate students and faculty; work well with research-oriented faculty; and relate well to colleagues and students in a small liberal arts environment. A leader will take the time to know the particular academic community, not only to provide needed services but to learn from, and perhaps collaborate with, the many talented individuals found throughout the campus in advancing the learning, teaching, and research goals of the institution. Librarians at any level within the organization can provide leadership and act as role models for colleagues in the development of campus relationships.

Excellent and productive campus relationships are based on a thorough understanding of the particular higher education environment in which librarians find themselves. In the past, public services librarians were more likely to develop campus relationships with those who came to the library, sought assistance, and recognized their own need to use library materials. Intimate knowledge of the complexities of the academy outside the library was not as critical. Now and even more so in the future, librarians from all areas of the library are expected to engage in active and purposeful outreach. Librarians need to know about the nuances of the campus, the delicate interrelationships between departments and areas of the college or university. Political savvy becomes an important skill for positive outreach efforts. Success in this area will benefit the library greatly by breaking down barriers and perceptions that various campus constituencies may hold about library staff and services. Leaders in this area can provide a wealth of information and direction for others in the library who are developing and building programs and services.

Collegiality and Effective Working Style/Personal Characteristics

Strong abilities to work positively, productively, and collegially with others are fundamental to the successful service provider. These qualities are basic to successful teamwork efforts as well as the ability to work on an individual basis with a wide variety of people. One job ad sought an individual who enjoys working closely with others and was a highly motivated and productive employee in prior work situations. Valued characteristics include collaboration skills, working closely and cooperatively as a member of a team, ability to foster teamwork, preference for working in a collaborative style with a strong team of professionals, demonstrated ability to work positively and productively in a changing environment, working collegially in a technically changing environment, ability to work effectively with colleagues, commitment to participatory management, and the ability to work well in individual as well as team situations. Collegiality is not limited to the library. The ability to work collegially and communicate effectively with internal and external constituents is also seen as important.

A number of factors contribute to the heightened importance of collegiality. As in other organizations, libraries have found it vital to enable staff to move more rapidly in advancing innovative programs, solving problems, and integrating new technologies and roles into day-to-day activities. The existence of teams or work groups is an increasingly common organizational approach to information services provision. The team environment provides excellent opportunities for collective leadership among a group of individuals with different backgrounds and expertise. The true leader within a team will have strong collaborative, planning, and implementation skills. Team participants should be able to join and leave teams as the work is completed or as new projects are launched. Thus, the ability to work with a wide variety of individuals in changing team configurations is also necessary. A challenge to individuals with strong personal leadership qualities is to avoid dominating and always "leading" the group rather than sharing roles and activities.

Though not often noted by individual employers, certain personal traits provide strength and depth to a librarian's professional abilities. Traits in this category mentioned by employers include creativity, sense of humor, energy, outgoing nature, self-motivation, evidence of initiative, and resourcefulness. Librarians who can communicate clearly and integrate their portfolio of professional expertise and their own unique personality are often leaders in major as well as more focused activities occurring throughout their career.

Innovation

Professionals who are excited about innovation are excellent candidates for public services assignments. This includes those who are comfortable around, and eager to experiment with, new programs and services as well as those ready and motivated to carry out and contribute to the innovative ideas of others. The capability of providing vision and direction to others in creating and diffusing innovations forms a major part of the leadership imperative. Although commonly thought of as important for a library director or administrator, librarians within departments can and do play major leadership roles in articulating vision and providing direction for implementation of vision. Individuals willing to experiment without knowing precise outcomes are valued in the new public services environment. Innovative librarians can help others to think more creatively and broadly regarding library programs and services, even if they do not hold official leadership positions.

Ability to Change

The ability to change is closely tied to innovative qualities mentioned earlier. Employers reflect the desire to recruit individuals who are comfortable or at least willing to work hard at dealing with change. Some employers indicate up front that the nature and scope of the position itself are likely to change. Therefore, the successful applicant not only exhibits the qualities expressed in the description of a particular job but shows a willingness, perhaps even an eagerness, to engage in a transformed job at some point in the future. Employers seek those with a clear understanding of the evolving role of the academic research librarian; flexibility and desire to work in a demanding, rapidly changing technological environment; experience in managing effective organizational change; and ability to thrive in an institution with rapid growth in new programs.

Diversity and Multiculturalism

Many employers are now explicitly noting their desire to recruit individuals with an understanding and commitment to diversity. This includes a demonstrated ability to work well with diverse populations, work effectively with colleagues and library users in a rapidly changing, complex, and multicultural environment, and experience/commitment in achieving diversity goals. Butler and DeSole (1993, 157) note that while academic librarians and library educators are committed to issues related to diversity, the commitment has not been adequately translated into sustained action. They note that ''too few of us have formed strategic alliances with other groups of professionals, with other educators on our own campuses, and within our own local communities to create long-term strategies.''

Librarians with experience and background relating to diversity can play a major leadership role within the library as well as on the campus. Individuals with the desire and commitment to learn more about diversity matters can help guide the library's service and recruitment programs to excellence in small and large ways.

Librarians at all levels and in all areas can work toward recruitment of a diverse staff (including professionals, support staff, and student assistants). The ability to develop and maintain positive relationships with multiculturally diverse campus populations is critical to the success of a library's programs and services. Librarians who can articulate their commitment in concrete terms, including what specific activities or actions they have taken to carry out diversity-related goals, are the most productive for the library and the campus in this area. Leadership from among all levels of staff in diversity matters is not only possible but essential in advancing a library's vision and overall excellence.

Management Skills

The existence of solid management skills is essential for successful librarians from all areas of the library. Management skills are sometimes considered important only for those supervising large departments or those who have many people reporting to them. At this point in the profession, all librarians must have some level of management skill in order to be successful. The true leader, among mid-or entry-level librarians, is an adept manager, if not of people, then of programs, services, and activities. Management skills articulated by employers included experience in planning, designing, and leading, providing leadership in the evaluation of library services, problem solving or evidence of the potential to solve problems, collaborative and individual problem-solving skills experience in designing and implementing a library instruction program, excellent analytical and organizational skills, initiative, project management, organizational skills, demonstrated talent for planning and managing in a complex and fluid service environment, ability to resolve conflict, and ability to identify operational needs and make appropriate recommendations.

New organizational structures emphasizing participatory management, team or work group management, or other collaborative models depend on a broad base of management skills among staff. Since the management toolbox is so large and deep, librarians with complementary skills in this area can provide strong group leadership for the library.

An important management skill noted by one employer is the ability to continually prioritize and perform multiple tasks in a constantly changing environment. Librarians exhibiting positive leadership from within the library almost always have this important skill. Those unable to break from working only in the linear, task-by-task mode will have an increasingly difficult time accomplishing the work and, I believe, will be increasingly marginalized from mainstream programs and service activities of the library. Those who can improve their tolerance for task diversity and adjustment as well as thrive in a fast-paced environment have internalized the leadership imperative.

ADDRESSING THE LEADERSHIP IMPERATIVE: A BRIEF HOW-TO GUIDE

Public services librarians can gain knowledge and skills needed to contribute in their own way to the leadership imperative in advancing academic library programs and services. From entry-level librarian to the reference librarian with decades of experience, all can engage in a purposeful and rewarding program of development for leadership. The concept of lifelong learning should be embraced by the successful public services librarian now, even if one's professional development program has been neglected in the past.

Professional Development

Most employers are looking for librarians with a commitment to active participation in the library profession as evidenced by a combination of activities, including research abilities through publications and presentations, potential for contributing to librarianship through professional organizations, and/or evidence of scholarly or professional achievement. Librarians must be in touch with the broader library and information science community in order to bring back and synthesize innovative programs and services. Librarians can no longer continue to reinvent the wheel in developing innovations. We must draw on one another's accomplishments in order to move forward quickly enough to adequately service a demanding and sophisticated user community. Certainly, in public services work, librarians are looking at transforming major service areas to include application of new technologies in order to reach more users in more locations. Leaders in this area are well grounded not only in relevant library and information science research and projects but also in related fields such as communication studies, education, and computer science.

Knowledge Bases

What constitutes a workable knowledge base for public services librarians? Employers specifically indicated a number of areas where knowledge was expected or preferred, including knowledge of issues and trends in information services; current knowledge of emerging information technologies and their impact on library users; understanding of academic institutions and higher education issues; knowledge of the application of new technologies in academic libraries; understanding and commitment of the role of electronic data and emerging technologies in the future of research libraries; understanding of, and commitment to, the important role of resource sharing, library automation, and new information technologies; trends in academic libraries; scholarly communication; and in higher education, knowledge of instructional and research methodologies, scholarly communication, and higher education in general.

This broad and wide-ranging knowledge base is further evidence of the need for librarians at all levels to maintain an active program of continuing education and professional involvement. The leader in this environment has broad interests and the ability to synthesize and critically evaluate information from a wide range of areas. The leader will bring back information and ideas and translate these into program possibilities for the library.

Intellectual Freedom

No employer mentioned the desire to seek a candidate with the commitment to, and understanding of, issues related to intellectual freedom. Public services librarians in academic institutions do need a strong grounding in the principles of intellectual freedom, specifically, *The Library Bill of Rights*. Given the variety of academic backgrounds, degrees, and educational requirements, it is essential that library staff who have not obtained a background in this area from library school gain it through other means. The academic environment values these freedoms, and librarians must be prepared to provide a strong leadership role in their articulation and presence.

The application of new information technology has further complicated issues regarding the preservation of privacy and freedom in its utilization. Conable and Gardner (1996, 71) believe that intellectual freedom, as a core value and ethical principle between the librarian and the user of library services, is under attack in the current technological environment, primarily by outside sources. Librarians seeking up-to-date information regarding specific issues and cases will find that these principles can be applied and upheld in the new information environments. However, many of us are not as up-to-date as we could be and need to take time to know the facts before making important decisions about access to information that could be in direct violation of our principles.

THE LEADERSHIP IMPERATIVE FOR PUBLIC SERVICES LIBRARIANS

Librarians at all levels in public services positions can and do provide strong and innovative leadership for the library and the campus. In fact, the library will fail if these qualities are not found in a significant number of staff from throughout the organization. Individuals have unique skills and abilities that will contribute to the leadership imperative, and, thus, each librarian does not have to have the full range indicated in this chapter. A true leader, I believe, will strive to broaden his or her knowledge and abilities in the qualities articulated here. A true leader will apply generously what is learned to advancing services and programs for library users and help others to do the same.

REFERENCES

Albritton, Rosie L. 1996. "A Path Analysis Study of Transformational Leadership Theory in University Libraries: Model Building in Library Research." Presentation at the *Library Research Seminar I: Partners and Paradigms, Library Research in the Information Age*. Florida State University, November 1–2.
American Library Association. 1980. *The Library Bill of Rights*. Chicago: American Library Association.
Avery, Chris and Kevin Ketchner. "Do Instruction Skills Impress Employers?" *College & Research Libraries* 57(3) (1996): 249–258.
Butler, Meredith A. and Gloria R. DeSole. "Creating the Multicultural Organization— A Call to Action." *Journal of Library Administration* 19(3/4) (1993): 155–174.
College & Research Libraries News. January–June 1996. "Classified Ads."
Conable, Gordon M. and Carrie Gardner. "Can Intellectual Freedom Survive the Information Age?" In S. Gardner Reed, ed., *Creating the Future: Essays on Librarianship*. Jefferson, NC: McFarland & Company, 1996.
de la Pena McCook, Kathleen and Tosca O. Gonsalves. "The Research University and Education for Librarianship: Considerations for User-Centered Professionals in Libraries." *Journal of Library Administration* 19(3/4) (1993): 193–207.
The New American Roget's College Thesaurus. Edited by the National Lexicographic Board. N.P.: Signet Books, New American Library, 1962, p. 205.
Nichols, Margaret T., Jeanette Sikes, Margaret M. Isselmann, and Rita Seelig Ayers.

1996. "Survival in Transition or Implementing Information Science Core Competencies." *Bulletin of the American Society for Information Science* (December/January): 11–15.

Nofsinger, Mary M. and Allan W. Bosch. "Roles of the Head of Reference: From the 1990s to the 21st Century." *Reference Librarian* 43 (1994): 87–99.

Radford, Marie L. "Communication Theory Applied to the Reference Encounter: An Analysis of Critical Incidents." *Library Quarterly* 66(2) (1996): 123–137.

Raelin, Joseph A. *The Clash of Cultures: Managers and Professionals.* Boston: Harvard Business School Press, 1986.

Shonrock, Diana and Craig Mulder. 1993. "Instruction Librarians: Acquiring the Proficiencies Critical to Their Work." *College & Research Libraries* (March): 137–149.

Sweeney, Richard T. "Leadership in the Post-Hierarchical Library." *Library Trends* 43 (1) (1994): 62–94.

Chapter 7

Every Instructional Services Librarian a Leader: Leadership in the Small Academic Library

Janet M. Hurlbert

According to Lao-tzu (1944), born in 604 B.C., archivist for the imperial archives at Loyang, "The leader is best when people barely know that he exists." Current thinking about leadership and problem solving in academic libraries seems to be incorporating this approach as we face the information challenges of the twenty-first century and consider those methods that will be the most effective. This sentiment endorses the leadership role of those who have chosen to remain in nonmanagerial positions as they lead other librarians, faculty, and students consistently and continuously by example. This chapter addresses the influence of instructional services librarians working within small academic settings and considers their leadership contributions to the area of information literacy, benefiting not only library operations but also the general instructional and curricular goals and well-being of a college.

THE ROLE OF INSTRUCTIONAL SERVICES LIBRARIANS—TODAY AND TOMORROW

The literature makes a careful distinction between a manager and a leader (Lee 1994; Cino 1995; Bechtel 1993; Gertzog 1992). Leadership is the ability to guide or move people in a particular direction and is a quality that must be able to induce, persuade, and motivate others to identify with the goals of an institution (Hightower 1990). Leadership also has a visionary quality embodying characteristics such as risk taking, good communication skills, and the ability to gain trust and lead by example (Cino 1995). Yet, we assume that a person who demonstrates qualities associated with a leader should, and eventually will, become a manager. There is an assumption in the literature that managers and would-be managers are the reading audience and that they are utilizing this information as they navigate within larger library settings. Cino (1995) challenges librarianship to develop leadership skills in its professionals and identify potential leaders early on in their careers. Is this because each librarian should be developed as a leader, or do we think good leaders should only become managers? What is harder to accept is that a leader may not want to be, nor should be, a manager. According to the Peter Principle, every employee tends to rise to his level of incompetence ("Peter Principle" 1995), a healthy warning to very competent librarians to properly evaluate the roles for which they are most suited. It is also a warning to library managers to recognize and reward leadership initiatives at all levels without pressure to assume managerial responsibilities. The tireless interview question "Where do you want to be in five years?" communicates that those who do not wish to aspire to administrative positions are somehow deficient. We must recognize that leadership comes in all forms and at all levels and mentor to persons at those levels. Also, goals may be set for the next five years that do not involve moving into administration but do involve applying leadership skills to many different types of positions and responsibilities.

One of the most visible and crucial areas for leadership, especially within the small liberal arts college environment, is instructional services. It is an area that looks forcefully to the uncertain information future and is crucial to the success of libraries in the twenty-first century, playing an important role in curriculum design for the college as a whole. Librarians working within this area must supply the information needed for managerial decision making on the library and college level. For a hundred years, libraries were very stable places where print materials were organized well and made easily available to anyone who took the trouble to learn the organization (Nelson, Killoran, and Dunham 1995). Even the advent of automated catalogs did not change the scheme or amount of information to any great extent. For 40 of these years, academic librarians have been concerned with integrating library instruction and information literacy into the undergraduate curriculum (Rader 1995). In the last few years, however, CD-ROM and now the Internet have brought about radical changes of which the young student has misconceptions. How information should be found and the integration of this information from differing formats and sources remain a difficult concept. We are no longer here to teach how to use the library but to teach about the very nature of information. Perhaps we should always have been doing this, but the need is now dramatically apparent. Instructional services librarians never viewed the library as a storage facility whose purpose was to be organized, yet they may not have viewed it as a laboratory to practice critical thinking and evaluation skills. As Rader (1995) states, "These are challenging and exciting times for academic librarians."

Every description of a library's future points toward those responsibilities of public services librarians, but especially those who work in instructional services. We see the future as opportunity, not threat; active, not passive; delivering, not just storing; services, not just assets (Lancaster 1993). There is no indecision in the literature that organizations exist in changing times, that change will be a constant, and that libraries are in the middle of these changes (Faerman 1993). Instructional services librarians are the real innovators who can actively shape the future and, by doing so, develop and choose a new philosophy of "information service leadership" (Penniman 1993). The teaching world and the information world must be integrated, especially since no library will ever be completely adequate, especially a small one. Yet the glut of information will swamp the staff and the students. We watch students having much more information but not becoming more capable of solving information-based problems or synthesizing all the information—accessing more does not mean accessing better. Perhaps no other phenomenon has so significantly affected the provision of reference services as has the Internet, which must now be integrated in most areas of librarianship and academic research. Once again reference staff are best suited to undertake this introduction and integration (Silva and Cartwright 1994).

What is the role of the librarian? Of primary importance is the need for librarians to assume a leadership position concerning instruction and navigation in the new electronic campus. To remain a vital part of the education and research process, librarians will need to emphasize our fundamental purposes while rethinking the methods of delivering library and information services in a climate of changing technology, budgets, and types of students. Not only are libraries without walls, but Breivik talks about librarians' becoming "beyond-library-walls leaders." As instruction librarians move beyond teaching about what is available and begin helping to shape the nature of informational resources and scholarly communication (Reichel 1993), our very job activity may need to be renamed. Bibliographic instruction is no longer appropriate, and library instruction may be misleading; perhaps it is research instruction or information instruction, but it is certainly the topic for many future discussions.

The current nature of librarians within instructional services lends itself to future challenges. These librarians tend to be flexible, to assess needs, and to change direction when necessary after careful evaluation. They have seen programs grow and expand and realize that today's groundwork determines what the future will be (Surprenant 1993). Their mind-set embraces many of the ideas in Hedrick Smith's *Rethinking America* (1995), as all of us look for new ways of thinking about how to work together more effectively, how to learn together as we search for answers to the unknown, and how to create environments where all feel safe to experiment (Chawla 1995).

THE SMALL COLLEGE LIBRARY AND DECISION MAKING

Although a library's direction must be negotiated from the position of director/manager, shared decision making is essential with instructional services. No area is more pivotal to the future of libraries and what they will symbolize in an information future. In the past, there has always been general acceptance of the fact that there would be a fairly traditional library at a small institution. It may or may not have been well funded or respected, but its existence was never challenged. Now, the library's role and association with the computer center bring into question what libraries really do and how valuable they are to an institution. Pragmatic questions concerning hierarchy and funding are asked by administrators who may or may not understand the nature of information themselves or the difference between computer literacy and information literacy, a very important distinction.

There is no real middle-management level in a small library, nor does it take much to be convinced that everyone is vital to the library mission. Sweeney (1994) reminds us that the new library will have fewer people, a constant learning structure, and a focus on customer service. In many small libraries, it is hard to imagine fewer people. However, it may be necessary to rethink job descriptions and manage technical responsibilities differently so that more staff and effort may be placed in instructional services. To reach these necessary managerial decisions, leadership must be revised to a new paradigm of employee empowerment through a collegial system where all are convinced of their leadership abilities and importance (Cino 1995) and allowed to gain confidence and improve their value to the unit (Bechtel 1993). The area of instruction showcases many of the characteristics of learning organizations described in Peter Senge's book *The Fifth Discipline: The Art and Practice of the Learning Organization* (1990). Librarians who view situations with new perspectives and seek individual fulfillment through personal mastery can act as followers while being leaders and focus on team learning.

THE SMALL CAMPUS ENVIRONMENT

The small college offers many role models as well as opportunities for leadership. Instructional services within the library and within the campus are no exception. The library in the small, liberal arts environment must assert itself to reestablish, often through instructional opportunities, the relevance of the library in this changing information world. Small libraries are not always aware of the opportunities they have, nor are librarians aware of the opportunities they have. Each librarian can play a dominant role on a small campus. What is often not recognized is that this form of leadership must be learned, and what may be missing is the insight on the part of managers or more experienced librarians to mentor those entering this arena into leadership roles unassociated with managerial responsibilities. Different situations require different leadership skills that are appropriate, compatible, and consistent with behavior equal to the demands and compatible with the task and with organizational realities (Hightower 1990).

A small campus is filled with those who may be leaders but not managers. Academic department heads are not hired as administrators but are teaching faculty who often rotate this administrative responsibility. Regardless, they serve on, and chair, committees, take stands on academic issues, and let their voices be heard on curricular matters. Within this setting, librarians must also let their voices, beliefs, and opinions be heard. In many cases, this is made easier by faculty status for librarians. What relationship does faculty status for librarians have to the degree of possible involvement on a campus? Faculty status for academic librarians is a topic that has consumed the attention of the profession for the last 40 years, with more being written about this subject than about any other related topic in academic librarianship (Kingma and McCombs 1995). The purpose of this chapter is not to examine the issue itself but to review some relevant conclusions from the pertinent literature. Bushing (1995) points out that it is difficult for librarians to understand the culture of a school if they are isolated within the library and so busy with their job performance that they have no time to become involved in the life and culture of the campus. She believes that a graduate education in library science does not provide an opportunity to imprint the academic culture and the role of the professorate in librarians. An academic job search is not necessarily guided by whether or not faculty status is part of the package—librarians often become faculty by accident of the marketplace rather than through an active choice.

How closely is faculty status tied to the effectiveness of a librarian, especially an instructional services librarian with teaching responsibilities, in terms of leadership roles as he or she relates to the campus? First, if faculty status is part of the position's responsibilities, it is much more than automatic membership on committees or attendance at faculty meetings. It entails making a meaningful impact on those who consider themselves your colleagues—influence on campus is earned (Shapiro 1993). Faculty status places librarians in the right places, but it is up to individuals to make an impact. Because of the teaching and public nature of instructional services librarians' positions, they may often be placed in the right places with or without faculty status. With or without faculty status, these librarians must be constantly aware of the influence that their programs can have. The library through public services should be reaching out to departments such as career development, retention committees, admissions, and freshman deans. Mentoring is absolutely necessary to show these librarians how to take advantage on an individual basis of opportunities to become meaningfully involved in the intellectual and administrative life of the college early in their careers.

CURRICULAR REFORM

Faculty status or not, instructional services librarians should be key players in the educational mission of the college. The new proficiencies that are becoming part of curricular programs—writing and oral communication across the curriculum, critical thinking, diversity emphasis, computer skills—all involve direct links to information literacy. Although many librarians may justifiably not totally accept "information literacy" as a term, the implication of teaching students how to work with information in a way that prepares them for lifelong education and problem solving is clear.

Creating and implementing information literacy programs and having goals and measurable objectives take true leadership skills. Shapiro and Hughes (1996) suggest rethinking the entire educational curriculum so that information literacy is a new liberal art, freeing the future citizen of dependency and fostering information leadership in the individual. Whatever the shape of the program, campus politics creates barriers for information literacy programs that only those librarians who have developed true leadership skills and a knowledge of an individual campus can overcome. Such situations require consistency and maturity in approach, time, and patience as well as continual, sustained, and subtle leadership while being aware of faculty sensitivities.

LIBRARY AS LABORATORY AND ASSIGNMENT DESIGN

Whether or not there is, or ever will be, a formal information literacy program on campus, instruction, the central mission of an undergraduate institution, is where librarians can be most effective. Librarians are challenged to be academic leaders, particularly in terms of teaching/learning aspects of campuses (Butcher, Hughes, and George 1995). To do so means transforming the library through outreach and leadership in teaching. In the library, students have the opportunity to enter into conversations about things that matter from the perspective of the past through such traditional gateways as books, periodicals, reference materials, and audiovisual resources. They can integrate this with electronic resources and then relate the perspective of the past to people in the present (Wild and Hurlbert 1995). A library and the information that it represents may also be a way for faculty members to improve the relevancy and quality of their program by inviting students to begin to take part in the dialogue of a particular discipline (Sterngold and Hurlbert 1996). Using the library as a laboratory, especially in the liberal arts, brings students into the library not to take tours or simply learn skills. An instructional services librarian must lead a campus community into a library program that continually integrates meaningful information content into many courses in differing ways over a four-year time span. In a transformed view of the contemporary library, the instructor and librarian are able to:

- Make the student's personal dialogue with information the center of the educational process;

- Engage students in active learning experiences involved with collecting, evaluating, and using information that model for students how to solve problems in whatever their fields of study;

- Allow students to discover through the experience of researching and using information how making decisions is a process of evaluating options and making choices within particular contexts;

- Develop critical thinking skills and the ability to make ethical choices and establish a sense of connectedness between past and present;

- Build interpersonal skills and create community among students, instructors, staff, and groups of individuals. (Wild and Hurlbert 1995)

To lead faculty into a view of the library as a laboratory with an educational mission, assignment design is paramount. Librarians who see information seeking as a developmental process that combines course goals and information/research goals are able to collaboratively work with faculty to create assignments that prepare students for jobs and for participation in the world community. The teamwork of teaching faculty and librarians' bringing their expertise to the assignment drafting board and moving away from the plagiarism-laden term paper assignments seeks to engage students from an information perspective and teach them real-life methods of using information (Hurlbert 1997). As well as a partnership, this demands risk taking and experimentation—and leadership on the part of instructional services librarians to explain the possibilities. As a support for these assignments, technological developments, educational reforms, and concern with preparation for success in the information age are beginning to enable academic librarians to once again integrate information and technological skills instruction into the undergraduate curriculum (Rader 1995). It is more than the cumulative impact of skills; it is a way of thinking.

Not only do curricular reform and technology serve as underpinnings for research instruction, but instructional methods in the form of active/collaborative learning, group processes, and experiential learning dictate how successful the program will be. The 21st LOEX Conference held an active learning workshop that not only taught a method of instruction but also focused attention on the fact that instructional services librarians often lead the way with these techniques. Librarians can be very much a part of the teaching effectiveness emphasis on a campus and, as such, should be taking part in workshops on campus and off, side by side with faculty in the disciplines.

Although managerial-level leadership is crucial to implementing a strong instruction program, the input of public services instructional librarians enables the manager to make strong decisions. This once again emphasizes the importance of team effort, increased communication (utilizing e-mail in new ways), and shared responsibility for learning and decisions.

As successful programs develop on campuses, the librarians involved have broader leadership responsibilities to share their successes and what they have gleaned from their failures. Leadership in instruction can obviously be disseminated within the library profession, but it is important to go further. One of the best methods is to coauthor publications with faculty and develop presentations at disciplinary conferences, seeking to communicate the ideas of assignment design and the crucial nature of information, not computer, literacy. In this manner, leadership reaches all those interested in curriculum integrity and reform, allowing them to consider information seeking through other perspectives.

CONCLUSION

Let us reexamine leadership qualities in relationship to research and information instruction. Leadership is the ability to guide or move people in a particular direction, to induce, persuade, and motivate others to identify with the goals of an institution. Leadership also has a visionary quality that embodies characteristics such as risk taking, good communication skills, and the ability to gain trust and lead by example. Such a librarian takes part in moving an academic institution to incorporate the value of information literacy formally and persuades and motivates others to incorporate these values within their individual courses or departmental operations. Librarians must communicate their values and lead with innovative teaching styles, sometimes experimental in nature but definitely reinforcing librarianship as a respected and integral part of the future of an academic institution. Such strong and effective leadership might eliminate the unique role of the instructional services librarian. At the 1996 LOEX conference, Lizabeth Wilson, in her keynote address, envisions a student-centered library in which instruction is the very nature of libraries themselves.

We return to the thoughts of Lao-tzu as we consider that faculty and students who learn to utilize information in new and meaningful ways for their research and in their personal lives often forget how they learned this important lesson and its underlying skills. "But of a good leader, who talks little, when his work is done, his aim fulfilled, they will all say, 'we did this ourselves.'"

REFERENCES

Bechtel, Joan M. 1993. "Leadership Lessons Learned from Managing and Being Managed." *Journal of Academic Librarianship* 18(6): 352–357.

Bushing, Mary C. 1995. "Academic Librarians: Perceptions of the Acculturation Process." *Library Acquisitions* 19 (Spring): 33–41.

Butcher, Karyle, Joy Hughes, and Melvin R. George. 1995. "Thoughts on Leadership: An Exchange." *College & Research Libraries News* no. 9 (October): 636–638.

Chawla, Sarita. 1995. "Introduction: Beginner's Mind." In Sanita Chawla and John Renesch, eds., *Learning Organizations: Developing Cultures for Tomorrow's Workplace.* Portland, OR: Productivity Press, pp. 1–10.

Cino, Catherine. 1995. "A Time of Change: The Need for Leadership in Librarianship." *Feliciter* 41 (September): 20–27.

Faerman, Sue R. 1993. "Organizational Change and Leadership Styles." *Journal of Library Administration* 19(3/4): 55–78.

Gertzog, Alice. 1992. "Leadership in Librarianship." *Library Trends* 40(3): 402–430.

Hightower, Monteria. 1990. "Thoughts on a Definition of Leadership." In Sheila S. Intner and Kay E. Vandergrift, eds., *Library Education and Leadership: Essays in Honor of Jane Anne Hannigan*. Metuchen, NJ: Scarecrow Press, pp. 19–26.

Hurlbert, Janet McNeil. 1997. "Library Instruction for the Liberal Arts: Dialogue, Assignment Design, Active Learning, and Outreach." In Linda Shirato, ed., *Proceedings of the Twenty-Fourth National LOEX Library Instruction Conference*. Ypsilanti, MI: Pierian Press, pp. 77–84.

Kingma, Bruce R. and Gillian M. McCombs. 1995. "The Opportunity Costs of Faculty Status for Academic Librarians." *College & Research Libraries*: 258–264.

Lancaster, F. W. 1993. "Introduction: Threat versus Opportunity." In F. W. Lancaster, ed., *Libraries and the Future: Essays on the Library in the Twenty-First Century*. New York: Haworth Press, pp. 1–4.

Lao-tzu. 1944. *The Way of Life according to Lao Tzu: An American Version*. Trans. Witter Bynner. New York: Capricorn Books.

Lee, Susan. 1994. "Leadership: Revised and Redesigned for the Electronic Age." *Journal of Library Administration* 20(2): 17–28.

Nelson, Bonnie R., Katherine B. Killoran, and Janice Dunham. 1995. "Electronic Information Literacy for the Criminal Justice Student." *Journal of Criminal Justice Education* 6(2): 235–258.

Penniman, David. 1993. "Libraries and the Future: Essays on the Library in the Twenty-First Century." In F. W. Lancaster, ed., *Libraries and the Future: Essays on the Library in the Twenty-First Century*. New York: Haworth Press, pp. 5–15.

"Peter Principle." 1995. *International Dictionary of Management*. 5th ed. Ed. Hano Johannsen and Terry Page. London: Kogan Page.

Rader, Hannelore B. 1995. "Information Literacy and the Undergraduate Curriculum." *Library Trends* 44(2): 270–278.

Reichel, Mary. 1993. "Information Use and Projections: The Importance for Library Instruction (and Dr. Seuss)." In Linda Shirato, ed., *What Is Good Instruction Now? Library Instruction for the 90's: Papers and Session Materials Presented at the Twentieth National LOEX Library Instruction Conference Held at Eastern Michigan University 8 to 9 May 1992*. Ann Arbor, MI: Pierian Press, pp. 19–24.

Senge, Peter. 1990. *The Fifth Discipline: The Art & Practice of the Learning Organization*. New York: Doubleday.

Shapiro, Beth. 1993. "The Myths Surrounding Faculty Status for Librarians." *College & Research Libraries News* no. 10 (November): 562–563.

Shapiro, Jeremy J. and Shelley K. Hughes. 1996. "Information Technology as a Liberal Art." *Educom Review* 31(2):31–35.

Silva, Marcos and Glenn F. Cartwright. 1994. "The Internet and Reference Librarians: A Question of Leadership." *The Reference Librarian* no. 41/42: 159–172.

Smith, Hedrick. 1995. *Rethinking America*. New York: Random House.

Sterngold, Arthur and Janet McNeil Hurlbert. "Using a Library-Based Research Project to Develop Students' Information and Professional Literacy." Submitted for publication.

Surprenant, Thomas T. 1993. "Welcome to Obsolescence." In Linda Shirato, ed., *What Is Good Instruction Now? Library Instruction for the 90's: Papers and Session Materials Presented at the Twentieth National LOEX Library Instruction Conference held at Eastern Michigan University 8 to 9 May 1992.* Ann Arbor, MI: Pierian Press, pp. 1–6.

Sweeney, Richard T. 1994. "Leadership in the Post-Hierarchical Library." *Library Trends* 43(1): 62–94.

Wild, Frederic M., Jr., and Janet McNeil Hurlbert. 1995. "Time, Place, and Community: A Developmental Strategy for Enabling College Students to Connect Course Content with 'Things That Matter.' " Unpublished working paper.

Wilson, Lizabeth A. 1997. "The Way Things Work: Teaching and Learning in Libraries." In Linda Shirato, ed., *Proceedings of the Twenty-Fourth National LOEX Library Instruction Conference.* Ypsilanti, MI: Pierian Press, pp. 1–11.

Chapter 8

Leading from Within: Leadership Within the Ranks of Academic Librarians

George Charles Newman

The word "leadership" is one of the most widely used terminologies in the world of academic libraries. By definition, leadership means to lead others, to inspire others, or to direct others toward a specific set of goals and objectives. Leadership can also be associated with achievement and accomplishment. Thus, individuals who have created change or innovation, in either higher education or, more specifically, academic libraries, can be considered leaders.

Leadership has traditionally been associated with the "elites" who manage organizations, educational institutions, or academic libraries. Within the academic library, leadership has generally been associated with the director or the head of the library, and it is undeniable that academic library directors have been leaders in the profession. In recent years, however, academic libraries have been flattening their organizational structures, partly as a result of the democratic/collegial process embodied in the governance systems of the teaching faculty and partly because of the reorganization efforts of the institution itself. Within this new structure, librarians are being empowered to make important operational and policy decisions, resulting in an increase in opportunities for leadership in the ranks (see Boisse and Bentley 1996).

This chapter explores the concept of leadership in the ranks of academic libraries, focusing first on three different areas where opportunities for leadership exist. The chapter then discusses the issues of recognition and reward for the leadership role played by academic librarians, followed by an analysis of what the changes occurring in academic libraries will mean to the profession. Through this discussion, academic librarians can learn how to seize opportunities for leadership and make a difference in the operation and success of their library.

AREAS OF LEADERSHIP

Although the possibilities for providing leadership within the academic library are as numerous as the number of librarians themselves, three areas in the library currently provide the greatest potential for leadership within the ranks.

Collection Management

The first opportunity for librarian leadership involves the building and maintenance of collections. It has been taken for granted in many academic communities that the teaching faculty and the librarians together have built the traditional collections associated with the library, since these collections often parallel the strengths of the academic programs and are modified as academic and library priorities change. While this is true to a great extent, library professionals have often taken a leadership position in creating balanced collections.

Academic library history is full of examples of individual professional librarians who, though not directors or a part of the library administration, were leaders in acquiring and building unique collections. Many of the treasures we find in academic libraries were acquired through the hard work, persistence, and scholarly ability of line librarians. Academic librarians tend to categorize these professionals as collection development or collection management librarians.

An example of this type of leadership can be found in the creation of special undergraduate libraries in the major research university library systems during the 1960s. The undergraduate libraries at the University of Michigan and Harvard University, for example, were developed under the leadership of line professionals who took it upon themselves to identify important books and periodicals for the collection. They also contributed to the design of libraries as distinct learning facilities and helped to organize and equip the libraries as such.

Books for College Libraries, which is a series of recommended bibliographies covering all major areas of study, has a core collection of 50,000 titles. Now in its third edition (published in 1988), it was inspired by the creation of the undergraduate library concept. The First published in 1967, *Books for College Libraries* came out of the University of California's New Campuses Program and drew upon the previous undergraduate resource lists developed at Harvard University and the University of Michigan Undergraduate Library. The journal *Choice*, which is a monthly review of academic library book literature, updates as well as provides continuity between editions of *Books for College Libraries*.

The scope of *Books for College Libraries* has remained the same between editions, with the emphasis on providing comprehensive and recommended lists of book monographs for liberal arts and sciences undergraduate library collections, although the most recent edition also examines recommended materials for business, computer science, engineering, and health sciences. While academic programs and other interdisciplinary curricula have brought new selection tools to collection development, *Books for College Libraries*, despite its arts and sciences orientation, has continued to be an important bibliographic tool for individual librarians charged with building collections.

Librarian leadership in collection management has always offered unique challenges. In the 1960s and 1970s, collection management was considered to be a developing concept. Academic librarians developed collections comprising books, monographs, serials, and journals. Microforms represented an important research resource, while nonprint media were beginning to be acquired by academic libraries. Academic librarians who were involved in ordering and building collections were usually referred to as collection development librarians.

Today, in the late 1990s, collection development has shifted from the creation of collections to the management of collections. This dramatic shift has come about because of several factors, both external and internal. The economics of higher education and proliferating formats for library materials have had major impacts on how academic librarians determine what goes into the physical collection. At the same time, internal library pressures to balance serials and journals with traditional book acquisitions have affected how collections are shaped. Added to this are the demands placed on the academic library both by the faculty and by new curricula. All of these factors have had an impact on the growth and development of the academic library collection.

The collection management librarian in today's academic library must carefully craft a collection from a variety of formats, including electronic databases such as CD-ROM technologies and Internet access, while at the same time maintaining a balance with the traditional core of the collection, that is, books and journals. The role of the collection management librarian has thus taken on a paramount significance in academic libraries.

In the future, librarians involved in collection management will provide the leadership that will bring the ''gateway'' concept to libraries in the form of electronic collections and resources. This, in turn, will enable academic libraries of different sizes and purposes to electronically access numerous resources that previously were not available to them. Such resources will enrich teaching and learning at the institution. Thus, the collection management librarian must be able to guide the library and the institution to recognize the importance of acquiring information and resources in all formats, both traditional and electronic, for the college or university library (see Olsen, 1997).

Library Instruction

A second type of leadership that has evolved from the ranks of the academic librarian has been in the area of library instruction. What began in the 1960s as a movement to provide more individual orientation toward the library in colleges and universities has grown into a comprehensive and ever-expanding discipline within every academic library. In large academic libraries one often finds a coordinator or head of library instruction and, in some cases, a staff of several librarians working almost solely on instructional matters.

The type of library instruction has changed over the past 20 years from mere library orientation to more specific instruction. In today's libraries, students need to know much more than simply where various library resources are. They now need to learn how to use computer technology to access resources both in the library and throughout the world. Because Internet access to numerous databases is changing the way library research is conducted, it is even more important that students be taught how to analyze and interpret both the sources and the information obtained.

The leadership for many of the successful library instruction programs has not come from the top of the organization. Although administrative support and resources have been forthcoming and, in some cases, substantial, the evolution of library instruction into a specific subdiscipline of academic librarianship has tended to come from individual academic librarians. These individuals have seen the opportunities for expanding the public service role of the library, and they have also seen the parallel between instruction and service (see Hirshon 1996). Academic librarians achieved faculty status on many campuses in the 1970s because they were able to provide convincing evidence that their work in the library, including library instruction, paralleled that of the teaching faculty.

Today the emerging technologies in all academic libraries are again providing new opportunities for academic librarians on the line to assert their leadership. Now the mission in library instruction is to teach students and faculty how to use technologies to expand and enrich research, scholarship, and teaching. As a result, academic librarians in medium-sized and large academic libraries may find themselves in the near future developing formal credit courses in library and information studies for undergraduates. It is not too far-fetched to predict that some of these institutions will certify minor and perhaps even major concentrations in library and information studies, taught by academic librarians. As a result, academic librarians may have the opportunity in the future to provide unparalleled leadership in curriculum development at the college level.

Library Technology

This leads us to the third area of importance in the unfolding of leadership opportunities for academic libraries: the field of library technology. Again, administrative support at the top of the academic library has been important to the growth and implementation of technology in many academic libraries. But the planning, design, and installation of the technology as well as of the instructional interfaces have generally been done by the academic librarians. Both individual librarians and groups of academic librarians from various areas of the library have studied and completed the implementation process as technology has changed the work and service patterns of the academic library. The training of support staff and the instruction of the user population (faculty and students) have also been done by individual academic librarians.

Today academic libraries have moved from the first generation of technology, which was the automation of traditional card catalogs and circulation functions, to a second and even third generation of technology. Lawrence Dowler has written: "Dramatic developments in electronic information and telecommunications are beginning to alter the way students learn and scholars do research" (see Dowler 1997). With technology being used by faculty to teach disciplines and by students to learn skills and gain knowledge, today's college and university curricula have become heavily interdisciplinary, and learning takes place in many forms, from group projects to use of interactive technology to fulfill course assignments.

In this environment, the academic librarian has a unique opportunity to provide leadership in the integration of technology with teaching and learning. Academic libraries today must do more than maintain collections and services; they must become key players in the teaching and learning environment. A good example would be the Cornell University Library Gateway, which, as of this writing, maintains 900 databases for its faculty and students. As technology impacts not only academic libraries but entire campuses, academic libraries have the opportunity to select as well as integrate technology resources into the curriculum and thus to shape entire curricula in terms of resources, teaching content, and student learning style.

In this way, the leadership of the academic librarian becomes more formally integrated into teaching patterns of higher education as faculty in the discipline turn to the academic librarians to help them define and design new courses and curricula.

THE STRUGGLE FOR RECOGNITION

As the responsibility for change in academic libraries has increasingly emanated from the professional ranks, academic libraries have moved from a hierarchical or a vertical management structure to a more horizontal one. Thus, new opportunities for leadership have become available for academic librarians. The delegation of authority and responsibility for change in academic libraries is evolving from the professional ranks of the organization, and new programs and services in many academic libraries are being presented to the greater profession through the efforts of line librarians.

The issue of leadership within the ranks of the academic library profession revolves around institutional and library politics and the reward systems these institutions employ. The politics of higher education and of academic libraries is conservative and oriented toward the status quo. Colleges and universities have traditionally been unable or unwilling to recognize leadership patterns in academic libraries other than at the administrative level. In most institutions in higher education, indeed, in academic libraries themselves, authority has been consolidated at the top of the administrative structure. Academic librarians have been expected to merely provide services and support to the academic mission of the institution, and as a result they have been reactive to issues and incremental changes that occur in the academic environment. In such a structure, the political status of the academic librarian affects the reward and recognition systems of the institution and the academic library. Teaching faculty—who are oriented around disciplines and judged for tenure, promotion, and compensation on the basis of teaching, research, and service—move in different circles from those of their colleagues in the academic library. Only when the academic librarian is able to demonstrate true leadership in the learning and teaching of the institution will the system be challenged to change.

The key factor within any organization, particularly in higher education, is to identify, nurture, and reward professionals for their valuable accomplishments. Although many academic library professional staff have the academic privileges of teaching faculty, they suffer from the lack of integration of the library into the academic decision making of the institution. Academic libraries do not recruit students, they have marginal impact on the introduction of new curriculum, and they provide little original research that enhances the reputation of the college or university.

Despite these constraints, which are created by the structure of higher education, the importance of the academic librarian has been heightened by the increased visibility of the library in the academic priorities of higher education and by the introduction of new levels of technology into the teaching and research functions of the institution. These changes, coupled with the empowerment movement in higher education and in academic libraries, have offered new avenues of visibility and advancement to academic librarians.

The advent of library technology has drastically changed the operation of libraries, and through technology the management of, and access to, information have become pervasive across the campus. This shift in operational structure has brought teaching and research faculty more into direct contact with academic libraries, and, as a result, the professional library staff has tended to develop new programs of instruction and services. Managers of higher education are keenly interested in the teaching and research potential of technology, and many institutions have seen the line academic librarian as a professional who is better prepared to understand and use instructional technology than many teaching faculty who continue to be constrained by the pedagogy of their department and discipline (see Massy and Zemsky 1995).

Where does this leave the issue of leadership and individual academic librarians? With the library profession challenged by economic, academic, and technology issues of serious dimensions, academic library directors must identify ways and means by which to foster growth and development among and through the professional staff. Academic librarians today are making great contributions in the literature to the changing role of the library in higher education. An examination of the presentations at national conferences in the field of academic libraries reveals a large number of presenters who come from the academic library faculty ranks. For example, the Eighth Annual Association of College and Research Libraries (ACRL) National Conference in Nashville, Tennessee, in the spring of 1997 featured 42 contributed papers, covering topics such as partnerships and competition, funding, changing work, roles, and organizations, learning and social responsibility, equity, and diversity. Of these 42 papers, 30 were developed and presented by academic librarians below the level of the administrative head or director of the academic library.

A survey of the 1997 ACRL program abstracts illustrates that academic librarians are keenly interested in the development, use, and organization of the World Wide Web, electronic publishing, the relationship of the computer center to the academic library, and the creation of the virtual library. Academic librarians discuss the use of these services in terms of customer-or client-centered libraries. How to incorporate the library into the greater campus community and how to develop an academic library in terms of openness, community, and diversity are other pressing issues. Fund-raising and its relationship to the library are not just the priority of library management but have also become an important concern of the academic librarian. Job change, work flow, and employee enrichment are important themes that reflect how academic librarians perceive their work climate (see Association of College & Research Libraries 1997b,c).

Thus, by looking at the larger picture, academic librarians have already taken the first step in integrating their contributions into the academic structure of the institution. The next and more difficult step is to change the perception of the institution, both faculty and administration, toward the role of the library.

THE POLITICS OF THE REWARD SYSTEM

In many academic libraries, the goal of the academic librarian since the 1960s has been to become coequal with teaching and research faculty. To date, however, this has been largely impossible to achieve. Not only are teaching faculty and administrators divided on the issue of the proper faculty status, responsibilities, and rewards for librarians, but so, too, are academic librarians (see Association of College & Research Libraries 1997a). Yet as long as librarians play a marginal, rather than an integral, role in the learning and teaching process, they will continue to be excluded from the reward system of the institution.

How can academic librarians succeed in a reward system that is oriented and weighted toward criteria that relate more to teaching and research than to the traditional functions of an academic librarian? The answer may be for the academic librarian to change the politics of the reward structure by providing leadership to the college through the use of technology. There has never been a more opportune time to challenge the merits of the politics of reward in higher education than today. The relationship of information technology to the academic disciplines and the teaching functions of any college and university offers the academic librarian the opportunity to pursue recognition and reward through political change.

The management of higher education has recently focused on the transformational aspects of change. At all levels in higher education, the methods of productivity, empowerment, benchmarking, and restructuring have been introduced as part of the transformational process. In this process of change, the administration and the faculty jointly discuss, analyze, plan, and initiate structural changes in the function and, in some cases, the mission of the organization (see Dolence and Norris 1995).

The same case can be made for changing the reward system. Academic librarians who use the power of persuasion, compromise, and negotiation to achieve recognition within the college or university environment have the ability to advance. The politics of reward is based on involvement in the governance of the institution. Academic librarians who become involved in the governance structure of higher education, such as serving on significant search committees, faculty senate committees, accreditation committees, campus planning committees, or committees that examine the academic curriculum or instructional issues of the organization, have greater opportunities to influence campus decision making. Because of the collegial nature of higher education governance, involvement in establishing college and university priorities has given individual faculty greater opportunities to assume new roles of influence in the direction of higher education, and academic librarians can do the same.

In general, most faculty and administration in higher education have little real understanding of how the academic library operates or of the power of technology in the management and retrieval of information. Because the academic library has a distinct designation in the institutional budget, it is viewed by many academic managers to be a required expenditure. Yet these same managers often also see the academic library as merely a depository for resources that appear to add little value to the institution besides complementing the academic curriculum. Furthermore, infusion of technology into the operation of library services is often viewed as making jobs easier for librarians but having marginal value to its users—the students, faculty, and research community. These views could not be further from the truth. Thus, academic librarians who work within individual academic libraries have unique opportunities to interpret present and emerging library services.

A proposed scenario of how the library and academic librarians might be integrated into the teaching process is the following:

A historian teaches a senior seminar for undergraduate history majors. Students enrolled in the seminar are expected to develop and write a historical paper using original and secondary library sources. The teacher, a well-respected scholar and frequent library user, has in the past instructed the students on the use of library resources, with the students consulting the academic librarians when needed. Based on recent personal experience in the library, however, the historian realizes that the process of retrieving historical information in the library has changed dramatically over the past few years.

As the new term begins, the historian asks a librarian who understands library technology and who has some knowledge of history to provide library instruction to the senior seminar. This provides the academic librarian with an opportunity not only to offer basic instruction on historical resources within the library but also to develop an instruction program that will show students how to access historical information, sources, and data through the use of library technology. During the semester, both the students and the faculty member are introduced to electronic retrieval systems that enable them to access journals not held by the library and to do so in full-text format; to access pertinent statistical data that are either not available or difficult to gather manually; and to access original documents that one might find only at a large research library. What the academic librarian has accomplished through this instruction, therefore, is to demonstrate to students and especially the faculty member the comprehensiveness of the resources that library technology has brought to the academic curriculum.

As a result of this type of subject-based library instruction, a dialogue is initiated between the academic library and the teaching faculty in history. Together with faculty from the other social science disciplines, they explore how to more fully integrate the teaching of the library into the academic majors of all the social sciences. After some discussion and a demonstration of the systems available, a decision is made to develop a credit-bearing course requirement for juniors and seniors majoring in the social sciences, to be completed before embarking on preparation of their senior paper. The academic departments representing the social sciences and the library also jointly decide that the course will be taught by the academic librarians and that these librarians will have joint appointments in one of the social science departments, based on their area of expertise.

In this scenario, the academic librarian is both recognized and rewarded for providing a unique teaching and curricular expertise. Through this process, the academic librarian becomes more than an adjunct member of the faculty; he or she also becomes a key member of the resource development of the teaching faculty. Combining one's academic library expertise with that of the teaching faculty will have a positive impact on the academic affairs area of a college or university. Whenever someone can point to a service that directly affects the curricular functions of an academic department, it will affect how the central administration reviews and rewards accomplishments.

Academic librarians have traditionally had strong working relationships with individual faculty members across the curriculum in any college or university. Today the technology as well as the expanded teaching and research support initiatives of the academic library offer librarians new mechanisms and new opportunities to become more directly involved in the development and implementation of specific courses and perhaps even entire curricula.

One of the criticisms of higher education today is the fact that many colleges and universities have failed to accurately publicize and promote what they are doing. Academic libraries, to some degree, share in this failure. Academic library faculty are frequently on the cutting edge of change, and it is important that they develop methods of promotion that create an awareness and understanding of these changes within the institution.

THE FUTURE OF THE ACADEMIC LIBRARIAN

In times of budgetary and technological change, the reorganization and re-structuring of higher education, and the general criticisms surrounding the accountability of higher education, the one element that appears to be of sustaining importance to any college or university is the personnel who constitute the teaching and support staff. Yet the future of academic librarians is by no means secure. They must be able to keep up with the changes occurring both in the profession and in higher education in general.

Perhaps the most important change occurring in the field of academic librarianship is in the area of library education. Rapid changes in technology and in its application to the teaching and learning process have necessitated changes in the education and training of academic librarians. At both the University of California at Berkeley and the University of Michigan at Ann Arbor, a complete reorganization and redesign of library education have taken place over the past three years (see Drabenstott and Atkins 1996). These changes are reflected in the renaming of the library programs at both of these institutions from the School of Library Science to the School of Information. What these two programs have identified is a broader context and redefinition of what constitutes academic preparation for professionals pursuing careers in all types of information and library environments. In the future, the emphasis will be on training academic librarians to have an in-depth knowledge of technology as well as the electronic dissemination of information. Both California and Michigan are preparing the academic librarian of the future to manage, retrieve, and manipulate information locally, through networks and across the Internet. They are placing librarians in a position to play a leading role in the dissemination of information.

These new schools of information have taken advantage of the fact that there has been an information and technology revolution over the past 20 years. Both programs are developing courses that will prepare professionals to work in an information environment mandated by technology, as well as to work in both the nonprofit and the profit sectors. These programs are highly interdisciplinary and require the student to develop an understanding of computer and network systems, public policy, economics, communication, and management theory.

What can be perceived from these changes in library education is the fact that technology is an enabling process. Through the use of technology, the academic librarians of tomorrow will recast the entire nature of libraries. With the digitizing of hundreds of thousands of materials and by working collaboratively, academic libraries will be able to provide access to an untold number of resources. This does not mean the disappearance of traditional sources of information such as books; rather, it means an expansion and management of information that can easily be retrieved electronically by the user.

Such a seismic shift in the goals and purpose of the library can have profound consequences for academic librarians. Already, these changes are apparent in academic libraries across the country. Through the introduction of a variety of automated systems, on-line, full-text databases, and the World Wide Web (Internet), there has been a flattening of the information field for all types of academic librarians. The small, private, liberal arts college library has direct electronic access to resources and collections that were inaccessible to nearly all academic libraries, except for large research universities, only a few years ago. This new expansion of information technology casts academic librarians in a new light. They must be continually retraining and analyzing the new retrieval systems and studying ways to incorporate technology access into the mainstream services of the academic library.

In the future, it will be increasingly important for academic librarians to become fully knowledgeable of the changes occurring in library education. The graduate schools of information need to examine the development of new curricula in light of offering continuing education and professional development to academic librarians. Summer institutes on the changes taking place in information education should be designed for professionals in the field. Some of the retraining of these professionals, given the sophistication of technology delivery, could even be conducted on-line. When there are more discussions and joint efforts to retrain the practicing professional, there will be a stronger interaction between the schools of information and the professionals in the field.

Given the dramatic changes occurring in technology, in higher education, and in the education of librarians, the librarian—rather than becoming obsolete—becomes increasingly important in the academic libraries of the future. Thus, these changes should be perceived as opportunities for enhancement and recognition. The academic librarian of the future has a vast potential to assume new and exciting leadership roles in the teaching, research, and service of higher education.

REFERENCES

Association of College & Research Libraries. 1997a. "ACRL Joins National Initiative on Faculty Roles and Rewards; Seeks Member Input." *College & Research Libraries News* 58 (January): 6.
———. 1997b. "ACRL Addresses the Future: Part 1." *College & Research Libraries News* 58 (June): 386–391.
———. 1997c. "ACRL Addresses the Future: Part 2." *College & Research Libraries News* 58 (July/August): 480–486.
Boisse, Joseph A. and Stella Bentley. 1996. "Reorganizing Libraries: Is Flatter Better?" In Irene Godden, ed., *Advances in Librarianship*, vol. 20. New York: Academic Press, pp. 27–45.
Dolence, Michael G. and Donald M. Norris. 1995. *Transforming Higher Education: A Vision for Learning in the 21st Century.* Ann Arbor, MI: Society for College and University Planning.
Dowler, Lawrence. 1997. "Gateway to Knowledge: A New Direction for the Harvard College Library." In Lawrence Dowler, ed., *Gateways to Knowledge: The Role*

of Academic Libraries in Teaching, Learning, and Research. Cambridge, MA: MIT Press, pp. 97–107.

Drabenstott, Karen M. and Daniel E. Atkins. 1996. "The Kellogg CRISTAL-ED Project: Creating a Model Program to Support Libraries in the Digital Age." In Irene Godden, ed., *Advances in Librarianship*, vol. 20. New York: Academic Press, pp. 47–68.

Hirshon, Arnold. 1996. "Running with the Red Queen: Breaking New Habits to Survive in the Virtual World." In Irene Godden, ed., *Advances in Librarianship*, vol. 20. New York: Academic Press, pp. 1–26.

Massy, William F. and Robert Zemsky. 1995. "Using Information Technology to Enhance Academic Productivity." Paper presented at the Wingspread Enhancing Academic Productivity Conference, Keystone, CO.

Olsen, Jan. 1997. "The Gateway: Point of Entry to the Electronic Library." In Lawrence Dowler, ed., *Gateways to Knowledge: The Role of Academic Libraries in Teaching, Learning, and Research.* Cambridge, MA: MIT Press, pp. 123–134.

Chapter 9

Expatriate Librarians and the Challenge of National Culture

Kenneth J. Oberembt

INTRODUCTION

In 1989, while living in Egypt, I had an experience of national culture that will serve nicely as an introduction to this chapter on library employment overseas, a career choice that has attracted, over the years, a large number of librarians of American citizenship. Placed in my hands one morning in late November was a press release (English translation) issued by the Egyptian government for publication, which read as follows:

> Prime Minister Dr. Atef Sedki passed a decision yesterday stipulating that the weekend at governmental bodies be Thursday and Friday of every week, instead of Friday and Saturday, to unify work time [in] all organs, in accordance with public interest.
>
> The decision is effective this week, in a manner not infringing upon work hours. ("Weekend, Thursday . . ." 1989, 17)

Because Egypt, at the time, had a wholly command economy, making the government effectively the chief employer and paymaster of the nation, the scope of the decision was enormous. No wide-ranging public debate of the efficacy of changing the weekend dates preceded the governmental decree, and no organized protest followed. Although grumbling about the stupidity of the authorities abounded, the energies of the general citizenry, as well as of the staff of the American University in Cairo Library, turned to accommodating the new reality. How would the children's school week be affected? The spouse's work schedule? The timings of the vegetable, fruit, meat, dairy, and dry goods shops for provisioning the daily needs of the household? Emergency leave from the workplace to seek answers and to make the necessary arrangements was both understandable and unavoidable. Within three weeks, however, the Friday–Saturday weekend was restored. Like the earlier decision, the later one, too, was deliberated in private by the Cabinet of Ministers and announced of a sudden by the Egyptian government. While no official reason was offered, rumor had it that people were manipulating the situation so as to extend the weekend from two to three days, and the government could have none of that.

Intrigued by the unilateral decision taking of the Egyptian government and the make-do response of the governed, I sought explanation and was assured, simply, "That's the system." Over time, what seemed at first to be a coy non-answer unfolded its hidden wisdom. At work in the 1989 remaking of the Egyptian weekend and its subsequent reversal and of everything in between were cultural assumptions about authority and human nature, activity, and relationships integrated into what can justly be called a *system*, a set of cultural assumptions neither better nor worse than alternatives, merely different.

The message from this that I first draw and then elaborate in this chapter is that libraries, whatever their broad similarities of mission and of operation, are embedded in different cultures, and those cultures infiltrate into every aspect of library business, affecting everything from the perception of what constitutes proper service to the preference for certain styles of management (and leadership) over others as offering the best means of meeting service goals. Because any library will receive and apply technology, develop its human resources, and transform organizational processes in ways most suitable to its own national culture and not to any other, those American librarians practicing their profession abroad (and others who anticipate working overseas) must expect national culture to be an ever-present reality in the workplace, visibly *and* invisibly influencing how work is structured, allocated, and accounted for and, as well, shaping the interactions of those who do that work. Expatriates must learn and adjust to the national culture of the host country if they are to be effective in their jobs.

In the following I review some contemporary research into national culture's impact, generally, on work-related values and then consider some of the effects of Arab national culture, specifically, on the library workplace I have observed in two countries (Egypt and Saudi Arabia) that profess Pan-Arab cultural traditions and values. Even as the Arab world is divided into various self-governing states—the work of European colonialists—a sense of single nationhood pervades the consciousness of Arabs living from the Atlantic to the Arabian (Persian) Gulf and from the Blue Nile headwaters to the Mediterranean. Although Arab world culture is here the national culture under scrutiny, my intent is to present conclusions that have, mutatis mutandis, global applicability.

NATIONAL CULTURE

The influence of national culture in the workplace forces itself on Americans who find themselves employed overseas, whether in an affiliate of a multinational corporation or in a state-owned library. It is a topic that has attracted researchers in organization and management science, a large sample of whose work Mead (1994) records in his fairly up-to-date bibliography. More than 25 years ago, Geert Hofstede (1980) began to publish the results of his study of work-related values in 40 (later in excess of 50) different countries and three geographical regions. Even accepting the fact that the more than 116,000 employees of a single multinational company (code-named HERMES, later identified as IBM) he surveyed worldwide might not be entirely typical of their respective national populations and that several of the target countries (Belgium, the United States, Switzerland, and former Yugoslavia, notably) are perhaps too heterogeneous to lend themselves to strict monocultural analysis, Hofstede confirmed the presence of clear "difference in mental programming and national character" (1983, 78). National culture in the workplace, he demonstrated, can be measured according to four continua, or, in his terminology, "dimensions":

1. Individualism/collectivism—the relationship between an individual and his or her associates as it gives priority to the individual or to the collectivity;

2. Power distance—great or small disparities among people at different levels of an authority hierarchy;

3. Uncertainty avoidance—strong or weak capacity for accepting the unpredictable future; and

4. Masculinity/femininity—differentiation of sex-related roles and, by extension, work orientations that stress achievement or nurturance.

The following two figures of paired dimensions (Hofstede 1983, 82, 86) reveal the great diversity among national cultures. Figure 9.1 combines power distance (the horizontal scale) and individualism/collectivism (the vertical) and plots values for each of 50 countries and regions. (See the Hofstede [1983] reference for the key to the graph legends.) At one end of an axis extending from lower left to upper right is a cluster of mainly Northern European and North American countries characterized by a low tolerance for hierarchies of authority and a high acceptance of the value of self-responsibility. At the other end is a large grouping of Southern European, Middle Eastern, and Asian countries of diametrically opposite character: high acceptance of both hierarchical order and group-centered responsibility. The second pair (see Figure 9.2) of dimensions—femininity/masculinity (the horizontal scale) and uncertainty avoidance (the vertical)—depicts along two different axes North American and Northern European countries, plus several of the Asian Tigers, clustered together by their tendency to promote risk-taking activity. Apart from the Nordic countries, the

Figure 9.1
**A Power Distance × Individualism = Collectivism Plot for 50 Countries and
Three Regions**

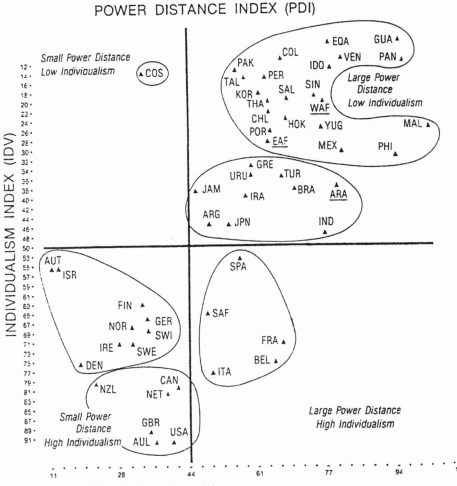

Source: Hofstede (1993), 82. Used with permission.

Figure 9.2
A Masculinity-Femininity × Uncertainty Avoidance Plot for 50 Countries and Three Regions

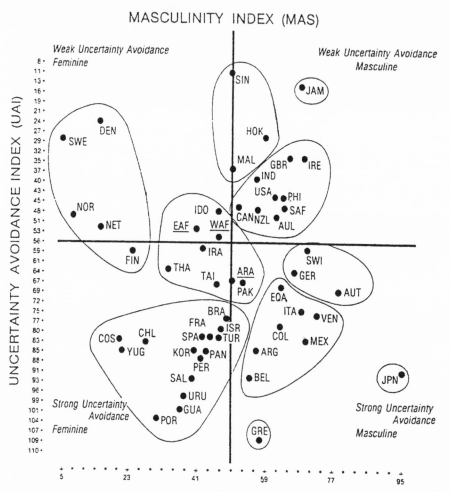

Source: Hofstede (1983), 86. Used with permission.

Netherlands, Africa, and Indonesia, they tend to encourage a more aggressive work orientation and to classify jobs by gender. All remaining countries/regions place a high premium on circumventing risk, though, at the same time, they show an exceedingly wide spread on the scale of dominant sex roles and work orientations, with Japan the most gender-biased in sexual division of labor in the workplace and the most marked by an achievement-oriented work ethos and with Costa Rica the least so on both counts.

Hofstede's dimensions are individual measures aggregated by nation to produce national scores. They have been judged by experts who have critiqued them, like Jaeger (1986, 181), "to have a reasonable representative validity of societal values and differences."

NATIONAL CULTURE AND THE WORKPLACE

That national cultures *do* differ is a point not lost upon even the casual traveler in foreign lands. The more profound point is that differences among national cultures *make a difference* when it comes to matters of the organization of the workplace and the management of it. National culture functions like a template on the mind, laying down patterns to be followed in structuring power and human relationships, in defining the value of work, and in systematizing inter-human responsibilities for the accomplishment of work tasks. Adherents to a national culture activate that template by rote, and repeatedly, in their socio-political lives outside the work environment, to impose order and to give meaning, they carry it with them into their places of work for the same purposes. It could not be otherwise, for that template and its patterns for organizing the human commonweal are an inextricable part of their socialization and their psychology and, in fact, their shared identity as one people distinct from others— what, in the final analysis, makes them *them*. It cannot be shucked off easily even by an act of will. It is, rather, an automatic overlay upon reality to make it manageable. National culture's template does not produce a rigidly uniform result within its force field everywhere or in every instance. It admits of variation and tolerance to experimentation, according to individual needs and situational possibilities. Nevertheless, it is stable over time and space, changing, for the most part, incrementally, and is measurable because it reveals itself and its assumptions and values through the ways a like-acculturated group of people think about, and do, things. This stability in time and fixedness in place make possible the study of national culture and the analysis of similarities and contrasts among various national cultures.

Drawing on my almost nine years of experience in Arab world libraries, as well as the collateral experiences of colleagues who have worked in libraries in this same part of the world, I focus on three issues currently important in contemporary librarianship in the Arab Middle East and the challenges Arab national culture poses for each: technological development, human resource development, and organization development. Each has some association with one or more of Hofstede's dimensions, and each is, equally, an issue being grappled with by librarians far beyond the Arab world. Nowhere, not even in the United States, is library development easy to initiate and to sustain, but in the Arab world, with its strong ties to an ancient Islamic culture more than 1,500 years old and with its sense of a lost *golden age*, the underlying cultural principles and values of which are still key to future development, there is so much more uncertainty than elsewhere about what needs changing and how any change will advance, rather than violate, the Arab national culture. The increasing global penetration through the borders of nation-states by what Benjamin Barber (1996, 60) has coined the *infotainment telesector* (the "wedding of telecommunications technologies with information and entertainment software") only adds to this uncertainty by its conveyance of an alien—and potentially threatening—Western culture that cannot be controlled, let alone easily filtered for Arab world consumption. As Mahmoud Amin El-Alem of Egypt starkly dissected the threat of global culture to the Arab world in remarks laid before a Pan-Arab assembly of intellectuals in Cairo early in December 1996, the globalizers (and their unwitting supporters) "seek to restructure societies to accept the one cultural, economic, political and social model which they wish to impose—this being the American model" (Abdel-Latif 1996, 1). Cultural hypersensitivity, heightened even by the twists and turns in the Middle East peace process, is a hallmark of the Arab world.

The Arab Middle East is hardly alone among the countries and regions of the developing world in knowing where, precisely, its best interests lie in an increasingly globalized information marketplace, and Arab world libraries, still perceived as playing the role of *cultural guardian*, must remain circumspect in the information policies they espouse and protective of national culture by screening for insensitive images and values the information to which they give their clients access.

Indeed, the deeply conservative Arab national culture opposes change that is overhasty and not carefully deliberated in advance. On the other hand, Arab national culture professes to encourage national development, of which change is the necessary precondition. There is actually no inconsistency here at all. The Arab world is only asking the outside world to understand that change must follow *their* Arab cultural agenda—must be compatible with *their* Arab modes of governing human activity and structuring human relationships, must be consonant with *their* Arab life and work values, and must proceed at a pace in tune with the rhythms dictated by *their* Arab way of doing things. *Their* culture, not *ours*, will lead the way! *Hesitancy to adopt change is no vice* is the Arab world's wise admonition. *Procrastination, the almost indistinguishable twin of hesitancy, is no virtue either* is, to be sure, the equally wise caution of the outside world.

How libraries in the Arab world are enabled by national culture to modernize technology, to upgrade human resources, and to remodel their organizations are subjects taken up in the pages following. The message is that of Arab national culture posing constraints to development but, at the same time, affording opportunities. Expatriate librarians working in a national culture different in important respects from their own do well to understand its autonomic ways and means and to use them advantageously.

Technological Development and National Culture

A recent essay (El-Bahrawi 1996, 8) in *Al-Ahram Weekly*, the national English-language newspaper of Egypt, has the rather striking—and revealing—subtitle teaser: "Purchasing Western Technology Is No Solution to the Arab's Predicament." The author articulates the concerns of many of his Egyptian (and regional) compatriots at the eagerness, from both without *and* within the Arab world, to introduce into Arab countries technologies of Western origin. It is nothing more than a renewal of the Western colonization of the Arab nation and of the subversion of the Arab culture by the West. In his judgment, the rush to adopt such technologies without first giving careful thought to the consequences is utterly reckless:

[T]he current concept of international relations limits scientific and technological production to the achievement of specific interests, i.e. the interests of the producers—who are, in the final analysis, the international capitalist centre and its immediate peripheries. In other words, the revolution in information technology becomes a tool for global hegemony within the new world order, not only over the formally colonised countries, but over the entire globe.

The expansion of communications networks, which carry the voice of the centre to all the peripheries, contribute[s] to this hegemony and allow[s] the cultural specificity of weaker parties to be undermined further. This constitutes a breach of one of the basic human rights: the right to maintain one's distinct identity in every aspect of one's interaction. (El-Bahrawi 1996, 8)

The Arab world is not alone in wanting, at one and the same time, to modernize *and* to preserve its ancient traditions. To do this requires a delicate balancing act: with too much emphasis upon tradition, modernization may well falter; with modernization too fast and too dependent on technologies bearing the values of an alien creator culture, tradition may be undermined. The fear expressed by El-Bahrawi is a real one in the developing world generally: a fear of foreign hegemony over intellectual, sociopolitical, and religious life such that the indigenous culture is marginalized. The Internet, potentially the most culturally invasive of contemporary information technologies, is a case in point. While even in the West it is not regarded as an unmixed blessing—the Internet can serve as a channel for pornography, for recipes to construct explosive devices, for libelous comments, for violations of copyright and patent rights, for seditious remarks, and the like—it is also intimately associated here with *democracy, individualism, intellectual freedom*, and *human rights*. In cultures with values diverging from these, the Internet is understandably cause for suspicion and concern. No less so are other technologies, such as satellite television, which the authorities in countries as culturally divergent as Iran and Singapore have seen fit to ban as countercultural.

One need only take another look at Hofstede's power distance graph (see Figure 9.1) to observe that Arab countries (the aggregate of Egypt, Lebanon, Libya, Kuwait, Iraq, Saudi Arabia, and the United Arab Emirates in Hofstede's survey) rank within the top eight in deference to authority and in tolerance for inequalities among their citizenry. In fact, 32 of Hofstede's 50 countries/regions display, in varying degrees, this very same value orientation. Democracy and the many virtues ascribed to it, whatever their intellectual and emotional appeal to certain elites living under one or another forms of oligarchic government, are not culturally embedded in nearly two-thirds of the world Hofstede surveyed.

If there is in the United States a perception that current communications technologies are essentially good but sometimes wild things that need taming, in Arab and other developing world countries they are, in the view of many, to be justified first and controlled later. The free flow of information into, out of, and within national borders, at least when some share of that information is judged to be culturally inappropriate, is not a winning argument in societies that favor a highly structured power hierarchy with great distances between successive levels in that hierarchy and that, likewise, elevate the collective over the individual good. The twined themes of state responsibility and protection of the commonweal are at the core of Saudi minister of education Dr. Muhammed Ahmad Al-Rashid's remarks to a United Nations Educational, Scientific, and Cultural Organization (UNESCO) meeting in Paris (October 1996) defending the right of governments to curb "unbridled use of information technology":

[W]e, in the Kingdom of Saudi Arabia are with the constructive freedom which is exercised for full sense of responsibility, respecting the dignity of man. We are for the freedom of every society in formulating regulations for exercising this freedom to fulfill the ambitions and objectives of its members. We are surprised when some people resent if the education and information agencies of a country supervise the incoming information in order to ensure the good of their citizens and to ensure the best use of technology to protect them against moral degradation. The forces of evil are rampant and they disdain the religious values and the distinctive qualities of different peoples. . . . Shall we give "freedom" to these people to thwart the efforts we are making to raise a pious and productive man fit to face the challenges of the twenty first century[?]. ("A Boon Turned Curse By Misuse" 1996, 9)

It seems clear that any technology fit for adoption outside the environment of its origin must be deeply rooted in the culture of adoption and addressed to its autochthonous values.

Of recent date in Saudi Arabia, with echoes in the wider Islamic world, there are people taking just this approach to the problem of technology transfer. Dr. Saud Kateb urges Muslims "to hook up into Internet as early as possible to make use of the information superhighway for spreading the message of Islam and countering false campaigns against their religion'' (''Muslims Urged . . .'' 1996, 12). Ihsan Abu Haliqa argues in a similar vein: ''Imagine in the African jungle, in Europe, America, and even in Alaska, people could learn a lot of things about Islam, Arab history and the Saudi economy. . . . A journalist in the United States, if he wants to write an article about our country, will have direct access to our sources and will no longer have to depend on biased sources'' (''Internet Can Be Used . . .'' 1996, 7). Speaking from within a cultural context where modernity evokes apprehension as well as appreciation, these two Saudis promote on-line networking as a technology appropriate for conveying accurate information about the national culture to an international audience and urge its adoption, for that reason, by their fellow nationals. Central to their argument is the religion that quickens Arab national culture: the Internet, in Islamic terms, is an opportunity for a Muslim to accomplish *halal* (action directed toward what is good); failing to seize, or even actively forgoing, that opportunity could well, on the other hand, be regarded as *haram* (action not supporting, or even opposing, what is good) for it leaves misinformation and disinformation victorious.

Libraries in the Arab world and in the wider developing world, too, intent upon staying current with the fast-evolving information technologies, must pace their development in terms of what national culture will support. Some Arab countries, for example, Egypt, are relatively more open to innovation than others, like Iraq, which is wholly closed to external influence. All, however, have a tradition of centralized authority that commands the allegiance of those at opposite ends of the power continuum, a dynamic between top-down action and bottom-up reaction that is accepted as part of the natural order of things. At the same time, all have Western-trained and Western-influenced elites in the academy, in government, in the security apparatus, and in the military requiring access to the best of international telecommunications and information technologies. Arab world governors have displayed a readiness, when pressured, to cater to elite needs. They have done so, nevertheless, with strict limitations on who can obtain access as well as what and where and when and how, libraries not excepted.

At this moment, the most advanced modes of communication technology are inaccessible to the general populace of the Arab world. They will remain so pending the day they become more accommodating to Arab national culture. This will require Arabized search tools (e.g., Web pages in Arabic) and extensive availability of culturally appropriate information content in the Arabic language. The English (and Western) language bias of technologies like the Internet renders them virtually useless for community-building purposes in Arab lands and elsewhere. Western technology's linguistic bias guarantees its perceived foreignness and, until that changes, inhibits the transfer of Western technology into non-Western cultures.

There is a role here for Arab world libraries and information centers to play as creators of linguistically and culturally sensitive information resources that can indigenize imported technology and ultimately ease the way for its acceptance into national culture. Even with the efforts in the Arabian Gulf of institutions like the Kuwait Institute of Scientific Research (KISR) and King Abdulaziz City for Science and Technology (KACST), too little has been done thus far to acculturate technology for the use of the general citizenry of the Gulf (and the greater Arab world by extension) and so to bring it into the cultural mainstream.

Human Resource Development and National Culture

A recent news story ("Bahrain Leads Arab World . . ." 1996, 14) proudly trumpets the fact that the Arabian Gulf is at the forefront of the Arab world in human resource development. As measured by the latest annual report of the United Nations Development Program (UNDP), Cyprus, Barbados, the Bahamas, South Korea, and Argentina are, in that order, the highest-ranking developing world countries, and the Arabian Gulf states of Bahrain, Qatar, and the United Arab Emirates hold down positions in the following tier. As testimony to the present-day acknowledgment of the importance of developing human potential—in Gulf region libraries specifically—the Arabian Gulf Chapter/Special Libraries Association (AGC/SLA) organized its 1996 annual conference in Kuwait under the theme "Human Resource Development in the Electronic Library Environment." The need as well as the appropriate strategies for exploiting the potential talents of Arabian Gulf nationals and marshaling trained and motivated Gulf citizens for service in the economies of their respective countries have particular meaning for the Arabian peninsula, which has achieved modernity and, in fact, a leading position in the developing world only in the past several decades. Although the (Arabian Gulf Cooperation Council AGCC) states have accomplished much, they recognize that they have far to go and must depend now, more than ever, on their own citizens to do it.

The countries composing the AGCC—Bahrain, Kuwait, Oman, Qatar, Saudi Arabia, and the United Arab Emirates—are singular in the Arab world for their heavy reliance on imported workers. Around one-third of the resident workforce in Saudi Arabia is expatriate, and in both Kuwait and the United Arab Emirates the figure is much higher. Mainly transhumant societies until the close of World War II, the AGCC countries rapidly developed modern economies in the wake of large-scale petroleum extraction and downstream exploitation. Their demand for experts (managers, technicians) as well as grunt labor has continued right up to the present day to exceed the supply of ready and willing natives. Beginning in the mid-1980s, a combination of fiscal crisis caused by a drop in the per barrel price of oil and nationalistic feeling precipitated by competition between natives and expatriates for jobs forced the issue of workforce nationalization. In all AGCC countries, there are now active plans for migrating jobs from expatriates to nationals. In Oman, for instance, a 15 percent ceiling has been set for expatriate workers in the economy by the year 2000. Workforce

nationalization is viewed not only as a means of securing employment for natives and of keeping more of the national wealth at home but also as an empowerment issue—AGCC citizens taking on more of the workload in their
several countries, thereby increasing ownership over their national destinies.
Empowerment, too, has come, most importantly in the United States, to be
associated with the new computer-based technologies now working their way
into the Arab world. These require workers with higher technical and knowledge
skills and, above all, entrepreneurial skills to exploit technology's potential. The
Arab world is coming to recognize this. Western-based (including Japanese)
quality management theories like total quality management (TQM) address the
issue of technology exploitation through worker empowerment. These have in
recent years also found an increasingly friendly reception in the Arab world
("Triumph of TQM . . ." 1996, 36).

Validating empowerment and implementing it are two quite different matters.
The gap between them must be closed by an educational system that, in the
words of Mona Ebeid (1993, 8), a member of the Egyptian People's Assembly,
"encourages research, the development of people's talents and a team spirit, not
memorization and the kind of rote-learning that dismisses rational thinking and
allows intellectual intimidation to take root." Her negatives are what she con-
demns in Egypt's education system, but memorizing and rote learning are the
hallmarks of primary, secondary, and university education in Arab (and other)
lands beyond Egypt's borders. Disempowering, they rob learners and, ultimately,
the nation of "capabilities in science and technology" (Ebeid 1993, 8). Em-
powerable citizens have such capabilities: more than knowing theory, they know
how to apply it; they have mastered problem-solving techniques; curious and
self-energizing, they probe for new verities behind received truths; they are not
bound by overly nice distinctions between hand tools and mind tools, preferring
to take a holistic view of the skills that will enrich life and work.

The dimensions of national culture plotted by Hofstede for the Arab countries
(see Figures 9.1 and 9.2) highlight the constraints that exist within Arab countries on empowerment of nationals in both civic life and the workplace: structured authority (very high), collectivist human interaction (higher than the world
survey mean), avoidance of uncertainty (higher than the world survey mean),
and a masculine concept of work (very high). Each of these has consequences
(cf. Hofstede 1980, 119, 135, 176–177, 186–187, 230–231, 238–239, 288–289,
296–297) for Arab world organizations, including Arab world libraries:

• Highly structured authority translates into more autocratic management, a greater reliance on consultation than participation in decision making, more attention to employee role and status, a greater valuation placed on job qualifications and employee
credentials, closer supervision by managers, lesser inclination for supervisees to question management decisions, a more intensive task-than process-driven work environment, greater exactness in defining jobs and responsibilities, and more emphasis on
seniority in making promotions;

- Highly collectivist human interaction makes for a stronger sense of the organization as like family rather than business, a greater need for outward display of loyalty and affection among coworkers, a higher level of conformity, more of an in-group-versus-out-group flavor to work relationships, more stress on organization-directed training than individual self-training, and more emphasis on work duties than fulfillment of the self in work;

- High avoidance of uncertainty means more structure to work activities, a more heavily layered and bureaucratic organization, more policies and rules and procedures and standards, a greater perceived need for micromanagement and close supervision, more ritual behavior among equals, less emphasis on promotion and climbing the organizational career ladder, and more anxiety about job security; and

- A highly masculine concept of work results in more organizational interference in the private lives of employees, more emphasis on salary and recognition, more sex discrimination in the assignment of jobs and compensation, a greater tendency in performance evaluation to value work quantity than quality, a more competitive and conflictual relationship among peers, greater job stress, and a higher regard for production than service work.

All of these consequences are relative rather than absolute, of course. While it is tempting to highlight what is negative about them and constraining to human resource development under Arab national culture, the better and more positive approach is to ascertain what kinds of developmental activities might nonetheless be productively pursued and how national culture can be enlisted to induce and then sustain these. Every national culture, wherever plotted on Hofstede's scales, is amenable to human resource development. Goals and strategies will, however, differ from culture to culture. Those for the great power distance, highly collectivist, and strong uncertainty-avoiding national culture of the Arab world cannot be the same as for the small power distance, highly individualist, and weak uncertainty-avoiding national culture of the United States. The resemblance, on the other hand, between Arab and Japanese national cultures—closely similar on Hofstede's power distance and individualism/collectivism scales and akin, though somewhat more distantly (i.e., plotted within the same quadrant), on the other two—would seem to justify budding Arabian Gulf interest in Japanese quality management theories.

The author has observed firsthand the worker empowerment program (for Saudis), modeled on Japanese practice, that the Saudi Consolidated Electricity Company in the Eastern Province (SCECO-East) of Saudi Arabia has undertaken and was impressed by that program's compatibility with national culture, by the ways it drew upon the dimensions Hofstede has identified with Arab national culture to support program empowerment goals. For example,

- Quality improvement initiatives devolved upon work groups (building on the national culture's preference for collective action) formed from a staff of nearly similar employment rank in the organization (preserving the national culture's high valuation of hierarchy);

- Work groups held regular communication meetings with management to report on progress and to receive feedback (respecting the national culture's reservation of final decision making to higher authority and its endorsement of risk avoidance); and

- Work groups focused on tasks/results rather than behaviors/satisfactions (complying with the national culture's more masculine work ethic) and derived conclusions through the application of TQM tools (flowcharts, Pareto charts, Ishikawa diagrams, etc.) designed to collect, compile, and interpret hard data (in tune with the national culture's predilection for certainties).

The SCECO-East staff development program is regarded as a test bed for quality management methods and practices, and other institutions in the Arabian Gulf are looking to it for guidance in developing more worker-empowering forms of workplace management.

For libraries and other organizations in the Arab world, human resource development would, quite reasonably, seem to invite a peer group approach (sustaining Arab national culture's inclination toward authority and collectivity) and a structured group task orientation (supporting Arab national culture's predisposition to shun risk taking and to advance masculine work values). Both of these are central to the Japanese quality managed workplace. Library-based human resource development programs in the Arabian Gulf are still in their infancy and, in the Arabian Gulf and the greater Arab world generally, still too little learner-centered. With their maturation and with a wider sense of what organizations like SCECO-East are accomplishing, training activities that really develop human potential and really empower people may begin to emerge and multiply.

Organizational Development and National Culture

Integral to every organization, W. Warner Burke (1992, 12–13) has emphasized, is a "technology subsystem," whether the production of something tangible or the provision of a service, and a "social subsystem," the body of people who interact to accomplish the work of the organization. The role of organization development (OD) is to initiate "change"—more exactly, "change in the organization's culture" and not necessarily or merely in its individual members as individuals. Modifying organizational culture is, under no circumstances, easy. The difficulty is certainly compounded when those elements in the organizational culture targeted for change are underpinned by the national culture in which the organization is embedded.

Following up Hofstede's work on national cultures, Alfred M. Jaeger (1986, 182–185) set out to determine what kinds of OD intervention (= a deliberately provoked disruption of an organization's business-as-usual, the provocation either internally or externally arranged) would best suit which cultures. He concluded that the national culture open to the full range of OD interventions was one that ranked low on Hofstede's power distance, uncertainty avoidance, and masculinity/femininity scales and at least at the median on the individualism/ collectivism scale. Only the national cultures of Denmark, Finland, Ireland, Israel, the Netherlands, Norway, and Sweden come close to the optimal. Nonetheless, he allowed that practically all national cultures are open to some type of OD intervention. Management by objectives works best where power distance is not too great, where uncertainty avoidance is not too strong, and where masculinity (i.e., a performance-oriented work ethic) predominates. Sensitivity training is most feasible where uncertainty avoidance is weak, and femininity (i.e., a nurturing work orientation) is dominant. Neither suits the Arab national culture profile—with its respect for authority, groupism, and assertiveness and its distaste for risk—but several OD interventions hold particular promise for application in the Arab world (cf. Jaeger 1986, 185, 187–189):

- Work humanization schemes that target the group rather than the individual, that define a new core of shared tasks and encourage group accountability for task outcomes meeting organizational objectives, and that build a modest measure of autonomy where authority continues to be largely a matter of role and status;

- Transactional analysis utilization for capturing in a most impersonal way data in perceived problem areas and for subjecting those data to review by groups of people similarly statused in the organization, so as to build group confidence in problem-solving skills and to neutralize clashes with authority and personal confrontations;

- Nurturant task-leading that matches a strong, but caring, leader with a group and that offers affection and protection as the continuous rewards for group accomplishment; and

- Third-party intervention for the application of expertise when an organization itself cannot sort out a problem, when warring organizational factions cannot reach a peaceful solution to a problem, or when higher levels of authority need persuasion by someone perceived to be wholly objective.

Successful OD activities in the Arab world, as elsewhere, must respect the values of the national culture, for organizational values allied to these are deeply held and change-resistant. Proactive rather than confrontational OD promises a warmer welcome and a happier outcome.

It must here be noted that certain non-Arab national cultures plotted by Hofstede have a larger presence in Arabian Gulf organizations than in those of the Arab world generally. With regard to Pakistan and the Arab world, differences obtain only on the Hofstede scales for power distance (lower for Pakistan) and individualism/collectivism (a far greater group orientation for Pakistan). Broadly speaking, the imported national culture reinforces the values of the native. Differences elsewhere are more contrastive. Between Indian and Philippine national cultures and the Arab, a major difference shows up on Hofstede's scale for uncertainty avoidance (significantly weaker for both India and the Philippines). Between United States and Arab national cultures, differences are revealed on three of Hofstede's dimensions: power distance (far smaller for the United

States), individualism/collectivism (far more value on the individual for the United States), and uncertainty avoidance (far weaker for the United States). Beyond the four countries just named, there are also, among those *not* surveyed by Hofstede, Bangladesh and Nepal and Sri Lanka, to cite three with especially large contingents in the Gulf, not to speak of Egypt and other Arab world countries also heavily represented that share the same national culture as the Arabian states but whose nationals hold non-Arabian citizenship and have a temporary contractual commitment to work in the Gulf that marks them off as foreign in the eyes of the natives.

For many Arabian Gulf organizations, including a fair number of libraries, the place of work is the meeting ground of sometimes incompatible national cultures. These exist alongside one another, each staunchly maintaining its own identity. The bridges across cultures tend, on the whole, to be created by individuals rather than by organizations. The typical organizational response to the cultural diversity in its midst is to ignore culturally inspired behaviors (work processes) and to focus on functions and duties (work tasks). Certainly, this is time-, effort-, and cost-saving for the organization to do, but it can be better understood and interpreted as a response fully in character with the masculine work ethic of Arab national culture. Task orientation is the national culture's ordinary means of avoiding or at least minimizing interpersonal and intergroup conflict applied, as well, to the extraordinary presence of sometimes contrary cultures and cultural values residing side by side in the workplace. To a cultural outsider, what can appear to be a human relations problem overlooked or neglected is, from the viewpoint of the Arab world, a potential problem defused and resolved in the national culture's tried and true way.

Even so, the multicultural diversity everywhere present in the Arabian Gulf raises interesting and largely unaddressed concerns about organization development. How should it proceed within the framework of workforce nationalization policies recently mandated by Arabian governments? If jobs are at risk, how can expatriate workers be won over to participate wholeheartedly in organization development efforts? How can the sometimes very different cultural values within a single organization be comprehended in a be seamless OD program? Satisfactory answers have yet to be found. Unfortunately, the questions are often too uncomfortable to ask. If the large expatriate workforce in the Arabian Gulf is only temporarily useful and, over time, expendable, OD programming will necessarily give it peripheral attention. If, on the contrary, expatriate workers are recognized to have long-term value to the Gulf region, and their role in organizations is to be maintained, OD programming will have to find ways to enhance their value.

For expatriate workers, nothing beyond their immediate future in the Gulf has been decided, but a final decision for the longer term depends on the continued dedication of expatriates to their work in the Gulf and the fruits of their labors that Gulf employers can expect to reap. It also depends on the direction that organization development—and, moreover, national development—will take.

CONCLUSION

Turning for a brief moment to the anecdote that opened this chapter—the back-and-forth change of Egypt's weekend in November 1989—one can see in the rhythm of action, reaction, and counteraction between the Egyptian government and the Egyptian populace Arab national culture at its most characteristic. Higher authority reserves to itself the risk of responsibility and the power of deciding, those of lesser authority adapt to what is handed down, higher authority revises, those of lesser authority again adapt, and so on adinfinitum. "That's the system," to repeat the words of my associate and interpreter. This dynamic is certified by national culture and repeated endlessly in sociopolitical life. It is replicated ceaselessly in the organizations influenced by national culture. It is perceived to be part of the natural order, as much as eating and sleeping and breathing. It gives to reality a satisfying uniformity and meaning.

How broadly or narrowly a national culture distributes power among its members and how tightly or loosely it mitigates uncertainty for those under its sway determine, for Hofstede (1983, 87), the shape any organization under its auspices will likely take. He couples the power distance and uncertainty avoidance dimensions of national culture (see Figure 9.3) to illustrate the organization preferences among different national cultures.

Hofstede identifies four organizational types or models dominant among national cultures worldwide:

- The Pyramid: "a hierarchical structure held together by the unity of command (larger Power Distance) as well as by rules (strong Uncertainty Avoidance)"—for example, France, South Korea, Turkey, and Uruguay;

- The Well-Oiled Machine: where "the exercise of personal command [is] largely unnecessary because the rules settl[e] everything (strong Uncertainty Avoidance, but smaller Power Distance)"—for example, Germany and Israel;

- The Village Market: "no decisive hierarchy, flexible rules, and a resolution of problems by negotiating (small Power Distance and weak Uncertainty Avoidance)"—for example, Canada, Great Britain, Jamaica, Australia; and

- The Family: "undisputed personal authority of the father-leader but few formal rules (large Power Distance and weak Uncertainty Avoidance)"—for example, India, East Africa.

North America (i.e., Canada and the United States) cultivates the negotiatory Village Market type of organization, and the Arab world cultivates the authoritarian Pyramid type. To the extent that an expatriate American's organizational experience at home is true to the cultural norm, she or he can expect to undergo disorientation (culture shock) in an Arab world library equally true to the model promoted by its culture. Less than one-quarter of the nations/regions Hofstede surveyed favor the Village Market model. By contrast, some 50 percent of coun-

Figure 9.3

A Power Distance × Uncertainty Avoidance Plot for 50 Countries and Three Regions

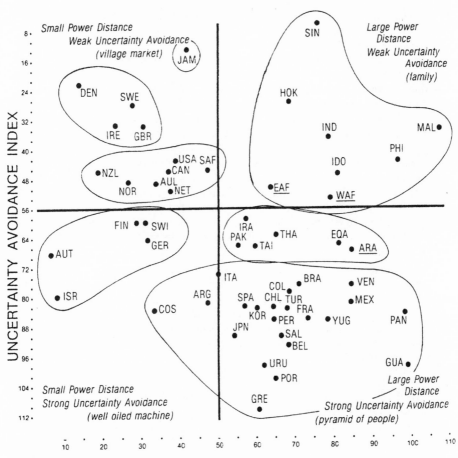

POWER DISTANCE INDEX

Small Power Distance
Weak Uncertainty Avoidance
(village market)

Large Power Distance
Weak Uncertainty Avoidance
(family)

UNCERTAINTY AVOIDANCE INDEX

Small Power Distance
Strong Uncertainty Avoidance
(well oiled machine)

Large Power Distance
Strong Uncertainty Avoidance
(pyramid of people)

Source: Hofstede (1983), 84. Used with permission.

tries/regions have a predilection for the Pyramid model, with the remainder split evenly between the Well-Oiled Machine and Family models.

What are the messages here for American librarians practicing their profession abroad?

- First, they themselves are carriers of a national culture that has formed, in ways beyond their overt consciousness, how they receive authority, face the capriciousness of the human condition, interact with their peers, and value work. Their new foreign work colleagues will likely recognize almost immediately what is culturally different about them, long before they themselves do.

- Second, expatriates can anticipate in a host country a national culture that stamps the workplace under its influence as different in important respects from the one they left behind. Whether that host culture is friendly or adversarial will depend, in the long run, on the expatriate's open-mindedness to the way organizational business is conducted and his or her flexibility in adapting to it. Wholesale abandonment to the prevailing culture—probably an impossible strategy anyway—is inadvisable. American librarians, the representatives of a more advanced librarianship, in the perception of foreign hosts, *are* expected to initiate changes in technique and technology. They cannot accept unreservedly everything as given and thereby risk rejecting their role as potential change agents. Neither can they allow themselves to be intimidated into immobility through fear of offending or violating the norms of national culture. At any rate, inviolable cultural norms are usually too obvious to be missed. In the Arab world (and, more broadly, in countries where Islam predominates), for example, *mercy* and *forgiveness* in civic and judicial affairs are given a special weight and soften sometimes the penalties for even the most serious transgressions. Arab national culture encourages reconciliation, despite the all-too-frequent misconceptions to the contrary among cultural outsiders.

- Finally, expatriates must come to recognize that libraries worldwide, for all their similarities, are embedded in very different cultures and will ineluctably receive and apply technology, develop the human resources of staff, and transform organizational processes and behaviors over time according to patterns laid down by their respective national cultures, and not to any other. This will come across to American expatriates more loudly and clearly than it ever could by staying at home, even in a country as diversely cultured as the United States.

All of these messages bear on the ability of the expatriate to survive in a foreign library work assignment. All, additionally, enable successful leadership in library work abroad—by promoting a more correct assessment of host library needs and receptivity to imported technological knowledge and skills and by fostering a recognition of those areas in the host organization where, given the cultural sensitivities present, change undertaken is most likely to succeed.

Is there any message for American librarians who do not venture abroad to work? There is one of some significance. The enthusiasm in the United States for globalization of information and the *virtual library* is not matched by an equal enthusiasm everywhere overseas. In fact, worldwide information networking has come to be identified in many foreign quarters with American political and economic hegemony—as something intrinsically subversive and threatening to national culture. American librarianship cannot, of course, stay its own development to suit those in other cultural environments unconvinced that it will serve their needs. National culture is autotelic, and American culture must and will pursue ends that drive its own needs. It is the same with American librarianship, guided by it own national culture. Nevertheless, an American library leadership capable of empathy with non-American cultures can expect a readier welcome abroad in developing a global information agenda. American library leadership rid of every trace of imperialism as possible will be welcome overseas as real leadership.

REFERENCES

Abdel-Latif, Omayma. 1996. "Culture of Resistance." *Al-Ahram Weekly* (December 5–11): 1.

"Bahrain Leads Arab World in Human Resource Development." 1996. *Saudi Gazette* (July 30): 14.

El-Bahrawi, Sayed. 1996. "Horizons of the Global Village." *Al-Ahram Weekly* (August 8–14): 8.

Barber, Benjamin R. 1996. *Jihad vs. McWorld.* New York: Ballantine Books.

"A Boon Turned Curse by Misuse." 1996. *Riyadh Daily* (November 8): 9.

Burke, W. Warner. 1992. *Organization Development; A Process of Learning and Changing.* 2d ed. Reading, MA: Addison-Wesley.

Ebeid, Mona Makram. 1993. "Rethinking Jobs and Education." *Al-Ahram Weekly* (June 24–30): 8.

Hofstede, Geert. 1980. *Culture's Consequences: International Differences in Work-Related Values.* Beverly Hills, CA: Sage.

———. 1983. "The Cultural Relativity of Organizational Practices and Theories." *Journal of International Business Studies* 14 (Fall): 75–89. [The countries and regions surveyed in the first report issued (Hofstede 1980) numbered 40. The number steadily increased to include by 1983 these 50: the Arab world countries of Egypt, Lebanon, Libya, Kuwait, Iraq, Saudi Arabia, the United Arab Emirates (ARA), Argentina (ARG), Australia (AUL), Austria (AUT), Belgium (BEL), Brazil (BRA), Canada (CAN), Chile (CHL), Colombia (COL), Costa Rica (COS), Denmark (DEN), the East African countries of Kenya, Ethiopia, Zambia (EAF), Equador (EOA), Finland (FIN), France (FRA), Great Britain (GBR), Germany (GER), Greece (GRE), Guatemala (GUA), Hong Kong (HOK), Indonesia (IDO), India (IND), Iran (IRA), Ireland (IRE), Israel (ISR), Italy (ITA), Jamaica (JAM), Japan (JPN), South Korea (KOR), Malaysia (MAL), Mexico (MEX), Netherlands (NET), Norway (NOR), New Zealand (NZL), Pakistan (PAK), Panama (PAN), Peru (PER), Philippines (PHI), Portugal (POR), El Salvador (SAL), South Africa (SAF), Singapore (SIN), Spain (SPA), Sweden (SWE), Switzerland (SWI), Taiwan (TAI), Thailand (THA), Turkey (TUR), Uruguay (URU), United States of America (USA), Venezuela (VEN), the West African countries of Nigeria, Ghana, Sierra Leone (WAF), Yugoslavia (YUG).]

"Internet Can Be Used to Promote Islam." 1996. *Saudi Gazette* (June 14): 7.

Jaeger, Alfred M. 1986. "Organization Development and National Culture: Where's the Fit?" *Academy of Management Review* 11(1): 178–190.

Mead, Richard. 1994. *International Management: Cross Cultural Dimensions*. Oxford: Blackwell.

"Muslims Urged to Hook Up into Internet to Spread Islam." 1996. *Saudi Gazette* (June 26): 12.

"Triumph of TQM at Carrier Saudi Arabia." 1996. *Saudi Gazette*, Special Edition (November 2): 36.

"Weekend, Thursday Instead of Saturday at Governmental Bodies." 1989. *Cairo Press Review* (November 20): 17.

Chapter 10

A Critique of Some Contemporary Conceptions of Reengineering-Based Library Leadership

Brian Champion

Where one stands on certain issues depends on where one sits at the table, meaning that those who sit at the head of the table likely have different stands on issues than those seated elsewhere. "Leadership" in academic libraries often assumes the appearance of a "motherhood statement"—something that no thinking person would disagree with. We all concede that leaders qua leaders are essential, but questions about direction, intent, and methods, especially in a collegial profession, usually catalyze the debate defining "leadership," to the extent that library leadership may arise from unsuspected quarters. Most often, this unanticipated leading orbits issues of workplace equity and fairness and, far from being tangential to library "leadership," may, in fact, be found to be core to the nature of both libraries and leadership.

The truism of taking a stand based on where one sits may be illustrated in the following story. During my tenure as president of the Association of Professional Librarians (APL) at a major university, the university chose a new director of libraries who, upon assumption of duties, implemented a daring and unorthodox library reorganization, revamping its previous administrative structure into a corporate/academic hybrid, initially compressing several midmanagement positions into only two divisions. In addition, other radical changes were planned for the library. Several positions would be eliminated, while others would be fused to create "new" positions and increased responsibilities, and the library would not administratively and functionally look as it had. To head these two new divisions, two librarians, who had previously held minor, mid-level management positions, were summarily appointed without benefit of open competition (understood by all librarians as a fundamental tenet of the librarians' collective agreement). Several of the APL membership communicated to me that such irregular appointments and the broad, autocratic nature of the proposed restructuring offended them—first, in their sense of workplace justice, fairness, and equity and second, as a threat to their individual careers in a previously collegial and participatory professional environment.

The APL executive questioned the legitimacy of the summary promotions and concurred in my interpretation of the collective agreement whose provisions specifically precluded such spontaneous elevations by the director. An opinion was sought from the executive director of the academic staff association (of which the librarians were a part), who endorsed the APL executives' collective conclusion. Membership of the APL included librarians in the law school; one who was consulted also had a law degree in addition to librarian's credentials and was asked for her opinion as to the bona fides of the APL case. After a thoughtful reading of the collective agreement, she concluded, as had the APL executive, that summary appointments breached the fair competition provisions of the contract. Having obtained these opinions, I then asked for, and was given access to, the academic staff association's legal counsel, who also concluded that the contract did not permit such appointments. Fortified with these opinions and with the vast majority of sentiment communicated to me from APL members who questioned the validity of the appointments and with the full confidence of both the APL executive and previous APL presidents, the association moved to grieve the appointment actions. Before the grievance could be officially adjudicated, the director capitulated and admitted that such actions were in technical violation of the contract and promised in writing not to make such appointments in the future. This last-minute compromise was accepted by the executive director of the academic staff association, and though APL ratification was barely majoritarian, it effectively curbed the director's anticipated massive reassignment of librarians.

While the new director of the library was spared the stigma of a grievance, the APL signaled very clearly through the actions of its executive that it could effectively fashion a form of library "leadership." The unspoken challenge for academic library administrators is to collegially harness the energy of such nontraditional "leadership" and cooperatively craft a vision of the library's future. Sadly, despite platitudinous affirmations, such collaboration is more honored in the breech than is regularly observed. This chapter argues that notions of library "leadership" that exclude or ignore the latent power of nontraditional leaders within academic libraries craft sham "leadership" that incubates cynicism and distrust, lethal to both sound administration and workplace fairness.

One effect of a job-related grievance was to signify to both the library and the university administration that librarians were concerned about their work environment and the ways in which senior management treated them. An action such as a grievance tends to fire-wall reckless administrative fiats from unintended consequences among the staff. Additionally, I submit that during periods of innovation and change, leadership may emanate from previously unidentified or unsuspecting sources—employee groups, for example, may be found to have within them leaders willing to challenge prevailing assumptions about the nature of change and suggest with whom senior staff should be collaborative in effecting humane and just change within the organization. In short, one conception of leadership consists of the effort to make senior management accountable for fairness and justice in structural reorganizations.

In a book on leadership, it is likely that a divergence of opinion exists on what, exactly, constitutes successful "leadership." Managers interpret and define leadership one way, while others use different benchmarks and descriptors. The purpose of this chapter is to explore an alternative conception of leadership through a critique of the current mode of leadership in libraries, with the intent that a broader recognition of "library leadership" might be factored into the larger library culture. However, the subtle nuance of leading, like the position one takes relative to one's locale at the table, may be open to interpretation. This chapter intends to suggest and explore some alternative facets concerning leadership. One major distinction between official and unofficial leaders is that there will likely be a wide divergence as to what the ultimate objectives of the organization are, what constitutes leadership and followership, and for whom (or what) one is acting. The act of reconciling such disparate worldviews may in itself be overt leadership.

Leadership, especially in the for-profit private sector, seems to be a recurring concern—judged by what one sees in business magazines and on business bookshelves, questions cyclically arise as to who has it, how one uses it, where one can find it, and how to train people to develop it. One of the highest accolades for a senior manager is to be deemed a "leader," yet how one actually "leads" eludes scientific description. Usually, "leadership" connotes a societal good, but frequently distressing or disruptive actions by senior staff are also deemed "leadership." For example, corporate officers who ruthlessly downsize occasionally are bestowed the honorific of "visionary leader" by the business press for such actions. But infrequently, such tactics create their own appellations— the "slash-and-burn" management style of the Chief Executive Officer (CEO) of Sunbeam Corporation earned him the nickname "Chainsaw Al"—and this at a time when executive compensation was reportedly paying handsomely.

Such disparity—that some lose their jobs, while others are well compensated for eliminating jobs—raises questions about workplace justice and fairness; what complicates this issue is that actions that exacerbate the disparity are perpetrated by those considered "leaders." That rank and file should be confused as to what authentically constitutes leadership should come as no surprise. For our purposes here, the preceding is preamble to the premise that higher education is not immune from some of the more lethal and anarchic aspects of the leadership cult of the private sector. A cautionary note is necessary for a number of reasons, not the least of which is that the academy and allied cultural institutions perform unique societal functions and should take care when adopting some forms of private sector management theory. For example, a bold "leadership" maneuver that results in improved profits for a private sector company potentially rewards "leaders" with some form of remunerative compensation; in contrast, academic and cultural organizations do not have equivalent operating capital to reward innovation in this manner—other surrogates must be found, and often in bureaucracies increases in responsibilities or in the number of persons reporting to the person rewarded substitute for cash bonuses. Thus, innovation motivation is more problematic, and this constraint tempers concepts of actual leadership, sometimes elevating persons with no leadership ability to positions of power. Second, in the private sector (where much of "leadership" is spoken and written), a particular "leadership" tactic that radically alters an organization, even dismantles traditional services, could be tolerated or even promoted if increased profits result. A similar radical move in the academy or in cultural industries may permanently ruin or unalterably change elements of a cultural or intellectual heritage, to the detriment of the larger host culture and surrounding intellectual tradition. Thus, those interested in, or charged with, preserving cultural and intellectual properties (such as librarians) must necessarily be less swayed by such for-profit sector management fads and fashions than their corporate counterparts. Therefore, skepticism about "leadership" should lead to some degree of caution in adopting current corporatist vernacular and practice.

One (of many) popular books on business leadership is Kreigel and Patler's (1991) *If It Ain't Broke . . . BREAK IT!* which more than suggests unconventional strategies for garnering greater business success. Like Hammer and Champy's (1993) *Re-Engineering the Corporation* or Osborne and Gaebler's (1992) *Reinventing Government*, the authors suggest things are so radically wrong organizationally that salvation of the enterprise can occur only if it is razed and then rebuilt, this time with fewer layers of management, fanatical attention to costs, addiction to nebulous "customer-driven" services, and an unremitting hunger for profits (or, in the case of governments, years of balanced budgets and low taxes). These books suggest that traditional organizations, regardless of function or social role, need to be eliminated and reconfigured for greater cost-benefit or, at the very least, become more like the private sector. They imply that institutions that do not conform to this view are doomed to extinction, because the "world is changing so fast" and will thus leave them behind, or they are doomed to perpetual failure and social embarrassment, with collateral increases in costs and inefficiencies because a new "management mind-set" or "paradigm" requires the adoption of radical restructuring. Admittedly, there is a cachet about such writing lending credibility to such ideas, which, by virtue of their vagueness, find wide adoption throughout the managerial world. Libraries and other cultural institutions are not necessarily immune from such contagious thinking, and nontraditional library "leaders" may have a role in evaluating and critiquing—perhaps fire-walling—some of the less applicable tenets of their philosophy.

Some recent writing on library leadership seems to have uncritically adopted the notion of reengineering the library and considers rakish change as the sole significant manifestation of leadership. Richard T. Sweeney's (1994) "Leadership in the Post-Hierarchical Library" purports to circumnavigate the future of libraries. Spurred on by the spirit of Tom Peters' (1987) management bible *Thriving on Chaos* and his *Liberation Management* (Peters 1992), where rapid, unanticipated, radical change is lusted after, Sweeney (1994, 63) urges every library worker to accept a new vision of the library where "empowerment" allows workers to take charge and do what has to be done, strongly suggesting that only those who do will be "real leaders" who then "possess, communicate and implement a vision for radically transformed and improved" libraries in a "post-hierarchical" organizational environment. According to Sweeney, there are two initial outcomes to such an epiphany:

Primarily, the post-hierarchical library will change the nature of library service, library work, and library leadership, and second, the post-hierarchical library, . . . will involve new information technologies, the emerging national information infrastructure and the electronic highway. (1994, 63)

In Sweeney's view, this new library is the antibureaucratic library—the antithesis of the hierarchical library—"a flattened organization with empowered cross-functional teams, . . . new knowledge and information infrastructures and reinvented and re-engineered work process focused on customized service"; it "may or may not have physical collections of books and other materials, or even a building" (Sweeney 1994, 64); a place where "user satisfaction is sacred—not the organizational structure" (Sweeney 1994, 65). Quoting Hammer and Champy's (1993, 94) best-seller *Re-Engineering the Corporation*, "Reengineering isn't about fixing anything. It's all about starting over from scratch." Sweeney (1994, 66–67) suggests "post-hierarchical library leaders must start planning as though they were starting with [nothing more than the] mission of the library . . . where only "the intended customers must judge the process to be of value or it is wasted no matter how well considered, intended or well established."

Sweeney (1994, 80) further advocates a more radical civilizational purge: "[T]he technology cannot be used to automate what now exists. The entire library needs to be re-engineered," and "the only solution" to satisfying users' demands "lies in re-engineering the entire library, focusing on customer satisfaction and relying less on buildings and collections" (Sweeney 1994, 78).

In Sweeney's incarnation of the future, libraries are no longer cultural or intellectual institutions but merely bottom-line–driven organizations concerned with throughputs and customer satisfaction. He proselytizes that "perhaps the single greatest reason that libraries must embark upon re-engineering is that the rest of the world is now in the information business" (Sweeney 1994, 81–82).

For a library leader to lash out so blindly results in thoughtful people's questioning his concept of leading.

To buttress his corporatist orientation, Sweeney quotes from Oracle computer company CEO Larry Ellison, someone not known to be sympathetic to the library's traditional cultural and intellectual heritage, about his company's current multimillion-dollar database project called the Alexandria Project: "It aims at nothing less than using computers to change the way human knowledge is amassed and stored." It seems that for Sweeney, the amassing and storing are the truly significant thing about Alexandria or about digital libraries, and he ignores the intellectual and cultural role such an institution has. Sweeney concludes that leaders in the posthierarchical library must be tough because "[r]-engineering is too traumatic to pursue as a nice idea without full commitment." He invokes a measure of anti-intellectualism in his preference for such library administrators. Pondering the qualifications of the consummate posthierarchialist, Sweeney asks, "Should the new library leader possess a doctoral degree in library and information science? Should this library leader possess experience as a leader in an ARL library or experience and training in information technology? These credentials may all be important but a candidate can possess all of these and not be the leader described in this article" (Sweeney 1994, 93). It seems that Sweeney thinks that a library administrator doesn't need formal training in librarianship or even to have worked in an academic or research library or even have a passing knowledge of cultural industries as necessary precursors to managing a library. What is really needed, he asserts, is someone who is, preferably, unknowing about libraries but well versed in both the techno-speak of the digital culture and a crackerjack for-profit manager to boot.

Another article, Susan Anderson and Joyce Burkhart's (1995) "St. Petersburg Junior College Reorganizes for the '90s," suggests another leadership example of using Hammer and Champy's radical reengineering. One hardly arguable rationale for making changes, cited as a justification, was to "simplify procedures and reduce duplications." To this end, they recommend staff cross-training and propose staff empowerment as a major tenet of reengineering. However, this management strategy has a reputation for resulting in reduced numbers of staff positions and having the survivors do more with less, suggesting that actions that catalyze these results need to be finessed within an organization. Too frequently, they are not. Anderson and Burkhart (1995, 541) admit they bungled a team-building workshop that "left some library staff, who had never met each other before, puzzling over spending a day together playing games." Despite the heartfelt intentions of administrators to unite staff, confusing actions like these only tend to increase staff cynicism and resistance to authentic change; frequently, unsuccessful gaming (or retreats or seminars) leave the impression of administrative insincerity, superficiality, and mere manipulation, not a genuine effort of managers to work with, and understand, employees. In at least one sense, such staff skepticism is warranted—bosses do occasionally try what values consultant Stephen Covey calls the "management flavor of the month," in lieu of substantive and meaningful planning, thereby telegraphing to workers (intentionally or otherwise) management's desire for a quick fix. Authentic leaders seek deeper understanding and are cautious in their tinkering with the work environment. But such finesse is rare.

One need not read too much into Anderson and Burkhart's first-person narrative, as their article is about how they implemented certain changes, not a textbook on how to improvise reconstructive management. Readers might infer from its laudatory tone that certain actions were or are acceptable leader initiatives and, for this reason, use them as a template for localized change.

Anderson and Burkhart recite vague management aphorisms as a catechism that, true of all catechisms, will be thought to be effective if only recited often enough. For instance, they note that with "automation" no new staff were hired except for the new "collegewide library director." This one event having then occurred, "opportunities for library leadership were abundant." It may be important to ask, For whom, or over whom? Was everyone self-led? A close reading of Anderson and Burkhart's achievements could suggest that the restructuring of their library took a less egalitarian turn. Administrative fiat replaced collegial forms of management—for example, of a sudden, with the loss of the systems librarian to coordinate the reengineering, "a campus librarian was selected to supervise each automation subsystem as it was implemented college wide. . . . One librarian became the 'leader' of the circulation system, another the 'leader' of the serials module, still another took the 'lead' for organizing the barcoding project" (Anderson and Burkhart 1995, 542). All these "new" duties sound pretty traditional—not much insightful reengineering here—except that now the library director could appoint "leaders" to effect the director's personal vision of the reengineered library. In fact, little of the library was reengineered, except for staff reductions and reassignments.

Indeed, a major part of this vision emanating from senior levels included the creation of two teams, each with its own "leader," again "selected" (by whom, and upon what criteria?) for those roles. Their "leadership" mandate was to trim away all those encumbering "other duties. . . . [r]educing the management responsibilities of campus librarians to focus their work on reference service and instruction was a long-term goal of the reorganization. With the long-term goal and short-term necessities in mind, management duties such as staff scheduling and adjunct librarian recruitment for all campus were assigned to the North and South County team leaders. These two leaders also assumed mentoring duties for new librarians as they were hired" (Anderson and Burkhart 1995, 543). This passage seems to say that other contributions to the organization by reference and BI librarians were eliminated by the consolidation into two centers of power (the North and South County leaders), which meant that desk librarians were given less responsibility, and the two team leaders had greatly increased management responsibilities, some of which now included the mentoring of newly hired librarians. In short, one might think such actions look like both a power grab and a decollegialization of professional librarians. Not only that, but restructuring, due to the liberation of technology, meant that "the management responsibilities of the librarian who is in charge of day-to-day operations of a site library will vary depending on the size of the facility" (Anderson and Burkhart 1995, 543). This seems to be pretty much like the traditional library.

"Traditional job descriptions and areas of responsibility break down as all staff work to meet the goals of service to users" (Anderson and Burkhart 1995, 543). Again, managers wish to have library workers as interchangeable as Lego blocks, each person suitable for changing wherever and whenever managers decree. Important intellectual decisions, such as collection development or reference service, can, in this view, be done by just anyone on the staff, no credentials required. In fact, as Sweeney noted, credentials can get in the way of the posthierarchical library leader. Like Sweeney, they note that it can be tough to make that posthierarchical omelet: "Library leadership can be an uncomfortable role because the leader must make public ideas, plans and projects and take responsibility for them" (Anderson and Burkhart 1995, 545). To assume this is a new "leadership" duty is to reflect unhistorically on the role of leadership. Anderson and Burkhart's major conclusion bears some scrutiny, in light of its implications for determining the effects of leadership. "Library leadership succeeds at SPJC [St. Petersburg Junior College] because library staff embrace change, realize the need for cooperation and support, and give each other the courage to lead" (Anderson and Burkhart 1995, 545). What does "embraced" change look like that makes it different from, say, "accepted change"? Does the realization of the "need" for cooperation and support equate to cooperation and support? Cooperation and support of whom or what? If everyone in the library is giving every other one in the library the courage to lead, who follows? This leads us to questions about some of the assumptions embedded within the article, especially if one wishes to seek greater fairness and equity in the library workplace.

Another text rich in messages on library leadership is Carla Stoffle, Robert Renaud, and Jerilyn R. Voldof's "Choosing Our Futures" (1996). The article begins with a major taxonomic distinction:

One view of the future proposed that little or no organizational changes are required. Proponents [of this concept] believe that current structures are adequate to implement the new services, information products, and work functions and tasks that will evolve. Change, where necessary, will occur incrementally. New services and products will be add-on rather than replacements for what is currently done. . . . This view posits that for the foreseeable future, the library will essentially be dealing with traditional formats side by side with new technology. The library will maintain its traditional activities in supporting teaching and research, changing only the tools used. (Stoffle et al. 1996, 213)

This is an organic conception of a library, vibrantly responding to external stimuli but preserving the essential cultural and intellectual core for transmission to succeeding generations. Librarians are embedded within this organic worldview, an "expert system" essential to the institution's adaptability and vitality. Absent librarians, and we are left with a used book store. But as we come to see, Stoffle et al. reject the organic notion of the library, substituting in its place a corporatist worldview, achievable only upon the principles of reengineering, complete with a lust for an "ability to identify, anticipate and quickly respond to constantly changing customer needs" (Stoffle et al. 1996, 213). Not only "must" libraries adapt to customer needs, but also, organizationally, they "must" "be able to anticipate those needs rather than wait for customer needs to be articulated fully" (Stoffle et al. 1996, 213). The library, therefore, is expected to fully respond to "customers' " inarticulate demands. Is this what cultural and intellectual institutions do? The implications are clear—if the Metropolitan Museum of Art, for example, discovered that Monet's impressionism was less preferred by museumgoers than illustrations of dogs with cigars playing poker, then, according to Stoffle et al., Sweeney, Anderson and Burkhart, and many others, it should display and promote all manner of dogs playing poker and shelve or even discard those difficult Monets. Back to libraries, it seems that Stoffle et al. would prefer academic libraries to stock multiple copies from the best-sellers list, rather than thoughtful works less popular. This seems to be posthierarchical rhetorical leadership run amok, and it conflicts with the cultural and intellectual intent of academic libraries.

As with Anderson and Burkhart, Stoffle et al.'s article warrants examination, because some of its implications relate to the notion of what constitutes leadership in libraries. As Stoffle et al. see it, not only must librarians divine user needs before they are fully known, but also libraries should, they suggest, discard things that actually work—librarians are, for example, to abandon formerly successful approaches to work, strategies, processing systems, and services that do not prove their value to customers (Stoffle et al. 1996, 213). How this proof is obtained or against which benchmark it is measured is not explained, but it raises the specter of library users not familiar with the catalog suggesting it be dumped, and librarians mindlessly complying. Perhaps the utility of the catalog could be proved, but the efficacy of MARC format records, no matter how well articulated to most patrons, eludes comprehension. Following Stoffle et al., this places MARC records in a category of items to be negatively assessed, as they fail to prove their worth to a capricious and unknowing "customer." A basic assumption Stoffle et al. make is that libraries do nothing well and must be rehabilitated into performing better. The facts are that libraries, in fact, do several things quite well and are highly responsive to their environments, that librarians provide added value, and that the central intellectual functions need not be at the mercy of efficiency or pedestrian whims.

To characterize libraries as mandating policies to serve misanthropic institutional urges is without foundation and unhistorical. One major research library where I used to work revised its serials circulation policy from liberal three-day loans to no loans, but such a change was not intended to vex library users; the intention was to equalize use and make library materials more accessible to a wider audience. A close reading of Stoffle et al. could lead one to wonder about their intentions; for instance, they report that "[t]o be successful under [fiscally stringent] conditions, libraries must reshape the prevailing corporate culture" (Stoffle et al. 1996, 213). But what is unarticulated is that one corporate culture must be replaced with another, one suspiciously like that of the computer companies that provide information technology to libraries. Though vaunting their ideas as progressive, such assertions open themselves to questioning by nontraditional library "leaders" who may prove that they are, in reality, only manipulative. Should this version of library leadership pass unquestioned, staff indifference and alienation could be reasonably expected outcomes, and an essential cultural and intellectual institution could be plundered in the name of technocorporatism.

What these samples of library management literature have in common is that they appear to have given little thought to the notion that the humans who work in them warrant any consideration at all. H. H. Rosenbrock's (1983, 127–128) words seem to be verified in the contemporary practices of library administrators:

When new technological developments are proposed, it is only in the rarest of cases that any thought is given, during the process of research and development, to the role of men and women in the system that will result. Usually it is the machines alone that are considered, and only when the development has been completed is any thought given to the essential contribution from people, without which nothing can be produced. The [machine's] contribution, not surprisingly, is often unsuited to human capabilities.

They do not seem to have reasonably considered the effects of indiscriminate adoption of both technology and corporate management.

Sweeney, Anderson and Burkhart, and Stoffle et al. do not seem to have integrated the place of people in their vision of the future. Sweeney (1994, 81) would like to see all aspects of libraries reduced to electronic formats, while Anderson and Burkhart gloss over processes of fairness in the assignment of work-related duties. Stoffle et al. interpret their experiment as such a success that they feel empowered to use imperatives to mandate nationwide library change. Do they reckon consequences with their actions?

Even in the private sector, where management frequently offers huge incentives for people to leave, thus "voluntarily" downsizing their workforces, not everything is sweetness and light. Edward L. Andrews' article (1995) on the reactions to buyout offers at Connecticut Mutual, a major East Coast insurer, reveals the high degree of anxiety employees face when confronted by radical employment change. At some point, it gets to be too much.

"A lot of people are fed up with the way they have been treated," said Shirley Brown, an administrative assistant in the real estate investment department who took the buyout and is leaving. "They have been screwing around with everybody's job for two years, since the transformation project, and people can only take so much.'' (Andrews 1995, C 1–C2)

Similarly, workers wonder what kind of leadership they toil under that moves to fundamentally change their organization when it is neither broken nor failing.

The concerns of ordinary working men and women continue to get short shrift. The outplacement firm Challenger, Gray and Christmas reported this week that more than half of the callers to its annual nationwide job search were employed. In other words, workers are so scared they are already looking for new jobs before getting the word that they have been fired. . . . A Presidential campaign that made sense would address the tyrannical power of great corporations and the effect that it is having on the working families politicians profess to care so much about. Instead we are led to believe that there is something inevitable about this unconscionable assault on the work force, and its steady erosion of the American dream. The staggering job losses, even at companies [or institutions] that are thriving, are rationalized as necessary sacrifices. . . . Little is said about the corrosive effect of rampant corporate greed, and even less about peculiar notions like corporate [or institutional] responsibility and accountability—not just to stockholders, but to employees and their families, to the local community, to the social and economic well-being of the country as a whole. (Herbert 1996, Al 5)

On what, then, do these putative library leaders base their reengineered world-views? The answer to this question may lie somewhere in the authors' foundational biases. They may be part of a phenomenon Michael Piore, a Harvard-trained economist, discovered and whose research is recounted in David Noble's book *Progress without People: New Technology, Unemployment and the Message of Resistance*. Speaking of Piore's work, Noble (1996, 91–92) writes:

The subject of [Piore's article] was what is known as relative factor analysis. According to neoclassical economics, businessmen decide whether or not to invest in machinery by comparing its cost with the costs of labour. According to this theory, if the cost of machinery is less than the cost of labour [*sic*], they will invest in machinery, and if the cost of machinery is more than the cost of labour [*sic*], they will stick with labour. This intrepid young economist undertook to test this theory in the field by conducting a survey of some sixty factories in the New England area. In each case he identified and talked with people who actually made such purchasing decisions and tried to find out how they did it. He discovered, first of all, that the majority of these people had technical backgrounds; they were engineers. He also found out that their actual purchasing behavior differed from what the theory suggested. When the cost of machinery was lower than that of labour [*sic*], they bought machines, but when the cost of machines was higher than that of labour [*sic*], they still bought machines (and sometimes fudged the justification accordingly). The economist concluded that there was a bias in favour [*sic*] of machinery (or against labour [*sic*]) on the part of these technically trained functionaires. Their enthusiasm for machinery was the major determining factor, not careful relative factor analysis.

Is it possible that the current mode of putative library leadership is biased toward technology—in all its manifestations—as opposed to a careful analysis of important human and social, if not cultural and intellectual, factors? Certainly, Anderson and Burkhart and Stoffle et al. strongly suggest that one of the ways the "library" will be "restructured" is for library "staff" to be cross-trained in all aspects of library operations ("Support staff assume new roles and responsibilities that cut across and diminish the traditional chain of command" [Anderson and Burkhart 1995, 543]. Such a move toward anemic and flattened organizations might look good on paper, and reengineering libraries to achieve such a goal might be considered by some as leadership, but one should consider the experience of labor sociologists who interpret "the impact of technological change on industrial work and on workers' attitudes."

After examining several industries, we became suspicious of the classless society theory. A cornerstone of the theory, the assumption of a simple correlation between technological progress and humanization of industrial work, turned out to be very weak. We found that the interplay between economic development, technological change, and work restructuring was much more complicated than we, like most of our colleagues, had assumed. Associated with the new, automated machinery being implemented at the time, . . . no simple tendency towards greater humanization was apparent. (Kern and Shumann 1992, 144)

Leaders sometimes assume that technical progress would necessarily partner a greater humanization in the workplace. Kern and Shumann point out this is not always the case; as a matter of fact, there is considerably less humanization of the workplace when technology is uncritically adopted. There are significant additional factors at play here, too—the link between staff and the economic efficiency of an organization operates in a very delicate ecology that can easily be put out of balance and made inefficient. But the prerogatives of all parties are not equal. As Thomas A. Kochan and Boaz Tamir (1989, 61–62) indicate, "the availability of new technologies increased the range of choice open to decision-makers in designing employment relationships." The introduction of new technologies (reengineering) serves as an opportunity for decision makers to "unfreeze" existing employment practices and arrangements in ways that will fundamentally alter the nature of the employment contract." Among important elements for consideration in recrafting work arrangements, Kochan and Tamir (1989, 67) suggest "extensive employee participation at all levels of the new organization, from the workplace to the business unit to the top level management staff committee . . . ; acceptance of the principle of consensus decision making as the model of operation; a flexible work organization system with only three to five job classifications; a wage payment system that provides for performance incentives and bonuses; . . . [and] an all salaried compensation system." Central to the concept of occupational fairness is the notion of consensual decision making, an element missing from Sweeney, Anderson and Burkhart, and Stoffle et al. Managers would do well to consider the advice from the Preface of James Boyle's (1966, xi) book on the information society—those who urge caution about rapid technological change "have argued persuasively that the fetishization of the computer may drive to social arrangements, educational theories and workplace experiences that are neither humane nor desirable, neither efficient nor equitable." It is precisely this concern that we should have for reckless reengineering in libraries.

Former Intel chief executive officer Andrew S. Grove in his book *Only the Paranoid Survive* may have some insights for library leaders. He makes two very important points that are germane to the present discussion. First, in contrast to the library examples cited earlier, he urges managers to cultivate and encourage wide-ranging debate on the nature of the organization's problems and on proposed solutions.

This kind of debate is daunting because it takes a lot of time and a lot of intellectual ergs. It also takes a lot of guts; it takes courage to enter into a debate you may lose, in which weaknesses in your knowledge may be exposed and in which you may draw the disapproval of your coworkers. Nevertheless, this comes with the territory and when it comes to identifying a strategic inflection point, unfortunately, there are no shortcuts. If you are in senior management, don't feel you're being a wimp for taking the time to solicit the views, convictions and passions of the experts. (Grove 1996, 115)

Then, Grove (1996, 116) urges engagement, creation of a dialogue within the organization:

If you are in middle management, don't be a wimp. . . . You owe it to your company and you owe it to yourself. Don't justify holding back by saying that you don't know the answers; at times like this, nobody does. Give your most considered opinion and give it clearly and forcefully; your criterion for involvement should be that you're heard and understood.

A second point is embodied in the title of his Chapter 8, "Rein in Chaos." The slash-and-burn mentality does little to abate chaos (in fact, it seems to cultivate it). It may be that a true leader in one who can effectively adjust institutional emphases while limiting the collateral damage of uncertainty that usually accompanies change. "Clarity of direction, which includes describing what we are going after as well as describing what we will not be going after, is exceedingly important" (Grove 1996, 137).

Thus, the true library leader may turn out to be someone who is very sensitive to the workplace ecology, to the nuances of work relationships and how important equity and fairness are in occupational roles. It may be the person who stands up and questions the directions of library managers, who appear to be uncaring about the library's traditional roles as cultural and intellectual institutions, and the persons who questions whether reengineering is a legitimate vehicle for sound change, being, as Grove suggests, part of the ongoing institutional "debate." To be a leader in libraries may take more than simplistically mandating change—leadership may manifest itself in openly questioning radical and abrasive reengineering practices and procedures. Or it may be evidenced in querying the use of jargonistic phrases, such as "cross-training" when the real intent is to have all staff do all jobs and thus allow for either or both layoffs or deprofessionalization. Leadership is shown in a willingness to consensually agree on patterns and practices of change and to collaborate on innovation. In short, we may find that the true library leader is one who stands on the principles of a collective agreement and who presses senior management to honor provisions honestly negotiated. The library leader may be one who recognizes the fundamental connection between employment and feelings of self-worth and who may be slow to tear asunder the links workers have to their jobs and their identities. Leadership in libraries may, surprisingly, be found in criticizing the adoption of management fads that heedlessly compress organizations and displace workers while entrenching senior administrators in their managerial niches.

It is possible to be outside the "management umbrella" or even be inside organized labor and be an institutional leader. This is the substance of Thomas L. Weekly and Jay C. Wilber's (1996, 86–131) book *United We Stand: The Unprecedented Story of the GM-UAW Quality Partnership*. Granted, the immediate objectives of such leadership may diverge from the objectives of senior management, but such differences can be negotiated and discussed; even if they are not immediately reconciled, they can be part of "the debate."

It is possible that Michael Hammer has begun to recognize that his initial radical razing of organizations was too heavy-handed. In his latest book, *Beyond Re-Engineering*, Hammer (1996) chooses a new metaphor for organizations. Instead of conceiving institutions as management versus labor, he now thinks the metaphor of a football team is more appropriate—11 people, each with specific duties, all working together at the same time, taking "plays" from one "quarterback" who consults with, and is himself directed by, a staff of coaches. This seems to be a much more enlightened model of leadership, for each team player can be a leader in his or her own position, under the direction of a quarterback, assistant coaches, specialty coaches, and, ultimately, the head coach. Leadership, in the end, may not be measured by how flat one manager gets the organization or by how much salary budget was saved by staff layoffs or other attrition; it should be measured by how fairly and humanely we take the group of people we have responsibility for from here to the next level. It should be measured against a standard of making things better, not merely different.

REFERENCES

Anderson, Susan and Joyce Burkhart. 1995. "St. Petersburg Junior College Reorganizes for the '90s." *College Research Libraries News* 56 (September): 541–546.

Andrews, Edward L. 1995. "Company's Buyout: Was It That Good? Rush to the Doors at an Insurer Shows Pitfalls in Cutting Staff." *New York Times* (December 15): C1–C2.

Boyle, James. 1996. *Shamans, Software and Spleens: Law and the Construction of the Information Society.* Cambridge, MA: Harvard University Press.

Grove, Andrew S. 1996. *Only the Paranoid Survive: How to Exploit the Crisis Points That Challenge Every Company and Career.* New York: Currency Doubleday.

Hammer, Michael. 1996. *Beyond Re-Engineering: How Process-Centered Organization Is Changing Our Work and Our Lives.* New York: HarperBusiness.

Hammer, Michael and James Champy. 1993. *Re-Engineering the Corporation: A Manifesto for Business Revolution.* New York: HarperBusiness.

Herbert, Bob. 1996. "Separation Anxiety: 'Cascade Bumping': Sound like Fun? It Isn't." *New York Times* (January 19): A15.

Kern, Horst and Michael Shumann. 1992. "New Concepts of Production and the Emergence of the Systems Controller." In Paul S. Adler, ed., *Technology and the Future of Work.* New York: Oxford University Press, pp. 111–148.

Kochan, Thomas A. and Boaz Tamir. 1989. "Collective Bargaining and New Technology: Some Preliminary Propositions." In Greg J. Bamber and Russell D. Lansbury, eds., *New Technology: International Perspectives on Human Resources and Industrial Relations.* London: Unwin Hyman, pp. 60–74.

Kreigel, Robert J. and Louis Patler. 1991. *If It Ain't Broke . . . BREAK IT.* New York: Warner Books.

Noble, David F. 1995. *Progress without People: New Technology Unemployment and the Message of Resistance.* Toronto: Between the Lines.

Osborne, David and Ted Gaebler. 1992. *Reinventing Government: How the Entrepreneurial Spirit Is Transforming the Public Sector.* Reading, MA: Addison-Wesley.

Peters, Tom. 1987. *Thriving on Chaos: Handbook for a Management Revolution.* New York: Knopf.

———. 1992. *Liberation Management: Necessary Disorganization for the Nanosecond Nineties.* New York: Knopf.

Rosenbrock, H. H. 1983. "Designing Automated Systems—Need Skill Be Lost?" In Pauline Maarstrand, ed., *New Technology and the Future of Work Skills.* London: Francis Pinter, pp. 124–132.

Stoffle, Carla, Robert Renaud, and Jerilyn R. Voldof. 1996. "Choosing Our Futures." *College and Research Libraries* 7 (May): 213–225.

Sweeney, Richard T. 1994. "Leadership in the Post-Hierarchical Library." *Library Trends* 43(1): 62–94.

Weekly, Thomas L. and Jay C. Wilber. 1996. *United We Stand: The Unprecedented Story of the GM–UAW Quality Partnership.* New York McGraw-Hill.

Part IV

The Professional Career and Leadership Behavior

Chapter 11

Leadership: In the Eye of the Beholder?

David R. Dowell

Leadership is difficult to define. In the preparation of this book, discussions between the editors and the chapter authors about such a definition have raised many questions but produced few answers. Is leadership the same as career advancement? Is leadership equated with the amount of compensation received from the organization? Is leadership in the eye of the beholder? The reader will not find succinct answers to these questions in this chapter. However, the models discussed may suggest answers that are, like most Web sites, still under construction.

If leadership is in the eye of the beholder, it is important to clarify who the beholder is. In this chapter we see that professionals may be perceived as leaders in one venue but not in another. It depends on who is defining leadership or career progression. It also has to do with the nature of the task and/or the venue in which activity is taking place. Three methods of defining leadership/career progression are discussed. In the first, the employing organization defines who is a leader; in the second, leadership is defined by professional peers; and in the third, leadership is defined by the individual professional.

When I entered the profession, accomplishment seemed to be measured by the number of staff one supervised. To be considered a successful librarian, one was expected to become a supervisor within five years. Success was sustained by increasing the number of staff one supervised. I am not sure where this myth originated or how widely it was disseminated. However, it would appear that most library salary plans gave this theory great credence. Managers have traditionally been the highest-paid employees in libraries. Does this mean they are also our leaders?

In the late 1970s, another perception of success, comparable rewards (Weber and Kass 1978), received increasing attention. Rather than replace the previous paradigm, it expanded on it. According to this model, there were two different paths to career success. In addition to compensating those who climbed the administrative ladder, one also should be compensated for increasing technical expertise. Both should be rewarded—often through parallel career (and salary) ladders. Comparable rewards was an appropriate model for those who advocated faculty status or at least academic status in which librarians could be promoted through the ranks without changing the position they occupied in the organization. However, is there any evidence to suggest that either of these models really rewarded librarians on the basis of their leadership contribution to their organizations?

FOUR STAGES OF PROFESSIONAL CAREERS

In the 1970s, a group of organizational designers began examining the relationship between age and performance among engineers (Dalton and Thompson 1971). In a study of 2,500 engineers in seven large organizations, they found a negative correlation, after age 35, between age and performance rating. The older the engineer, after the mid-30s, the lower his performance rating was likely to be.

After some reflection, this finding should not be too surprising. After all, we all have heard of the relatively short half-life of technical training. Therefore, it should not be too surprising that those with recent technical training are highly valued.

But what accounted for the fact that not all the older engineers had low ratings? The top third of the engineers over 50 were almost as highly regarded as the top third in any age group. Although more of those in their 40s and 50s had low ratings than did younger engineers, many engineers had remained highly valued contributors for the duration of their careers. Why had some professionals remained high performers over the years, while others had not? What had they done differently? Could this phenomenon be explained by continuing education courses taken by the older engineers who continued to progress up the career ladder?

Further research (Dalton, Thompson, and Price 1977; Dalton and Thompson 1986) showed no relationship between the performance ratings of the older engineers and the completion of continuing education courses. After reexamination of the data from several previous studies, the investigators began to detect a pattern that seemed to explain the varying value placed on the performance of older engineers. This observation led to the formulation of a theory of four stages of professional development. As long as engineers progressed through the four stages in a timely manner, their evaluations continued to be good. If they lingered in an early stage of professional development, their ratings began to fall. In fact, if they bogged down in the first stage, they were not likely to remain long with the company.

The four stages of professional development were, roughly speaking, as follows:

(1) apprentice; (2) independent performer; (3) mentor; and (4) mover and shaker.

In each successive stage, the professional took on a wider organizational role. Sometimes that wider role was temporary or informal. In other cases, it was formal and permanent (i.e., a supervisory or management position). Although this paradigm was developed during a series of studies of large engineering firms, it was subsequently validated in other organizations that employed large numbers of professionals. This generalization of the study results included the observation of professors in universities. The four-stage model appeared to apply to all these organizations.

Stage 1

Apprentices are new professionals right out of school. They have the book knowledge. However, they need to learn how to apply that knowledge to practical situations in an organizational context. They also need to build credibility because others do not know how much they can rely on the newcomer's professional judgment. During this stage, new professionals are expected to have a single, dependent relationship or a series of dependent relationships through which they follow directions and help a more experienced professional as they learn the values and processes of the organization. In other words, it is critically important that they learn "how we do things good here."

At first, the assignments involve rather detailed work under close supervision. As a helper of senior professionals, ambitious new professionals often become impatient—wanting to demonstrate what they can really do for the organization and its clients. However, this eagerness to be an independent performer can undercut some wonderful opportunities to learn from more experienced co-workers. The sometimes boring work is the trade-off for the chance to demonstrate that one has the competence to work independently and to secure a mentor in the organization who can be useful for years to come. In addition, it is an opportunity to learn judgment and instinct based on experience—lessons that cannot be learned from a textbook.

It is important that new professionals also are given the opportunity to demonstrate innovative ways to solve problems. Studies have shown that such assignments early in a career have an impact on career development as much as seven years later.

Within three to four years, "apprentices" need to demonstrate that they can pull their own weight as independent performers. If this is not established, the individual will make an early exit from the organization. Therefore, career stagnation does not become a problem.

In a library setting, Stage 1 would apply to a newly minted M.L.S. Although the new librarian may have better technology skills than many more seasoned colleagues, there is still much to learn on the job. There are a vast number of areas in which the new librarian must learn the local interpretations and even the exceptions to the professional principles that were presented in graduate school. A seasoned colleague can facilitate this learning of how the tension between professional and bureaucratic values can be addressed productively.

Stage 2

The key to progressing successfully to Stage 2 is to develop a track record as a technically competent professional who can work independently and produce significant results. Generally, at this stage, professionals are assigned their own areas of responsibility. They are allowed to work within those areas of responsibility and make decisions without constantly checking with their supervisor. Although it is critical to demonstrate the ability to work independently, this must be balanced with the ability to coordinate projects and activities with others. Skills are polished, and often an area of specialization is developed.

In this stage, librarians need to establish their expertise within the area of their work assignment. This may be in a single area such reference, children's services, or cataloging. Or in a smaller library, the specialty may be the ability to juggle multiple activities but at less depth than is required for librarians whose assignments are more narrowly focused. In either case, librarians must demonstrate that they are able to pull their own share of the workload within their area(s) of assignment. They must demonstrate that they can be relied on by the organization and by their peers to produce competent professional work.

At Stage 2 many professionals plateau. If they are truly competent producers within their specified areas of responsibility, they are of value to the organization. However, they will not receive the increasing rewards of professionals who progress to Stage 3 and beyond.

Stage 3

"We have sometimes called Stage 3 the mentor stage because of the increased responsibility individuals in this stage begin to take for influencing, guiding, directing, and developing other people. It is usually persons in this stage who play the critical role in helping others move through Stage 1" (Dalton et al. 1977, 29). Within the library setting, this would mean helping the new M.L.S. holders learn how to apply their professional education within the local organizational setting.

In addition to assuming responsibility for other professionals, there tends to be a broadening of the area of concern. To succeed at this stage, one must understand other specialties and often other organizations. Three roles are characteristic of this stage: informal mentor; idea generator; and/or manager. An important point to note is that one did not need to become a formal manager or supervisor in order to reach Stage 3. In fact, only about one-third of the professionals at this echelon were assigned to such positions. Two-thirds were performing at this level by virtue of temporary assignments or informal roles. Such temporary assignments might include special projects or task forces in which they were expected to play a leadership role. Most managers in Stage 3 were first-or second-level supervisors. Twenty-nine percent of professionals were found to be in Stage 3. If Stage 3 professionals are not yet leaders, they are certainly leaders in the making in the eyes of the organization.

In addition to mentoring new librarians or becoming a supervisor, librarians can move into Stage 3 by expanding on the area of professional expertise they mastered in Stage 2. This might be accomplished by demonstrating knowledge in related areas of library service (e.g., expanding from cataloging to all aspects of technical services). This might also be accomplished by becoming knowledgeable of cataloging practices of other libraries. This increased professional expertise is often demonstrated by making major contributions in temporary roles on task forces and committees. These roles may be within the employing library or in professional organizations.

Stage 4

Professionals at Stage 4 of their careers exercised influence "in defining the direction of the organization or some major segment of it" (Dalton et al. 1977, 32). A majority occupied line management positions, but 26 percent did not.

Each had come, in his own way, to be a force in shaping the future of the organization. . . . This influence is in fact more widely distributed among key people than is commonly thought. They exercise this influence in a number of ways: negotiating and interfacing with the key parts of the environment; developing the new ideas, products, markets, or services that lead the organization into new areas of activity; or directing the resources of the organization toward specific goals. (Dalton et al. 1977, 32)

Those who were not in line management positions exercised influence on the basis of their expertise. While Stage 3 professionals help Stage 1 professionals adjust to the organization and learn to apply professional skills, professionals in Stage 4 select and groom the future leaders of the organization.

Often those in Stage 4 had reputations that extended beyond their organizations resulting from their accomplishments and/or publications. Increasingly, their time was spent on determining where the organization should be going rather than concentrating on day-to-day management activities. Ah, it is beginning to sound like leadership!

Table 11.1
Frequency with Which Librarians Were Listed as Major Contributors

	Listed at least once	Listed more than ten times
Contribution to the library	67.8%	4.3%
Contribution to a university-wide committee	57.1%	7.0%
Contribution to the profession	43.7%	5.4%

Stage 4 professionals made up about 17 percent of the group according to Dalton et al. Later in this chapter, this finding will be compared with data on academic librarians in large universities.

WHICH LIBRARIAN IS MAKING THE GREATEST CONTRIBUTION?

The second study this chapter examines attempted to measure contribution based on the judgment of professional peers within the same organization. In this case, the organizations were large academic libraries, most of which employed at least 50 librarians.

As part of a study that examined differences in salaries paid to male and female librarians (Dowell 1986; Dowell 1988), each librarian was asked to list:

- librarians at their university who were making the greatest contribution to achieving the *mission of the library*;
- librarians at their university who could make the greatest contribution to a *university-wide committee*; and
- librarians at their university who were making the greatest contribution to the *profession of librarianship*.

This was an attempt to come up with a "qualitative" measure to consider along with the many "quantitative" measures such as years of professional service, number of librarians supervised, number of degrees completed, number of articles and books published, and number of years of service in professional organization. Self-nominations were allowed.

As can be seen in Table 11.1, more librarians were seen as contributing, at least by someone, when the focus of consideration was the local library. As the arena being considered expanded to the entire campus, the number of individuals receiving nominations decreased. At the same time, there was more consensus concerning who the leaders were. A larger number received more than 10 nom-

Table 11.2
Average Times Men and Women Were Listed as Major Contributors

	Men	Women
Contribution to the library	2.9	2.6
Contribution to a university-wide committee	3.0	2.5
Contribution to the profession	2.3	1.6

inations. When the venue became the profession of librarianship, only about two-thirds as many were nominated as had been for contributing to library goals. Overall, 429 of the 513 librarians received at least one nomination in one category or another.

Men were slightly more likely to be listed than women; but the differences were not statistically significant. As is seen in Table 11.2, the difference was virtually nonexistent when contribution to the library was the question. However, the gap widened as the focus shifted to the university. The difference increased even more when profession-wide contribution was evaluated. In the latter case, statistical significance was approached but not achieved.

The pattern of responses demonstrated that leadership, like art, is in the eye of the beholder. When the data were processed so that it was possible to see who was listing whom, blatant sexism was demonstrated on both sides of the gender gap. To give some perspective to this, one must assume that leadership is exercised randomly by women and men in a manner equal to their respective presence in the library. Based on this assumption, women listed women about 11 percent more frequently than their numbers would justify when contribution to the library was being considered. In other words, the percentage of women named on the lists by women was greater than the percentage of women in the libraries. This, however, was more than offset as a result of the men's listing men about 24 percent more than would be expected if men and women were listed in proportion to their relative presence on the staff. The net result of this gender preference was not as devastating to women as it might first appear. There were almost twice as many women as men employed as librarians in these universities. Therefore, there were almost twice as many women "overranking" women as there were men "overranking" men. This almost offset the more exaggerated gender contribution gap as viewed by the men.

As the focus shifted to university-wide and profession-wide areas, the "over-rating" of women by women diminished and then disappeared. The "underrating" of women by men, however, continued with almost equal strength. The overall result was that women were not listed in these two categories in the proportions that their numbers in the workforce might suggest (Figure 11.1).

Figure 11.1
"Overrating" ("Underrating") of Women from Percentage of Women in Workforce

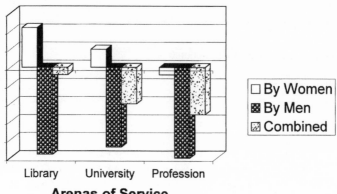

Arenas of Service

As mentioned earlier, there was some blatant sexism at work. One recently divorced, middle-aged woman seemed to make a political statement with her lists. She wrote in the margin, "See, I didn't put any blankety-blank man on any of my lists!" An older man looked back at his lists in apparent self-discovery and perhaps some sadness as he realized he had not included any women. Others kept their thoughts and political agendas, if any, to themselves.

Sexism appeared to increase with the age of the rater. While this finding is not surprising, it gives cause for concern. Older professionals typically make most of the decisions concerning the hiring, promotion, and rewarding of other professionals. However, further analysis of the data indicated that the overrating of one's own gender seemed to peak at the first-line supervisor level. Librarians at the top management levels displayed more balanced judgments.

Dalton et al. found approximately 11 percent of their professionals to be in the top echelon of Stage 4. In Table 11.3 the top 11 percent of academic librarians are distributed by organizational level. Their rankings were determined by a composite of all three peer ratings scales: contribution to the library, contribution to a university-wide committee; and contribution to the profession of librarianship.

For comparison purposes, the levels of department head through director certainly could be considered managers in the four-stage model. Based on this assumption, only 15 percent of the librarians listed as high contributors are below the level of department head. This compares with 26 percent in the four-stage model.

If only contribution to the library was considered, the following distribution was found (Table 11.4). Based on this assumption, only 15 percent of the librarians listed as high contributors are below the level of department head. This compares with 26 percent in the four-stage model.

Table 11.3
Librarians by Organizational Level in Top 11 Percent Based on Composite of All Three Peer Ratings for Contribution

Organizational Level	Number of Librarians
Director	7
Associate Director	6
Assistant Director	11
Department Head	23
First Line Supervisor	3
Front Line Librarian	5

Based on this assumption, 25 percent of the librarians listed as high contributors are below the level of department head. This is almost identical to the 26 percent in the four-stage model. However, it does not clearly answer the question of whether or not leadership is what is being measured.

THE PROTEAN CAREER

Over the last three decades, Douglas Hall has been writing a book every 10 years on careers (Hall 1976; Hall et al. 1986; Hall et al. 1996). In the first of the trilogy, Hall predicted that "there would be a new form of career that is driven more by the individual than the organization. This career would call for frequent change and self-invention and would be propelled by the desire for psychological success rather than by externally determined measure of success" (Hall and Associates 1996). In the 1980s, contrary to Hall's expectation, careers became even more intensely organizationally defined. However, in the 1990s there is evidence that his prediction is beginning to come true. More people seem to be taking the attitude, "If I can't get to the top or make a big financial killing, I might as well do what I really want to do."

It is still too early to see with any certainty whether the trend that Hall observed in the first half of the 1990s will have a long-term impact or whether it was merely a slight hiccup in his data. The protean attitude about career progression is certainly nothing new. To some extent, it has been around as long as there have been people pursuing careers. It certainly was expressed by some in the 1960s. However, there may be forces in the workplace that will accelerate and institutionalize this model well into the next century.

Table 11.4
Librarians by Organizational Level in Top 11 Percent Based on Peer Ratings for Contribution to the Library Only

Organizational Level	Number of Librarians
Director	6
Associate Director	8
Assistant Director	9
Department Head	20
First Line Supervisor	9
Front Line Librarian	5

The rapid change taking place in organizations has eroded the expectation of lifetime employment (except perhaps in academe). Many companies today no longer make a pretense of promising lifelong employment. They can't promise how long they will be in business, that they won't be acquired, that there will be room for promotion, that your job will exist until you reach retirement age, or that money will be available for your pension. Both the organizations and the content of individual jobs within them are changing.

"Protean" is derived from the name of the Greek God Proteus, who could change his appearance literally from animal to vegetable to mineral at a whim. As applied to careers, "protean" would be described as follows:

The protean career is a process which the person, not the organization, is managing. It consists of all the person's varied experiences in education, training, work in several organizations, changes in occupational field, etc. The protean career is not what happens to the person in any one organization. The protean person's own personal career choices and search for self-fulfillment are the unifying or integrative elements in his or her life. The criterion of success is internal (psychological success), not external. In short, the protean career is shaped more by the individual than by the organization and may be redirected from time to time to meet the needs of the person. (Hall 1776, 201)

"Thus, whereas in the past the contract was with the organization, in the protean career the contract is with the self" (Hall et al. 1996, 20). Instead of the rational, understandable, and linear progression through stages of a career (Dalton et al. 1977), all workers must find the unique path that is the right one for them. The protean career may have many zigs and zags and even several changes to other lines of work. Some of these twists and turns are driven by "quality of life" concerns, but some may be driven by economic necessity. "Downsizing" has become a major fact of life for professionals and middle managers as well as laborers. Also "outsourcing" and the extensive use of temporary employees are becoming more and more common in spite of continuing debate over some of the social policy issues involved.

But what does this trend toward an individual-defined- and-driven career progression, if it continues, have to do with leadership?Perhaps the most important aspect will be the increased importance of listening skills. If the individual, not the organization (or even peers), defines what the path should be, leaders and "want-to-be" leaders will have to listen carefully and continuously to every individual. This will not be easy, because individuals often will not know with certainty where they want to go. Furthermore, what they think they know today may be very different from what they thought yesterday or what they may think tomorrow.

Organizations will continue to need leaders who are fulfilling the mentoring roles and direction-shaping roles discussed in Stage 3 and Stage 4. However, those roles, particularly the mentoring role, will have become more complicated. No longer can young professionals pattern their careers after those of successful senior professionals, because what it takes to be successful is changing. No longer can new professionals perfect the tools of their trade in Stage 1 and demonstrate them in Stage 2 and then move on to other matters. Throughout their careers, professions will need to continue to learn and grow because of the accelerating rate of change—both within organizations and within professions. However, perhaps the problem can become part of the solution. This ability to learn continuously becomes the model new professionals must incorporate into their behavior if they are to be successful.

Leading the whole person will be another shift in focus. In the past, when the organization defined the appropriate pattern for career progression, personal matters were supposed to be kept out of the workplace. When personal needs drive career progression, both the personal and professional persona must be unified and dealt with simultaneously. Many examples of this evolution could be cited. However, one of the most prevalent at this time is the attention many pace-setting employers—dare I say leading employers—are now providing for employees with on-site childcare facilities. Leaders of the future will have to be willing to help employees address problems once thought to be personal, but at the same time must avoid prying into matters the employee wishes to keep private. This will be a very delicate balancing act indeed.

WHO LEADS?

In traditional models, leaders were defined by the organizations. Even in that setting, they may exercise leadership either formally or informally. That is, leaders were likely to be managers, but often they were nonmanagers. Professionals could be temporary leaders as the primary shapers of special projects. Senior professionals, in order to receive the full range of organizational rewards, needed to assume at least some of the roles and responsibilities of leaders.

Even within the organizational model, to some extent, leaders were in the eye of the beholder. Gender has been one of the filters through which we view leaders. Coworkers may be seen as leaders in one venue but not in another.

As increasing focus is placed on individuals' taking charge of their own careers, very subtle shifts are taking place. The organizational model is still alive and well. It will likely remain robust for some time. However, it is not the only game in town, and it probably never was. Some have always looked to their peers rather than to their employing organizations for validation that what they were doing was worthwhile. We also have had others who moved to the beat of their own drums. Are the proportions really shifting in any fundamental way? Have they all been there all the time, and we just did not notice? Do we need to unify these paradigms or is one supplanting another? Only time will tell. For now, one-dimensional definitions of leadership definitely do not fit all.

REFERENCES

Dalton, Gene W. and Paul H. Thompson. 1971. "Accelerating Obsolescence of Older Engineers." *Harvard Business Review* 49 (September–October): 57–67.

———. 1986. *Novations: Strategies for Career Management.* Glenview, IL: Scott, Foresman.

Dalton, Gene W., Paul H. Thompson, and Raymond Price. 1977. "Four Stages of Professional Careers." *Organizational Dynamics* 6 (Summer): 19–42.

Dowell, David R. 1986. "The Relation of Salary to Sex in a Female Dominated Profession: *Librarians Employed at Research Universities in the South Atlantic Census Region.*" Diss., University of North Carolina at Chapel Hill.

———. 1988. "Sex and Salary in a Female Dominated Profession." *Journal of Academic Librarianship* 14 (May): 92–98.

Hall, Douglas T. 1976. *Careers, in Organization.* Glenview, IL: Scott, Foresman.

Hall, Douglas T. et al. 1986. *Career Development in Organizations.* San Francisco: Jossey-Bass.

———. 1996. *The Career Is Dead—Long Live the Career: A Relational Approach to Careers.* San Francisco: Jossey-Bass.

Weber, David C. and Tina Kass. 1978. "Comparable Rewards: The Case for Equal Compensation for Nonadministrative Expertise . . .". *Library Journal* 113 (April 15): 824–827.

Chapter 12

The Advancement Dilemma of Academic Library Directors

George Charles Newman

Career advancement is usually defined as the act of upward mobility from one position of leadership to another, and it is associated with achievement, accomplishment, and reward. People seek advancement for a number of reasons. For some, it may be the lure of increased power or more money; for others, it may be the challenge of a new position or even a chance for renewal of a career. Indeed, as a person's needs change at different stages of his or her career, so, too, does the attitude toward advancement. A person who is very career-oriented with a goal of moving up the ladder may, at a later time, be equally fulfilled by mentoring others as they move toward positions of leadership (see Hoffman 1988).

This chapter examines the concept of advancement as it relates to academic library directors. Particular emphasis is placed on the factors of advancement as they relate to the unique goals and objectives facing higher education in the late 1990s. To more fully understand the concept of advancement for academic library directors, one must first look at the organizational structure of colleges and universities today and the role library directors play within that structure.

Colleges and universities are traditionally organized around principles and roles that relate to either function or intellectual process. On one side of the organizational structure, one finds the academic or intellectual process of the institution. Through the governance structure of colleges and universities, the administration and the faculty work toward consensus in the implementation of intellectual process at the campus. In academic decision making, faculty have historically shared politics, policy, and power with the administration, but the balance within this partnership has shifted in most higher educational institutions as a result of the variety and acceleration of change coupled with economic, political, and social forces. Although faculty remain committed to providing influence through traditional governance structures, in reality, most, if not all, colleges and universities have shifted academic planning and the intellectual process of the institution to a central management team that consists of the Board of Trustees, the president, the provost, and other vice presidents. The academic deans remain a part of the process, but their role has changed to one of communication with the faculty and implementation of institutional academic change, rather than being the initiator of changes in the curriculum and the faculty.

On the other side of the organizational structure of colleges and universities are those areas that provide specific functions. Although certain mythmaking people (particularly presidents) are fond of describing the library as the centerpiece of the scholarship of an institution, in reality, today's academic library remains on the periphery of the academic structure. This is one of the challenges academic library directors face—to convince the president and, indeed, the entire central management team that the library must be a vital and integral part of the academic plan to meet the current and future needs of the faculty and students as well as the curriculum itself.

Academic libraries are "the gatekeepers and the gateways" to the knowledge and scholarship that support the teaching function and curriculum of higher education. They are expected to provide to students, faculty, and the community those services and operations that support and parallel the academic goals of the institution. Thus, the academic library director is charged with making sure that the library can deliver traditional services as well as the new technological services of the information age to students and faculty (see Dowler 1997).

The functional role of the academic library has placed the director in the position of middle manager, and, as such, the institution relies on the academic library director for very specific management roles. Academic library directors are responsible for both professional and clerical staff; they manage budgets that represent 3 to 6 percent of the total institutional budget; they plan services and operations and maintain physical facilities. The directors are expected to supervise their staff within a cooperative and consensus-building style, yet at the same time they must report to a vice president or provost within the administration. In addition to being skilled at communicating up and down the organizational structure, academic library directors must be adept at communicating across the structure and working with other middle managers such as computer center directors, student affairs officers, and so on.

Sometimes the institution does very little to bring these middle managers together for purposes of communication or planning and instead leaves them outside the loop (see Kraus 1983). When this occurs, the library director must work with other middle managers to facilitate communication and bring about needed changes. Additionally, meaningful communication with the administration of the institution and inclusion in decision making outside the library are both critical to the future course of any academic library. Now and in the future, academic library directors must facilitate effective communication and information sharing, particularly with those to whom they report.

CONSTRAINTS AND OPPORTUNITIES

What does this tell us about career advancement for academic library directors? An appropriate analogy can be found in the business world. As professionals move up the ladder in complex corporations, they are faced with a narrowing of opportunities. The merger, downsizing, and reengineering forces in the corporate sector during the past decade have affected traditional avenues of advancement. In the past, middle managers with strong traditional work records were usually identified for advancement into upper management and groomed to eventually provide executive leadership to a corporation. Now, however, advancement in the business world has begun to shift to a more broadly based process where individuals who have unique problem-solving, planning, marketing, and technological skills can move to the top of the organizational hierarchy, although they may do so at another corporation.

These same changes are now occurring in higher education, and, as a result, career advancement for academic library directors is changing as well. There are two ways academic library directors can advance their careers: (1) they can move from the directorship of one type of academic library to the directorship of another, with each move representing a larger organization and a different set of responsibilities, or (2) based on their experience, skill, knowledge, and accomplishment, they can be appointed to a different academic position in either the same or another organization. Overwhelmingly, directors who want to advance in their careers are forced to choose the first method, as they are competing with faculty and administrators for upper-level administrative positions.

Many of the barriers to advancement for the academic library director, particularly outside the "directorship to directorship" mode, are similar to the "glass ceiling" that women and minorities have faced for many years. While a case can be made for a library director to become an administrator because of the complexity of the operation of a library system and the transferable skills of operation and organization, the peculiar dynamics of the world of higher education have usually prevented this kind of transference of skills (see Garten 1988).

The prevailing philosophy of academic culture today binds higher educational decision making to traditional and conservative lines of thought. Thus, advancement in higher educational management occurs through a supposedly collegial selection process where academic faculty select individuals who are like themselves to solve very complex issues in today's changing academic environment. As a result, large numbers of other professionals who are perceived as nontraditional or outside the scope of the specifics of the position are excluded. At a time when institutions are striving to find solutions to complex problems and issues, most are locked into conservative, status quo positions.

With both public and private higher education today facing some of the most critical financial, political, and academic issues in the history of higher education, it has been said that higher education cannot "continue to do business as usual" and that the support bases are not there or are quickly eroding. Public judgment has shifted to critical challenge. Higher education has to change itself or be changed by forces and groups outside its domain. What better time, therefore, to challenge the traditional incremental/across-the-board concept of institutional management and to pioneer new forms of leadership from the ranks of middle management.

It can be argued that academic library directors in the 1990s are probably more qualified to advance to other administrative or academic posts in higher education than faculty members because of the unique issues they have had to face and broad scope of their responsibilities. Unlike the dean of a particular school or discipline, who assuredly has a good understanding of a specific discipline but not necessarily the breadth of understanding of the entire institution, the academic library director is experienced in dealing with the total institutional environment. The director must manage enormous collections that parallel all academic programs and must be familiar with the new emerging technologies. (In fact, academic libraries are often at the cutting edge of technological innovation when compared to the rest of the institution.) In addition, he or she works with complex budgets, manages a large and diverse staff, both clerical and professional, and has expertise in planning, fund-raising, and physical facilities. Despite these qualifications, academic library directors often find it difficult to assume new and different career challenges in either their present institution or another (see Woodsworth 1989).

A study of career mobility of academic library directors was conducted by the author.[1] The data are not surprising in that they reflect the status quo career patterns for a majority of academic library directors. Although there were a few instances where a director made a change in type of position, for the most part, career changes for the directors in this sample were lateral in nature—simply moving from one academic library to another. This analysis also showed that a number of new academic library directors came from other library administrative posts, such as assistant and associate library directors, reflecting the traditional career path in the library profession as well as in higher education in general.

Certainly, assistant and associate directors of today can look toward a somewhat different set of career opportunities than in the past. With the rapid technological changes in academic libraries today, these assistant and associate directors can acquire unique skills that will take them beyond their present role. As they acquire administrative experience within the library, they may become more ambitious and aspire to senior roles in the administration of the institution. While such administrative positions require a somewhat different set of skills, this new type of academic library director, being more management-oriented and adept at harnessing the changing nature of the academic library and the information needs of the institution, will be in a better position to assume greater upward career mobility in higher education (see Giesecke, Michalak, and Franklin 1997).

NEW HORIZONS FOR CAREER CHANGE

In the past, practical library experience and educational credentials were thought to be the appropriate career criteria for advancement in the profession. As academic libraries have changed, so, too, have the fabric of higher education and especially its management and administrative needs. Academic library directors today must balance the traditional mission and operation of an academic library with the new, emerging technologies that are available to the public, while higher education searches for ways to manage complex academic and informational sectors.

All of this offers the academic library director a variety of unique opportunities. The individual, not the organization, is responsible for his or her career, and thus the director must be willing to create opportunities to move in a new direction. There are three areas within the library where the library director can make an impact within the institution and thereby exhibit skills that would enhance the possibility of advancement into nonlibrary-related positions. These three areas are institutional planning, fund-raising, and technology and teaching.

Institutional Planning

One opportunity for achieving success for the academic library and the director as well is presented by institutional change. As higher educational institutions struggle to develop a meaningful institutional plan in the face of rapid change in both technology and society, academic library directors need to identify unique contributions that the library can make to the institution. With the library staff and faculty, the director can prepare planning documents for the library that more fully integrate the library into the academic plan of the college; such a plan could also serve as a model for other academic and nonacademic areas of the campus. This planning strategy is similar to what the office of institutional research provides globally for the college or university. The library director, however, would focus on the needs and initiatives of the library.

Preparing a comprehensive library plan requires an identification of library goals along with documentation of library needs. Perhaps the preeminent document used by academic libraries in this planning process is *Standards for College Libraries*, developed by the Association of College and Research Libraries (ACRL) in the 1950s and updated periodically thereafter. This work provides both quantitative and qualitative standards for libraries and covers such areas as goals and objectives, physical facilities, personnel, and budget and expenditures.

It is an excellent tool through which a library director and staff can gather pertinent data for a comprehensive planning document for the library (see Newman 1979).

Once the planning document is complete, it must be promoted within the institution, not only to gain acceptance of the plan but to raise the consciousness of the administration and the faculty as to the true mission of the library and its new role in higher education. How is this accomplished? First, a document of this nature must be accepted by the office of academic affairs. Once acceptance at the administrative level is gained, a strategy should be devised to discuss the plan and the library with the deans and department heads. This approach would inform the faculty and administration of the specific needs and accomplishments of the academic library and enlist their support in implementing the plan. It might also serve as a model for planning that could be applied to other areas of the institution.

Institutional research and planning are much more than the mere gathering of data. Their true purpose is to enable an institution to identify its mission and its goals and to redirect itself toward the most appropriate course of action. Thus, each unit in the institution, including the library, must be willing—and able— to periodically review its operations and develop a plan of action. By initiating this planning process within the library, the library director can provide leadership with the entire institution and thereby open up new career opportunities in higher education.

Fund-Raising

At no time in the history of higher education has the issue of institutional advancement been more important than during the decade leading to the twenty-first century. One can scarcely pick up a major newspaper or *The Chronicle of Higher Education* without noticing stories of any number of colleges and universities' embarking on a major fund-raising campaign (see Nicklin 1997). Some of the large research universities have completed or are completing billion-dollar campaigns in the 1990s, and it is not unusual for a new campaign to be announced almost as soon as one is concluded. Institutional advancement is more than endowments, however; it also represents the "value-added" resources that will sustain and enhance a college or university. In some ways, institutional advancement is reshaping the structure of higher education.

Just as the admission and retention of students must be a campuswide effort in order to be successful in today's competitive environment, so, too, must the fund-raising process involve all sectors of the institution. While the president or vice presidents will often be the ones to "close the deal" in fund-raising efforts, much of the groundwork can—and should—be done by the faculty and middle managers of the college. These people thoroughly understand the curricular and program issues of the institution and can convey them to potential donors.

The concept of fund-raising and academic libraries is a relatively unexplored area, probably because of the conservative nature of higher education (see Grace 1993). Presidents, provosts, and vice presidents of institutional advancement traditionally have viewed academic libraries merely as physical facilities, storehouses of large and diverse collections. Academic library directors have had few opportunities to change this concept, but bringing libraries into the fund-raising process offers an opportunity to do so and offers benefits to both the academic library director and the office of institutional advancement.

Fund-raising provides academic library directors with a new vehicle for potential success and recognition for the library. It requires that academic library directors be aware of campus initiatives, and fund-raising planning and implementation should be integrated into the work of both the director and the librarians. By doing so, the opportunity for the director and the library to be included in future campaigns is greatly enhanced, if not assured.

Convincing the institution to accept the library director as a player in the fund-raising process may not be an easy task, however. Although some institutional advancement officers will welcome help from any area of the campus, others may resist advances by the library director to participate in the fund-raising process. This resistance could occur because they do not want the library initiatives to be in competition with what they feel are more pressing campus needs, or it may simply be because they do not understand the library and its role. The library director who wants to participate in the development process of the institution must therefore convince the administration, particularly the office of institutional advancement, of the wisdom of including the library director in the planning and implementation of its campaigns. Once this is accomplished, the library director must then make an effort to play an active role in the process.

The planning for any major campus fund-raising initiative begins many months in advance of the presentation of the campaign initiatives to the public. In these early stages of discussion and analysis among the Board of Trustees, the president, and the chief administrative officers, a consultant is often brought to campus to assist in the preparation of the campaign. During this period of preparation the academic library director should bring the initiatives of the library to those responsible for identifying key components of the campaign.

First, however, the academic library director and key staff within the library need to identify a series of initiatives, a wish list, if you will, that addresses both the present and future needs of the library. Data gathering and planning are critical to developing and presenting the initiatives of the library to the administration of the institution. These initiatives should be broad in perspective, such as enhancements to the building, funding to incorporate and advance the library's technological structure, funding or endowments for areas of the collection and/or for library positions (endowed chairs), special discretionary funding for professional development, and staff enhancement. Cooperative proposals that enhance faculty and student research through library resources and technologies should also be considered. These library initiatives should then be ranked, with greater weight being given to those that would be jointly valuable to faculty, the curriculum, and the mission of the library.

Once the initiatives have been identified and agreed upon within the library, they need to be incorporated into a planning document that presents the current status of the academic library and describes why inclusion in the college or university fund-raising campaign will be beneficial to both the library and the institution. The planning document for library fund-raising must present a positive and progressive picture of the library and identify initiatives that will elevate the library to a higher plateau. Most importantly, it must show how fund-raising for the library will improve and enhance not only the library but also the reputation of the college or university.

The library director must then begin a dialogue with the administration to determine which initiatives the library should pursue. Some initiatives may be funded through regular institutional budgeting, while others are more appropriate for a fund-raising campaign. By working together, the library, the administration, and the office of institutional advancement can reach a consensus that benefits both the library and the institution as a whole.

In fund-raising, the identification of sources of funding—foundations, corporations, and individuals—is crucial to the types of initiatives a college or university will pursue. It is not unusual, in fact, for the library director or even a library department head to work with the grants office in identifying and writing library-related grant proposals. In the same way, the academic library director should identify some of these sources in the library's fund-raising proposal. It would also be useful to make a case for pursuing particular foundations or corporations by identifying what these organizations have provided for other academic libraries. Be very specific as to what was funded and the amounts given, as well as any joint fund-raising that was required.

It is a more complex and political issue to identify particular individuals who might donate to the library. Since the institution may already be soliciting a certain individual to support other initiatives, it is probably better to suggest individuals but let the institution decide whom to pursue. Then the library director can, if requested, work with institutional advancement to make contact with the targeted individuals.

Fund-raising for the library offers the academic library director the opportunity to promote the library and, in addition, to provide special expertise to the institution with respect to library initiatives. Most institutions are too busy trying to promote and manage complex campaigns to focus on the library and its needs. The person who demonstrates a unique set of skills through a comprehensive plan for fund-raising becomes more valuable to the institution and thus creates new opportunities for advancement in nonlibrary administrative positions.

Technology and Teaching

The third area where academic library directors can make changes in the campus perception of the library is in the use of technology to improve teaching.

Library technology has come full circle in the past 20 years. Originally, technology was primarily used to manage and process the library's collections, coordinate circulation of resources, and manage the financial accountability of library budgets. Today the opportunities exist to incorporate technology into the teaching process (see Lowry 1997; Wilkinson 1997). Library technology has moved to an access approach through local and wide area networks, which provides a number of new methods for accessing information (such as the Internet) as well as for incorporating information resources into the teaching process.

Academic libraries stand at the threshold of the technology instruction movement in higher education, and academic library directors can seize the opportunity to integrate library technology into the teaching process. One way is to bring the teaching of technology into the library. With the advent of large-scale technology implementation on many campuses, the library director can negotiate to have the academic library as the preferred location of the "electronic" or "smart" classroom by emphasizing that it is merely an extension of the technology used throughout the library to manage and retrieve information.

Another way is to take a fresh approach to the traditional methods of library instruction and encourage staff to incorporate learning theory into the adoption of library technology and the teaching process. In many cases, especially in the comprehensive, open-door institution, the students' first use of technology in the curriculum may come when they use the library to access information. By providing a hands-on approach to technology instruction, the library can play an integral role in the teaching of technology on campus. Access to on-line databases, full-text journal and periodical retrieval systems, and the World Wide Web through a variety of Internet search engines provides a broad array of resources, and academic library instruction should reflect this new information environment.

As it stands now, library instruction in a majority of academic libraries is limited to library orientations or single class presentations. This was fine while the library was in the process of becoming automated, as it allowed librarians to teach students and faculty about collections, services, and access. But today the greatest opportunities for library instruction lie in the area of formal course instruction. Orientation to library services has traditionally had little impact on students except perhaps to show them where the library is located on campus. Formal library instruction, however, can be developed around particular information sectors such as the humanities, social sciences, and the sciences, with some consideration offered to other information skill areas such as the processing of information, searching on the Internet, software development, and information management for the professional. This type of instruction could be taught as a joint endeavor with a faculty member, focusing on a particular discipline. Becoming more directly involved in the teaching process offers librarians and library directors the perfect opportunity to become directly involved in the institution's curriculum and planning. Integrating information skills into the curriculum is a good way to raise the visibility of the library, librarians, and the director.

CONCLUSION

The dilemmas facing academic library directors in their quest to advance beyond the confines of the library should be viewed in terms of opportunity rather than constraints. Many of the building blocks needed to change academic institutions' perspectives on their library directors and their abilities to succeed in other positions of responsibility exist within the present framework. As this chapter has illustrated, planning, fund-raising, and technology and the teaching process are three areas where academic librarians can and should be involved. Academic library directors must be willing to take the initiative in these areas and work with their administrations to make their libraries active and integral players in the academic process. In doing so, library directors have the opportunity to develop, with input from the library staff, methods of disseminating to the faculty and administration information about the library's role and needs.

The academic library director who seeks unique ways to contribute to the mission of the institution has the opportunity to enhance the library and be in a position to assume new and greater responsibility in other areas. The professional who can develop a planning process has the potential to reshape the academics of an institution and made a significant contribution. Directors who prepare a proposal, devise a fund-raising strategy, and achieve the funding to implement proposals that enhance both the library and the institution have greatly increased their expertise. Academic library directors who can reallocate internal resources to create an information skills curriculum using the emerging library technologies to integrate information skills into the institution's teaching and learning patterns have made a distinctive impact on the academic nature of their institutions.

As middle managers in a time of change in higher education, academic library directors should look beyond years of experience, traditional library accomplishments, and educational credentials as prerequisites for career advancement. Instead, they can and should prepare themselves for other challenges and opportunities. By actively working with the administration and the faculty on a variety of issues, library directors can develop a track record of accomplishment that can pave the way for advancement into other areas of academe and have a lasting impact on both their institution and their career.

NOTE

1. The author analyzed the profiles of academic library directors who were identified in *College & Research Libraries News* (1990–1996) as having changed positions. While admittedly an unscientific sample of career change in the academic library profession, it is a reflection of where academic library directors move in their careers.

REFERENCES

Dowler, Lawrence. 1997. "Gateways to Knowledge: A New Direction for the Harvard College Library." In Lawrence Dowler, ed., *Gateways to Knowledge: The Role of Academic Libraries in Teaching, Learning, and Research*. Cambridge, MA: MIT Press, pp. 95–107.

Garten, Edward D. 1988. "Observations on Why So Few Chief Library Officers Move into Senior Academic Administration." *Library Administration and Management* 2 (March): 95–98.

Giesecke, Joan, Sarah Michalak, and Brinley Franklin. 1997. "Changing Management Roles for Associate Directors in Libraries." *Library Administration and Management* 11 (Summer): 172–180.

Grace, Judy Diane. 1993. "Trends in Fund-Raising Research." In Michael J. Worth, ed., *Educational Fund Raising Principles and Practices*. Phoenix, AZ: Oryx Press, pp. 380–388.

Hoffman, Ellen J. 1988. "Career Management for Leaders." In Anne Woodsworth and Barbara von Wahlde, eds., *Leadership for Research Libraries: A Festschrift for Robert M. Hayes*. Metuchen, NJ: Scarecrow Press, pp. 166–185.

Kraus, John D. 1983. "Middle Management in Higher Education: A Dog's Life?" *Journal of the College and University Personnel Association* 34 (Winter): 29–35.

Lowry, Anita. 1997. "Gateways to the Classroom." In Lawrence Dowler, ed., *Gateways to Knowledge: The Role of Academic Libraries in Teaching, Learning, and Research*. Cambridge, MA: MIT Press, pp. 199–206.

Newman, George C. 1979. *Institutional Resources—Shafer Library, and Profile*. Vols. 1, 2. ED314072.

Nicklin, Julie L. 1997. "Bull Market Helped Endowments Earn Average of 17.2% in 1996." *The Chronicle of Higher Education* (February 14): A34, A35.

Wilkinson, James. 1997. "Homesteading on the Electronic Frontier: Technology, Libraries, and Learning." In Lawrence Dowler, ed., *Gateways to Knowledge: The Role of Academic Libraries in Teaching, Learning, and Research*. Cambridge, MA: MIT Press, pp. 181–196.

Woodsworth, Anne. 1989. "Library Directors as Middle Managers: A Neglected Resource." *Library Administration and Management* 3 (Winter): 24–27.

Chapter 13

Postleadership Career Paths for Academic Library Directors

George Charles Newman

During the past decade, corporate America has seen thousands of chief executives and middle managers lose their positions as a result of downsizing, mergers, reengineering, or simply the politics of change. As the century ends, higher education is experiencing many of the same forces. From the president down to middle managers such as the academic library director, the organizational and administrative structure of colleges and universities is being reshaped. As a result, many academic library directors may find themselves departing from their positions, either voluntarily or involuntarily.

What happens to the heads of academic libraries when they leave the directorship and find themselves facing an uncertain future? This chapter discusses the changes occurring in higher education and the effect that leaving a leadership position has on an academic library director. It then provides strategies for setting up a plan for the future. Exploring the variety of career paths that are available to academic library directors when they leave their positions of leadership, the chapter focuses on what the future holds for these highly skilled, educated, and experienced professionals.

THE WINDS OF CHANGE

Job loss or job departure through reorganization, reengineering, or downsizing has become a frequent occurrence in the business world, and some social critics believe that this cycle of events will continue to occur well into the twenty-first century (see Fram 1994). Lifetime employment within one organization has become a vanishing concept, given the changing environment, the impact of costs and economics, the ever-changing technology, and the shifting political nature of bureaucratic organizations. Such upheavals in people's lives and careers are now showing up in academe, as colleges and universities begin to solve issues of costs, clientele, and technology (see Guskin 1996). With the addition of such external factors as educational and management accountability, higher education is in a change mode that most experts feel will only accelerate and continue for several years.

Academic libraries and their staff mirror all of the elements of change and accountability that we find in greater society. Technology, which 20 years ago first began to shape a new future for academic libraries through the automation of operations and services, has accelerated this change, and libraries are now attempting to come to grips with the transition from traditional library services to the concept of the virtual library. These elements of change are generally influenced and directed by the director of the academic library, and it is therefore not surprising that the director often becomes a lightning rod for any resistance to the rapid changes taking place in the library field.

Thus, in today's academic world, remaining in a leadership position may be beyond the control of the individual. Middle managers, such as academic library directors, are especially vulnerable. Pressures from the administration and/or from the ranks of the faculty and staff may result in changes in leadership. An example of how the fortunes of an academic library director can change is illustrated in the following scenario:

A woman with a considerable amount of line and management experience as well as a doctoral degree was hired to head a library system at a major research university. She was considered by her peers to be an excellent communicator and knowledgeable about all of the major issues facing academic libraries. One of the first issues the new university librarian addressed was the low morale of the library staff as well as the need to create improved communications with the university administration. She then began working with key members of the university library staff to create an internal review of the organizational structure, function, operation, and services of the university library. This internal review process took nearly two years.

During that two-year period, a number of changes occurred in the leadership of the university. A new university president was hired by the Board of Trustees. Six months later, the new president asked all the vice presidents, including the provost, to submit their resignations, as he preferred hiring his own vice presidents. It was the provost to whom the university library system reported, and the appointment of a new provost had a great effect upon the relationship between the library and the administration.

The university librarian had had open and good communication with the former provost, who had generally been enthusiastic about her future plans for the university library. Six months into the tenure of the new provost, however, there were strains between the provost and the university librarian. Much of this was fostered by the results of the internal library review and the resulting discord in the ranks of the university library system. Since the internal review proposed sweeping changes in the library system, many of the librarians and staff were threatened by the prospect of these changes and by the direction they felt the library was headed. They became disenchanted with the leadership of the university librarian.

As a result of this disenchantment, a group of librarians and staff members initiated a number of meetings with the new provost and his academic affairs staff. Some of the deans of the largest programs at the university were also included in these discussions. Despite the efforts of the university librarian to educate both her librarians and staff and the members of the administration about the merits of the internal review and the changes proposed, the new provost and administrative team saw only the discord that had resulted from the review. To eliminate the "problem," the provost elected to terminate the university librarian. For the next year, until her contract expired, she was assigned to a faculty position in a discipline related to her educational credentials.

The university librarian in this scenario was a progressive and capable leader whose ability to lead was affected both by a change in the administration of the institution and by a political struggle with the academic librarians. These factors combined to cause her to lose her position. Does that make her any less able to be a leader in another environment? The answer clearly is no. But the university librarian now faces a crossroads in her career, and how she copes will determine how successful she will be in her postleadership role.

THE DEPARTURE

Whether an academic library director is dismissed or voluntarily steps down from his or her position as the administrative head of the library, the loss of a position of power and influence is significant. Library directors have often spent a number of years accumulating appropriate experience and earning advanced degrees to attain an administrative position, yet they now find themselves separated from the very position they have striven to reach.

The departure may be even more strained because tremendous political, economic, and academic changes in higher education have had major effects on all middle managers, including the academic library director. Furthermore, personnel decisions regarding a library director are often debated within the administration and thus drawn out over a period of time. Some type of internal and, occasionally, external assessment is often made of the performance of the academic library—and of the director as well. Because of the collegial nature of higher education, library staff and faculty also often play a role in the determination of a director's fate. As a result, by the time a library director decides or is asked to leave his or her position, no matter how capable or successful, the director's confidence may be shaken.

When an administrator also has a tenured faculty position in an academic department, he or she can sometimes make a rather smooth transition back into the role of teaching and research. Some former administrators have even been known to tell colleagues that they were really always faculty members and that they assumed administrative responsibilities because no one else was willing to take on the task of management. Although this attitude is sometimes a defensive mechanism, it also reveals the mixed allegiances and lack of understanding many faculty have of the complex responsibilities involved in the administration of colleges and universities.

Although some academic library directors do have tenured academic appointments, many are less fortunate and may have no other option except to exit the institution, sometimes before they find another position. As with middle managers in the world of business, academic library directors may need from one to two years to obtain new employment, and the process of obtaining another academic library directorship or choosing another career path can be very emotional and time-consuming.

Professionals such as academic library directors who are separated from positions of power go through many of the emotional changes that any employee would. First there is a period of shock, anger, and disbelief, particularly if the loss of the position has been sudden and involuntary. But even if the decision has been made by the individual or has been long in coming, there is still a sense of loss—even though there may be a sense of relief as well. Then comes a grieving period. Next to the loss of a family member, the loss of one's employment or professional position marks a major transition in one's personal and professional life, and experiencing some form of grief over this loss is natural. This is also a period of emotional upheaval, ranging from anger to loss of self-esteem. Even the fact that the removal or departure of other academic middle managers is becoming more commonplace does not diminish these feelings for the individual.

The individual eventually comes to a realization that nothing will reverse the events that have taken place. At this point, one begins to develop a concept of what happened and to put it into the proper perspective—that he or she was given a job to do and did it to the best of his or her ability. At this point the former library director begins a process of renewal. This process may take many forms, from discussing the situation with colleagues or attending professional development programs to reading pertinent literature or seeking professional counseling. During this period, the person begins to evaluate and examine new career opportunities. Here is the beginning of the postleadership period of one's career. Once full closure is brought to the previous departure process, a new and more dynamic period of growth takes place.

STRATEGIES FOR A NEW CAREER

While training, education, and work experience determine much of the course of the unfolding of new professional responsibilities, how an individual looks at the options that are available and creates new opportunities for success will determine what the new career path will be. As the former library director moves into a process of developing a new career, many of the strategies used by job-seeking professionals in the business world can be most useful (e.g., see Bolles 1996). Perhaps the most important first step is for the person to look honestly within himself or herself and identify both skills and interests at this stage in his or her career. The individual must then determine whether and where these skills and interests fit into today's academic environment.

After this analysis, the former library director may decide that a new library directorship is the appropriate career path and then apply for positions at other institutions. Others may see this as an opportunity to provide leadership in another part of the college or university. The following two examples illustrate how library directors seized the opportunity to make changes in their career paths.

In the first example, the library director's skills in the area of technology were easily transferable to a new position.

The academic library director at a regional university heard that the university was planning to change its administrative structure and that his position would be eliminated in favor of a vice president for information; this new position would combine the library, the computer center, and the instructional resources unit under one administrator. Having successfully introduced technology into the management of library services and operations and possessing a doctoral degree in higher educational administration, he felt qualified for this new position. In fact, the academic library director was currently working closely with the vice president of academic affairs and the academic deans to create a collegewide technology network. Part of his work included coordinating with the computer center director and his staff to create "electronic classrooms" for each of the academic areas of the institution as well as working with the vice presidents of business and institutional advancement to develop an external funding proposal for campus technology access.

During the next year and a half, while the university worked on revamping its administrative structure and creating the new position, the library director made an effort to maintain a visible presence with members of the administration as well as to keep in regular contact with the academic deans and department chairpersons. When the vice presidency was finally created, and a national search had begun, the library director was in a strong position to be a candidate. He applied for the position and was ultimately selected to be the new vice president for information.

This case illustrates that the transition from an academic library directorship to another academic position is a process of identifying opportunities within one's position of responsibility and successfully molding this experience into a new set of challenges. The academic library director in this case seized the opportunities that library technology provided and became an expert for the college. This expertise then brought the person into contact with campuswide authorities and decision makers. He was ultimately rewarded for his expertise and knowledge by being offered the new administrative position.

In the second example, an academic library director was able to change her career path even more dramatically within her own institution.

When the provost suggested that the library be a center for a major university campaign in the mid-1980s, the academic library director was appointed to the campaign coordination committee and thus became directly involved in the planning initiatives of the university campaign. As part of her work on the committee, the library director prepared a fund-raising plan for the library initiative and presented the plan to the committee.

Over the next two years, the university successfully met its fund-raising goals, and the vice president for institutional advancement—who headed the campaign—was subsequently recruited by a neighboring higher educational institution. The president of the university, who was impressed with the library director's fund-raising initiatives, skills, and enthusiasm, suggested that she apply for the vacant vice presidency. The library director realized that not only was she good at fund-raising, but she actually enjoyed the greater contact with the public than that afforded by remaining in the position of director of the academic library.

She applied for the position, and, because of her prior success in fund-raising for the university, she was selected as the new vice president for institutional advancement. During the next decade, she was able to raise millions to support the university endowment. She also created the first endowed academic chairs as well as provided funding for other enhancements to the academic reputation of the university.

This person was successful not only because she was able to find a leadership position that would merge her skills and interests but also because she was willing to take a risk and move to a new and dramatically different position within the university. Risk-taking skills are important for any academic, but particularly for those who have few options for career change such as academic library directors. While this library director conceivably might have had a more difficult time obtaining a fund-raising position at a different university, her current administration had seen her work in fund-raising and were able to see her as a leader in the development area.

What if the library director, as in the case of the first scenario in this chapter, is removed from the position of leadership? While the same career strategies apply, in these circumstances the person is often not able to transfer his or her skills to another leadership position within the institution. What is essential, therefore, in obtaining a new position is a network of friends and colleagues throughout the profession and the academic world. How this can occur is best shown in a continuation of that first scenario:

Throughout her career, the university librarian had contributed to the literature of the profession as well as participated in the activities of national associations in the library and higher education fields. She had also established a network of associates and colleagues who were a source of support and a bridge to renewed contact with the profession. Prior to being removed from her directorship, this library professional had agreed to be a consultant to two university libraries. Thus, during her year as a faculty member, she worked on these consulting projects. In one consultantship, she worked with a university library search committee to select a new university librarian; in the other, she worked with the university library staff to identify and implement a new organizational structure for the library. The university librarian heard through one of her consulting contacts that a regional urban university was looking to fill a faculty position at a library and information studies school. She decided to apply, emphasizing her recent consulting experiences as well as her continued research and scholarship. To her great joy, she was selected for the position.

Within a year of joining the library school faculty, because of her previous experience, the former university librarian was asked to coordinate a six-month study of the present and future status of the library school. Shortly after she embarked on this project, however, it was "deja vu all over again"—a new university president and provost were hired by the university. This time the outcome was different. At the conclusion of the study, the library school faculty rallied around her and supported her recommendations. Furthermore, the university administration was impressed and enthusiastic.

Together, the administration and the library school devised a three-year plan that would reallocate university resources to expand and reshape the library school curriculum to include technology in all course components. When the dean of the library school retired a year later, the library school faculty nominated their colleague, the former university librarian, for the position of dean of the program. She accepted the new deanship position and went on to successfully implement the new library school curriculum.

This individual used her networking, scholarship, and consulting skills to move into a new career. Yet sometimes even the most diligent efforts do not produce a new opportunity for leadership in the academic world, and a former academic library director is left with no choice except to be a faculty member or line librarian. Such a situation offers new, albeit different, opportunities for leadership, as shown in the following scenario:

A library director at a small public college had many accomplishments during his tenure, including the funding and implementation of library technology and the creation of strong professional and staff development programs. However, during a period of massive turnover throughout the administrative ranks of the college, the director was asked to step down from his leadership position.

In the period of transition, he did apply and was interviewed for several academic library directorships. But despite having a strong record as a manager, innovator, and academic, nothing materialized in terms of a new job offer. Having tenured faculty status within the library and the college, he then chose to continue on the library faculty and to work in areas related to public service and teaching.

During his years as a middle manager and head of academic libraries, the director had maintained a strong interest in both teaching and research. He also, after reflection, realized that his new role would provide him with opportunities to use the technology he had brought to the library in new teaching initiatives as well as to explore through research and continuing scholarship several important library and higher educational themes he had not had the time to pursue at an earlier point in his career.

Although the transition to a nonleadership position was initially somewhat difficult, he soon immersed himself in the public service aspects of his new position. He found that his increased contact with the students and the rewards of assisting them with the library technology were preferable to the isolation of his role as a middle manager. Working with students and other library patrons, he was able to use—and illustrate by example—the same "client-centered" approach to public service he had espoused as the director. He then turned his efforts to teaching, developing his own hands-on library instruction modules for students to teach them how to use the library and its technology. Over time, the other librarians gradually began to implement some of the public service and teaching techniques he utilized.

This scenario illustrates how one academic library director made the successful transition from administration of a library to a successful career as a teacher and researcher and in the process provided continued leadership to the library and the college. He also acquired new skills and competencies and was able to put his philosophy regarding public service in academic libraries to actual use.

What all of these case studies have shown is that there are many career paths available for former academic library directors who are perceptive and who seize new opportunities as college and university environments change. Timing, luck, and knowing the right people have always been important in making a career shift, but the playing field has shifted such that new career opportunities do exist beyond the academic library directorship.

A PRESCRIPTION FOR THE FUTURE

What do the case studies in this chapter tell us about the career development of academic library directors? The universal theme throughout is leadership. Whatever the circumstances, no matter how difficult a job departure, resignation, or termination, a person's ability to provide leadership does not disappear. These case studies illustrate the courage and determination required to rewrite one's career aspirations and goals. Despite setbacks and obstacles, the academic library directors described in this chapter were able to analyze their strengths and identify important factors in their career goals and thus make a successful transition to a new stage in their career development. Each identified new opportunities and took risks, and as a result each was able to provide new leadership, although not necessarily within the academic library field.

The changes taking place in colleges and universities today are providing increasing opportunities for professionals such as academic library directors to successfully change from one career goal to another. The academic library's leadership role in technology on many campuses is but one opportunity upon which an academic library director can build a new career. Institutional change always presents opportunities to those who can perceive and visualize the future.

Having the appropriate educational credentials and work experience is certainly important for academic library directors in formulating a midlife career change. Another key element for successfully changing one's career direction is networking with other colleagues in the library field. All professionals should maintain an active membership in one's principal professional association, and those who become leaders in these associations at a regional or national level have created important bridges to new careers.

Because of the tenuous nature of the work of all middle managers in higher education today, many—if not most—of today's current library administrators may find that their present job will not be their last. Academic library directors have a number of unique opportunities from which to select a new career orientation, but they must be willing to address changes in their personal and professional life as well as assume risks in dealing with these changes. The academic library directors described in this chapter all successfully dealt with the postleadership issue and reshaped their careers and life goals for this decade and the twenty-first century. By learning to recognize opportunities and being unafraid to take risks, current academic library directors can prepare themselves to do the same.

REFERENCES

Bolles, Richard N. 1997. *What Color Is Your Parachute? A Practical Manual for Job-Hunters and Career Changers.* Berkeley, CA: Ten Speed Press.

Fram, Eugene H. 1994. "Today's Mercurial Career Path." *Management Review* 83 (November): 40+.

Guskin, Alan E. 1996. "Facing the Future: The Change Process in Restructuring Universities." *Change* (July/August): 27–37.

Part V

Other Academic Settings and Leadership Roles

Chapter 14

Leadership Roles in Other Academic Settings

Dennis E. Robison

Librarianship is one of those curious professions that seem to equip their practitioners with universally applicable skills, particularly for the information age.
Whether or not leadership can be defined as one of those skills is problematic.
While leadership skills tend to be universal and applicable to any situation, I
believe they come about through experience as much as formal training. They
are not difficult to identify. Library shelves are full of materials pointing the
way to successful leadership. Two authors who have appealed to me are Warren
Bennis (1976, 1989) and Robert K. Greenleaf (1977). Bennis is a distinguished
business administration professor at the University of Southern California and
critic of the failure of leadership among corporations and government in the
1970s and 1980s. His list of leadership qualities are enduring—integrity, dedication, magnanimity, humility, openness, and teamwork. Greenleaf, a management consultant and teacher, is an advocate of the servant leader. His comment
on the uses of power are compelling. Power, Greenleaf observes, is something
all leaders possess. A servant leader is anxious to divest himself or herself of
centralized power. It is something to be shared, to be used for growth in a
collegial group. Power is benign when in the course of using it, both the user
and the subject grow as persons. It is a malignant force when people are coerced
by it.

When I have taken Bennis and Greenleaf to heart, those whom I've been
entrusted to lead have achieved great things; when I have not, success was and
is illusive. If you are seen as one who has integrity and can gain the trust of

those who report to you, your peers, and those for whom you work, you will have a chance. Without it, failure is inevitable not only for you but for those who work for you. They become victimized due to your untrustworthiness. If you are not dedicated to what you do, are not passionate and enthusiastic about your organization, are not willing to give of yourself to its mission, why would anyone want to follow or fund you?

LEARNING TO LEAD

Successful leadership is also the result of mentoring, of being nurtured by individuals who are willing to share what they know. It is important to be magnanimous, forgiving, above revenge or resentment. If you are seen as petty and small-minded in your relationships with others, respect will evaporate. It is also important to understand that it isn't "your" organization. It is the product of many individuals. A successful leader is seen as a team leader rather than a lone ranger, one who is willing to listen to other ideas and suggestions. Successful teamwork is not the abdication of responsibility or groupthink but the sharing of power advocated by Greenleaf.

Successful leadership also has to do with taking advantage of opportunities that may or may not be within one's control. In my career, I have worked at three institutions—the University of South Florida (USF) and two universities in Virginia, the University of Richmond and James Madison University. I would not wish to suggest that I was prescient in my seeking positions in each of these places, but hindsight suggests some similarities. One was experimentation and the setting of new directions. When I joined the library at USF as a young professional in 1962, it had existed only two years. It was the first newly chartered institution of public higher education in Florida in this century. When I arrived, there were fewer than 2,000 undergraduate students majoring in the liberal arts. When I left 12 years later, there were 22,000 students and 73 master's and 6 doctoral programs offered in colleges as diverse as business, medicine, engineering, and the liberal arts. Thus, the first third of my career was tempered by rapid change, dynamic growth, and the excitement of new experimentation and taking of risks.

At first glance, it would seem that the only thing the University of Richmond and the University of South Florida have in common is that they are both institutions of higher education. South Florida is a large, comprehensive, public university, whereas Richmond is relatively small (3,000 undergraduates with modest graduate programs) and private with denominational ties to the Virginia Baptist conference. South Florida was less than 20 years old when I left it in 1974; the University of Richmond could trace its roots back 144 years. In its early years, Richmond's primary mission had been to educate the poor Baptists of Virginia. In 1969, the University's endowment was enriched by $50 million, thanks to the generosity of alumnus Claiborne Robins (Robins Pharmaceuticals) and expanded its role to become a premier regional and national private university. The infusion of these resources caused enormous changes and encouraged the faculty and administration to explore new directions. I was fortunate in being a participant as the newly appointed university librarian.

James Madison University (JMU), when I arrived in 1985, had by that time been led for 12 years by Ronald E. Carrier, arguably one of the most dynamic and visionary leaders in higher education in Virginia. During his tenure, JMU had moved from Madison College of 2,500 students to nearly 9,000 and from a predominantly female teacher's college to a coeducational, comprehensive university. It was and still is considered to be a highly innovative university where change and exploration of different methods of accomplishing its mission were and are encouraged.

In addition to a willingness to challenge the status quo, these three institutions have another similarity—quality leadership. During my time at each of these universities, I was fortunate to work with and for individuals who were creative, mentoring, and willing to allow me the latitude to expand my horizons. They also instilled in me a strong sense of purpose in meeting the information needs of the university community as well as the broader objectives of educating students.

During my time at these three universities, there were dynamic changes happening within academic libraries. Three, I believe, are worthy of further comment. Two of these, which were to have a major influence on library services, were the bibliographic instruction movement and the adaptation of computer technology. The third, while not unique to libraries, was a move away from an autocratic, top-down management style to one more participatory.

EARLY INCENTIVES TO LEADERSHIP

The librarians at the University of South Florida were very active in participation in university functions, including governance. They were considered peers to the faculty, even though they did not "officially" have faculty status. Librarians were expected to serve on university-wide committees such as those concerned with curricular development. In the early 1960s, the bibliographic instruction movement was just getting under way. The reference staff became enthusiastic promoters of the library's role in the teaching and learning process. We took a proactive role in working with faculty to incorporate course-related library instruction into their departmental curriculum. As a result, we became full partners in the learning/teaching process.

The acceptance of this role and obligation early in my career was influential in my role as a library director at Richmond and JMU. I became a dedicated and enthusiastic proponent of not only the importance of bibliographic instruction but the parity of librarians and the library with other university groups and units. I was becoming sensitive to the need to be a strong advocate of what the library could offer to students, faculty, and university administration rather than playing a passive role of letting them come to us. We were also encouraged to develop a strong service position in our support of the academic program.

During my 11 years (1974–1985) as the university librarian for Richmond's Boatwright Library, bibliographic instruction became a major program and part of the University of Richmond's (UR) curriculum. It also gained legitimacy at the national level when it was accepted as a part of the mission of the Association of College and Research Libraries. At about this same time, computers were beginning to make a major impact on academic libraries. Those of us now used to high-speed pentium computers and fiber-optic networks may find it hard to believe, but searching Lockheed Dialog and BRS with a Texas Instrument's Silent 700 terminal with a 300 baud modem represented an exciting technological breakthrough. On-line searching became a part of our regular services and was folded into our course-related library instruction program. Around 1980, the Friends of Boatwright Library funded the purchase of the first microcomputers in the library, which were also among the first on the campus. OCLC (Online Computer Library Center) moved from being an Ohio success story to national and international prominence as a bibliographic utility. I was fortunate to be elected to the SOLINET (Southeast Library Information Network) Board from 1974–1977 at a time when that organization was attempting to find its identity. I'll confess, however, that even then I didn't quite realize the enormity of the impact that automation and computers would have on our profession.

From my predecessor at Richmond, I inherited a grant from the Council on Library Resources/National Endowment for the Humanities to form a Library Faculty Partnership. The purpose of this was to develop library-centered instruction in the curriculum. We also established a liaison program assigning librarians direct responsibility to develop services and serve as library contacts with academic departments in the social sciences, business, sciences, and humanities. The result of these two efforts was a dramatic increase in the role of the library to the teaching and learning mission of the university plus a heightened visibility of librarians on the campus. The central administration, which heretofore had resisted awarding faculty status to librarians, did so in recognition of the contributions they were making to the academic programs.

The lessons I learned at Richmond had little to do with computing technology. They did, however, strengthen my administrative and leadership skills. I learned the value of a good mentor, whom I had in Dr. Charles Glassick, the provost and vice president for academic affairs. He was extraordinarily supportive of programs we wanted to implement as well as very forgiving of some idiotic decisions made by his neophyte head librarian. I was also fortunate to be selected to be trained by the Association of Research Libraries' Office of Management Studies (OMS) as a process consultant. OMS has always been an active proponent of empowering library staff through advocacy of participatory management techniques and carefully crafted self-studies. In 1980, it began an ambitious program of training 100 librarians as consultants. This opportunity came at a very critical time in my development as an administrator. OMS training encouraged the development of good listening and group-processing skills. It also provided a new way of looking at the environment of the organization and gave new insights into creative ways of encouraging those who work in libraries to take charge of their own destinies. Soon after the OMS training experience, I was invited to participate in my first Southern Association of Colleges and Schools (SACS) reaffirmation of accreditation visit. I know the OMS experience made me a better visiting team member. I have subsequently been invited to do SACS visits every year since 1983.

Richmond also gave me opportunities for growth beyond that of university librarian. As with many institutions, the chief library administrator serves as a peer with the academic deans and is considered an officer of the university. I was encouraged to take this role seriously and often found myself immersed in concerns over student recruitment, fund-raising, and faculty–administrative relationships. In the latter role I sometimes found myself in the middle between faculty and administration. I believe one of the measures of success of a library director is to be accepted as a member of both the faculty and the administration, two groups that are often at loggerheads over governance and other issues.

In 1985, I accepted the position of university librarian at James Madison University. As I reflect on these past 13 years, I am persuaded that my career and the change in academic librarianship have been on parallel tracks. Obviously, I brought with me what I had learned at South Florida and Richmond. Moreover, there were dramatic changes occuring in academic libraries that were to profoundly affect the ways librarians would deliver their services. I was extremely fortunate that the librarians, staff, and the central administration of the university were willing, even eager, to anticipate the changes and accept the risk of sometimes being on the cutting edge.

MEETING AUTOMATION'S CHALLENGE

The rapid rise of digital technology beginning in the early 1980s has become the dominant factor in changing academic libraries. This includes the advent of the personal computer, OCLC's expanded services, and the Internet. During this period JMU's library installed two different integrated library systems and went from on-line literature searching, to CD-ROM-based, stand-alone computers, to fully networked scholarly workstations with access to the Internet via Netscape. In 1985, there were two personal computers in the building; in 1996, there were over 150. Without question, the library has become the most intensive user of computer technology on the campus. What has the impact been on the librarians and staff of this kind of change? How has it been managed? What new leadership skills, if any, were brought to bear on the transition? Finally, has the change brought about more benefits than problems?

To understand the answers to these questions, it is important to know something about James Madison University. JMU is considered one of the preeminent, comprehensive institutions in Virginia. It has a strong regional reputation and is frequently listed as among the top regional institutions by *U.S. News and World Report*'s annual rankings. It is considered among the top 10 percent of the colleges and universities in the nation by the *Fiske Guide*. It achieved this reputation, in no small part, because of the strong vision and long tenure (over 25 years) of its president, Dr. Ronald E. Carrier. In addition to having an un-canny talent for positioning JMU where it ought to be within the state and the nation, Carrier also strongly encourages innovation and the taking of risks.

Hindsight suggests that he was the ideal president to have at this time in the development of the "electronic" library. His enthusiasm for the emerging digital technology was infectious. It is difficult to capture Carrier's leadership style. He can be very autocratic if he senses a need to get something done for the better-ment of the institution—process be damned. On the other hand, I have never felt him to be a micromanager. If he trusts your judgment and believes you have the best interest of the institution, you have an absolutely free hand to pursue your own vision. He will support it to the fullest extent possible. How-ever, he is not a patient man or one to let JMU or those who are in his admin-istration rest on their accomplishments. While I have found this environment to challenge and foster growth for me, it has been stressful to others who wish for a more bottom-up, participatory governance structure. I am of at least two minds about this. I think Carrier is a unique leader who has had and continues to have the right vision for the university. He has been proven right so often with ex-traordinarily positive results that he is able to be authoritarian and get away with it. Any lesser being would have undoubtedly lost the confidence of the faculty and the board by now. While library and Integrated Learning Resources have flourished under his leadership, it is not a style I would emulate. Whenever I have fallen under this spell of full speed ahead regardless of consequences, I have found myself in deep trouble with those whom I would lead. But then, I'm no Ronald Carrier.

As many academic libraries learned when they brought up the first CD-ROM indices, giving students and faculty rapid bibliographic access to information was hardly enough. They wanted the information as well. At JMU, this resulted in highly irritated and vocal students who refused to understand or accept the argument that JMU was not a research institution and therefore should not be expected to have everything they wanted. The criticism reached such a crescendo that the president found himself under fire for not adequately "supporting" the library. Rather than spend any time assigning blame to someone for this negative publicity, President Carrier decided to establish a Commission on the Library of the 21st Century for the purpose of reviewing options by which the library could meet the information needs of the future using new technologies.

The commission, which I chaired, had representatives from the faculty, stu-dents, administration, and the university's Office of Information Technology (OIT). Since OIT was responsible for supporting all computer operations—both administrative and academic—it was critical that it be directly involved in supporting directions the library might wish to take. The president offered to fund the commission's recommendations up to $100,000.

Outcomes from the commission were to have a lasting impact on the future of the library. They included:

- increased recognition of the relatedness and interdependence of the library and OIT;
- the encouragement of a more collaborative working relationship between the library and OIT;
- the implementation of a rapid, 48-hour delivery of periodical articles at no charge to JMU students and faculty through the use of telefacsimile (now Ariel) arrangements with the University of Virginia and Virginia Tech (VPI&SU);
- a solidification in the minds of students, faculty, and the administration of the library's dominant role in the imaginative use of technology to meet the university's information needs.

At about the time the commission was completing its work, there was an emerging concern about the use of digitally based instructional technology in the classroom as a method of teaching and learning. Who was going to be responsible for helping faculty to learn what was available? If instructional technology was adopted by a faculty member, who was going to equip the classrooms, train the faculty, and maintain the infrastructure of computers, networks, and so on? As a way of moving forward with instructional technology, President Carrier charged OIT with the task of creating a state-of-the-art, technologically equipped classroom. Twenty-five faculty were sent to the University of North Carolina's Institute for Academic Technology (IAT) for training. This initiative by the president brought the challenges of instructional technology to a new level of concern. For example, the library also included the Media Resources Center (MRC), which was responsible for nonprint resources and the delivery and maintenance of audio visual (AV) equipment. MRC staff had not been involved in the new classroom design. Being left out was a blow to their pride and left ownership and development of future mediated classrooms far from clear.

In 1992, President Carrier established a task force to develop a plan to address the university's needs in instructional technology and telecommunications. He appointed the dean of the College of Arts and Sciences and me as cochairs of the task force. We invited a number of faculty representing the different colleges of the university to join us. We visited institutions that were blazing new trails in this area, notably Miami University of Ohio, Indiana University/Purdue University at Indianapolis (IUPUI), and Appalachian State University (ASU), an institution in North Carolina similar to JMU. We read widely in the field and held several hearings on the campus to attempt to understand the needs of the faculty. We also sponsored a forum, inviting those whom we met at Miami, IUPUI, and ASU to address the faculty and demonstrate some of their achievements.

It became increasingly apparent that two recommendations were going to be made to the president. First, there needed to be a concerted effort to develop an organizational structure to bring the work of OIT and the library closer together to coordinate, manage, and plan to meet the university's future information technology needs. Second, a professionally staffed and expanded faculty support center needed to be established to assist faculty in incorporating the new technologies into their teaching. Politically, these could be some troublesome recommendations. OIT reported to the senior vice president for administration and finance; the library reported to the vice president for academic affairs. OIT was responsible for university-wide technology support. It had been recently reorganized into telecommunications, systems development, technical services (networking, personal computer [pc] repair, mainframe operations), and customer services (help desk, computer laboratories, consulting services). OIT was also woefully understaffed, which I believed often resulted in unjust criticism for not meeting its obligations.

The task force recommended that a new, yet-to-be-defined organization be formed that would bring the library and OIT under a common leadership. Further, it was recommended that this organization report to the vice president for academic affairs. In addition, the task force recommended that the existing faculty support center be expanded and professionally staffed with experts in the field of multimedia and instructional design to work with faculty to develop and use instructional technology in their teaching. Once the recommendations were made public, the anxieties among computing and library staff rose to new heights. Many had observed that there was a trend nationally to merge computing and libraries—sometimes under the direction of the library, sometimes under the direction of computing. As with any merger, not all the participants are especially pleased.

There were other models considered. One was to form a new vice presidency and establish a Chief Information Office (CIO) model that would include the library and OIT. Another was to continue the collaborative model but strengthen it with a clearly understood mission statement and agreed-upon goals. It should be noted that, at this time, the university was also deep into the process of selecting a new integrated information system for administrative computing. This, coupled with the need to create a center for faculty development, caused the central administration to take a different approach. The technical support for computing was separated from the service support by forming two entities—Information Technology (IT) and Integrated Learning Resources (ILR). IT would retain responsibility for systems development, technical services, and telecommunications. In addition, there would be a Technology Planning office established. ILR was to consist of the library, Media Resources and OIT's Customer Services (renamed Computing Support), and the newly expanded Center for Multimedia. I was appointed dean of ILR as well as retaining direct responsibility for day-to-day library operations. Within a year a director of libraries was appointed when it became apparent that my energies were being spread far too thin. IT came under the wing of the associate vice president for resource planning.

TODAY'S LEADERSHIP CHALLENGES

To be perfectly honest, I didn't know what to make of this new organization. Several of the computing personnel who now were in ILR had already been reorganized at least three times in my tenure at JMU and were becoming a bit jaded. I was so confident that this was truly an interim solution that I suggested that all of computing would be back together in 12 to 18 months. Understandably, Computing Support eased into neutral and didn't see themselves as a part of ILR. They merely had to bide their time and put up with this new, but probably temporary, organization and its dean. They were not alone. All four units were a bit shaken by the reorganization. My immediate challenge was to develop what became the Center for Multimedia and try to persuade myself and those in ILR that this was going to be a viable and reasonably long-lasting organization.

It has now been several years since this reorganization took place. ILR now has a firmly established Center for Multimedia for faculty development. Media Resources has taken on a new mission of having primary responsibility for mediated classroom development in addition to the traditional audiovisual services. What has been lacking, as one librarian recently observed, is the "integration" part of ILR. The library and Computing Support still work fairly independently of the other units. We hope to bring it all together through the development of college-level Teaching/Learning/Technology Roundtables (TLTR), an initiative developed and promoted by Steven Gilbert, director of technology projects for the American Association for Higher Education (AAHE). Membership of each college TLTR will include representation from ILR, faculty, staff, and the college administration. It is hoped that the TLTR will encourage a meaningful dialogue about teaching and learning and develop a technology plan for the college as well as help ILR focus its resources.

It has been an exciting, enervating, and sometimes exhausting period. Librarians have responded admirably to the challenges of the new age. They, like many others in our society, often stagger under the weight of having to keep up with the unrelenting changes in technology, the information explosion, and a myriad of other tasks.

CONCLUSION

What have we learned about the leadership skills derived from the experiences of the past 30 years? I would submit the following observations for consideration:

- As I stated at the outset, I'm not sure I changed careers to a nontraditional setting but rather changed as my profession changed—the University of Michigan is staking a new curriculum on this assumption (for further information see the University of Michigan School of Information Sciences project (http://www.si.umich.edu/cristaled/)

- In the years that I have been an academic librarian, an active, even proactive, involvement in the teaching and learning process by librarians has been a dominant service component. This is not true of computing. Up until about 10 years ago the computing profession was dominated by the mainframe with its centralized control. The symbolism demonstrated by an open and approachable reference desk in a library and a glass wall of a computer center with its push-button security locks is not lost on the user. During this same period, computing professionals had to emerge from a culture seen as mysterious and forbidding to one of proactive service.

- The information highway is a far from a user-friendly environment. Opportunities abound for librarians and computing professionals to work together. They are the most knowledgeable on most campuses about accessing information. Together, we need to work diligently to make certain that faculty and the administration know that regardless of our cultural differences or to whom we report in the organization, we're pledged to meet a common goal of achieving information and computer literacy.

Finally, leadership is not management. Good management will see that a task is completed effectively and efficiently; leadership provides the vision that led to the task. While I advocate, and I hope practice, an open, participatory administrative style of management, I certainly have worked for individuals who did not—still, they were very successful leaders. I think leadership can be summed up in one word—vision. If you are someone who is seen as visionary, who has a record of putting the organization in the right place at the right time, I believe people will follow and support what you want to do in spite of what might be autocratic management. The value of an open administrative style is that it empowers those who work with you, often creating and emboldening the visionary leaders of tomorrow.

In the midst of writing this chapter, I had the good fortune to attend the Second Summer Institute of the AAHE's Teaching, Learning and Technology Roundtable. Alfredo de los Santos of the Maricopa Community College System spoke and ended his presentation with part of a poem by Adrienne Rich (1978) which begins ''The rules break like a thermometer...'' (taken from Rich's book *The Poems of Adrienne Rich*) and which in a way describes the vision attempted here. De los Santos used it effectively, and I recommend it to readers of this book. On most days I think this sums up the current state of our changing profession.

REFERENCES

Bennis, Warren G. 1976. *The Unconscious Conspiracy: Why Leaders Can't Lead.* New York: AMACOM.

————. 1989. *On Becoming a Leader*. Reading, MA: Addison-Wesley.

Greenleaf, Robert K. 1977. *Servant Leadership: A Journey into the Nature of Legitimate Power and Greatness*. New York: Paulist Press.

Rich, Adrienne Cecile. 1978. *The Dream of a Common Language: Poems, 1974–1977*. New York: Norton.

Chapter 15

Choosing the College Presidency: Extending the Career Ladder

Elaine P. Adams

Academic librarians traditionally have viewed the director of libraries position as the pinnacle appointment for an academic librarian. Higher education's career ladder, however, can extend for the academic librarian all the way to the college presidency. This is particularly so when academic librarians enhance and market their recognized talents for information retrieval and analysis, creative problem solving, supportive collegiality, and structural organization.

In this chapter, the career path that led one academic librarian to a college presidency is explored, a comparison of that individual career path to that of typical college presidents is made, and recommendations on how librarians can facilitate access to the college presidency are provided.

It should be borne in mind that senior administrative posts other than presidencies are also rewarding and available. Those committed to the pursuit of the presidency should be prepared for "longer-than-average work weeks, significant social and professional involvements, and above average to high levels of job risk and job stress" (Vaughan, Mellander, and Blois 1994, 40).

CHOOSING LIBRARIANSHIP

Librarianship has always been a love/hate affair for me. I was drawn to the field at an early age because of a deep fondness and admiration for a cousin, a public librarian who later became an academic library leader. A most regal person, she spoke with great pride about the wisdom that she discovered among the books that surrounded her and how important librarians were in helping individuals find needed information.

I sensed that those like her who cared for the library and its contents were privileged people—that they had been given charge of a rare and precious treasure. Since librarians, particularly African-American librarians, were relatively scarce in my community, I also concluded that librarianship was a fairly exclusive profession that only a select number of individuals could enter. I wished to be anointed.

During my youth, the libraries in my hometown of New Orleans were segregated. Besides my cousin, a second source of inspiration for me to become a librarian was the Dryades Street Branch Library, which sat at the head of the city's main shopping street for African Americans. On hot, humid days, the library was a majestic oasis at the end of a long bus ride for many youth of color, where you could sit at the polished wood tables under the cool high ceilings and let books take you to faraway places.

My first impressions of librarianship were constructed from these happy memories. Later, my interest in the field was stimulated by encounters with librarians that were quite contrary to the open and pleasant experiences of my childhood. As libraries in the city desegregated, and my family changed addresses, my visits were frequently to neighborhood libraries where librarians peered at readers like me with suspicion. The joy was replaced with depression and anxiety.

During that period, the contradictions among librarians in terms of their behavior posed a career challenge. Why were some librarians sharers of the literary wealth and others withholders? It seemed that a professional dichotomy existed. Librarians fell into either one extreme or the other—grand book people or the stereotypical shushers and fine collectors.

A good student through elementary and high school, my options in terms of a career were limitless, although I was unaware of that fact. Like many young women during the 1950s, I knew that I could become a teacher or social worker, a nun or a nurse. Because of my father's efforts to recruit at least one of his daughters to follow in his footsteps as a pharmacist, I also knew that I could enter that profession. However, my desire to become a librarian prevailed, and I knew that it would be my chosen profession.

My mother, a very practical woman and an educator herself, did not wish her bright, oldest daughter to enter a profession that might lead to starvation. She knew that with a teaching degree, one could always find work. By that time a single parent, my mother also made it very clear that one degree per daughter was all that would be financed from parental support. It was expected that the degree would lead to immediate employment upon graduation. After meeting those requirements, the sky was the limit. You could be all that you could be— as long as you paid for it yourself.

Thus, after college, I began an enjoyable, four-year tenure as a foreign language instructor at a local inner-city high school and worked my way toward a master's degree in library science at Louisiana State University (LSU) during summers. Having attended Xavier University, a small, private, historically black university, for my undergraduate degree, the library at a large state university was a delight with its rows and rows of well-filled stacks. Ironically, LSU, although conservative in most aspects of campus life, had a very liberal book selection policy, particularly in contemporary social politics and African-American studies. Academic librarianship gained my respect and admiration.

After receiving the master's degree in library science in January 1966, I returned to the public school system and joined a team whose assignment was to centralize the scattered classroom collections of various elementary schools in the Orleans Parish School System. This federally funded project provided an in-depth opportunity to work in technical services and expand my familiarity with children's literature. However, since the team was based at an off-site processing center, contact with students was lacking.

I decided to return to my undergraduate alma mater for the 1966–1967 school year and serve as a reference librarian. Clearly, in the academic milieu, instruction commanded high esteem. Recognizing this fact, I accepted the challenge to provide bibliographic instruction to every freshman student at Xavier University. The enormous class filled the campus auditorium; however, with engaging assignments, students began to appreciate more the role librarians and libraries could play in their college matriculation. During this year, I was also able to revive the university's undergraduate minor in library science, preparing chiefly elementary school librarians for the libraries that were blossoming on their campuses.

Although I returned to the school system the next year to fulfill a year's assignment as an elementary school librarian, I had a sense of underachievement. I learned that the federal government was funding fellowships for individuals to pursue the doctorate in library science and that the annual fellowship paid approximately the same salary that I was earning as a public school librarian. I applied for the Higher Education Act (HEA) Title II fellowship at the University of Southern California and fancied myself sitting under palm trees engaged in Socratic dialogue with faculty wise persons. That was not quite the reality of doctoral study in 1968, however.

The social behavior of librarians continued to fascinate me. Therefore, when the time came to select a dissertation topic, I seized the chance to perform a study that examined the connection of personality to the performance of public services in school librarianship. While personality studies are a rarity in library science research, several factors encouraged such research during the 1970s. School librarians still operated singly in many school libraries; centralized technical services for these librarians often were provided by their school districts; simple, self-administering personality scales were available; and most importantly, the School Library Manpower Project had produced a task analysis survey of the activities of school librarians.

The dissertation research, which required travel throughout three California counties—Los Angeles, Orange, and San Diego—was predictive of another factor that began to affect my professional life. Having married a corporate manager, corporate transfers were a fact of life during the 1970s for my family and me. From 1971 to 1975, we lived in four states and five cities. I learned quickly that I had to be open-minded about the available jobs and my ability to perform them. I also recognized that I would have a limited time in which to demonstrate my professional skills on a job. Hitting the ground running would be a requirement for me to build a professional reputation of accomplishment.

In the San Diego area, I found a position as a district catalog librarian managing a centralized processing center for a high school district. By the next year, my family and I were living in Pittsburgh, where I served as a middle school librarian. These assignments accompanied the writing of the dissertation. In August 1973, after receiving the Ph.D. in library science with a minor in instructional technology, my career path became fixed more solidly in higher education.

CHOOSING THE PRESIDENCY

My first assignment in higher education after obtaining the doctorate was an adjunct faculty position at the University of Maryland in the fall of 1973. Pittsburgh, where we were living at the time, had a saturated market in library science educators. Having learned about commuting marriages from a television interview conducted by Barbara Walters on the *Today* show, I wrote all the library schools within an hour's commuting time by air, soliciting a faculty assignment. It was my good fortune to receive a request to interview from the University of Maryland.

At Maryland, I taught various undergraduate library science education courses, giving special attention to field trips where the students could connect with the practical reality of librarianship. I also assisted with minority recruitment. In California, while a student, I had been active in library reform movements, such as Congress for Change, and I continued my interest in the aspects of librarianship that addressed social responsibility.

By the time the fall semester ended at Maryland, my husband had already been transferred back to California. My next assignment was as a media specialist at the University of Southern California's (USC) Health Sciences Campus. With the encouragement of an innovative library director, I developed the initial media center in the Norris Medical Library. The staff worked in a very proactive manner with the USC health sciences faculties and with staff from the affiliated county hospital. Norris Medical Library became a leader in the utilization of nonprint media and in the provision of other nontraditional instructional support.

After Los Angeles, in 1975, my spouse's assignment took the family, which now included an infant son, to Houston, Texas. For nearly four years I worked in half-time library positions at Texas Southern University (TSU) in order to spend time with my young child. Initially, I revamped a cluttered Pharmacy Library and made it usable for faculty and students. While my skills as a professional librarian came in handy, the bulk of the job focused on discarding outmoded furniture and equipment and consolidating and restoring order to the library collection.

Six months after my arrival, the director of libraries requested that I move to the central library on the campus as coordinator of the Learning Resources Center. TSU had been awarded a significant Title II grant that enabled the university to analyze its core curriculum and compose a menu of classroom instruction interwoven with related learning resources. Students could move through courses at their own pace. Learning resources in a variety of formats facilitated the progress of rapid learners as well as learners needing more skills development. During summers, I taught library science education courses at the University of Houston at Clear Lake.

As the 1980s began, I returned full-time to the workforce. Seeking to enhance the range of my professional skills, I opted to enter the business/industrial sector. I applied for, and obtained, an interview for a librarian's position at Getty Oil Research Center. During the interview, I was able to convince my future manager that a staff expansion would provide the sophisticated library services needed by the company during this period of growth in the oil industry. Over the course of time, technical training also became a responsibility, with the staff developing annual personalized training plans with on-site employees and coordinating training services for off-site employees.

By 1983, I had a desire to return to the higher education arena—I was again missing the dynamic interactions with faculty and students. I became associate vice president for academic services and planning at Prairie View A&M University, a historically black institution. This was an exciting period for the university because of enhanced state funding. In my role as associate vice president, I developed several new projects, including the Benjamin Banneker Honors College, the first honors college at a historically black institution of higher education, and a $16 million new library building. I also served as the senior line officer for the library and other academic units, such as admissions and records.

By 1985, my assignment at Prairie View had assumed more student services components and was expanded to the role of vice president for student affairs. Counseling, financial aid, residential life, school relations (recruitment and precollege programs), and student activities fell under my charge. Admissions and records and the library remained with the vice president for academic affairs. For the new role, it was helpful that I had taken graduate minor studies in the guidance area while pursuing the master's degree in library science.

Wishing to broaden my credentials in higher education, in 1989 I applied for, and was hired to serve as, assistant commissioner for educational opportunity planning for the Texas Higher Education Coordinating Board. My assignment addressed the implementation of the higher education desegregation plan for the state of Texas, specifically focusing on the recruitment and retention of minority students. During this period and for several prior years, I also participated on accreditation teams for the Middle States Association and the Southern Association of Colleges and Schools, specializing in the library and student affairs components of the institutional analysis.

Encouraged by the commissioner and other supportive mentors, in 1991 I was appointed the founding president of the Northeast College of Houston Community College System, administering a budget of approximately $10 million. During my tenure from 1991 through 1996 as president, I developed from a renovated department store the nation's largest community college center located in an active regional mall. I also secured one of the first federally funded School-to-Work Urban Opportunities Grants in the state of Texas. While coordinating the development of a facilities master plan that envisioned the college's first new campus construction, I administered the college's 10 existing instructional sites.

PATHWAY FROM LIBRARIANSHIP TO THE PRESIDENCY

For librarians considering the college presidency as a career goal, it may be helpful to examine how factors in my personal and professional background compare with those of other community college presidents. Fortunately, in 1994, George Vaughan, Gustavo Mellander, and Beverly Blois published a study profiling community college presidents—*The Community College Presidency: Current Status and Future outlook*. The report is based on responses to the Community College Presidency: Career and Lifestyles Survey completed by 837 of the 1,097 presidents of the nation's public community colleges and is used to develop the comparison.

Family Background

Community college presidents are considered a classic example of upward mobility. The Vaughan et al. study points out that "as a group, community college presidents have far exceeded the occupational categories and educational accomplishments of their parents in the overwhelming majority of cases" (Vaughan et al. 1994, 7). My personal experience in achieving a community college presidency is that presidential selection is based far more on skills and talents than on elements of personal background, with the exception of race and gender. Whites and males constitute a significant portion of the presidents, with survey percentages indicating 89 percent in both categories (Vaughan et al. 1994, 13).

As a minority female president, however, findings in the Vaughan et al. study revealed that my family background followed the trends for those particular subsets related to female and/or minority community college presidents:

1. *Parents' Educational Attainments.* Although the majority of the parents of community college presidents never attended college, the percentage of parents of female or mi-

nority presidents attending college exceeded that of the nonminority male presidents. Both my parents were college graduates.

2. *Father's Occupation*. Fathers of female presidents were more likely than fathers of male presidents to be among the self-employed or from fields such as public administration, law, medicine, and the clergy. My father was a registered pharmacist who operated his own drugstore, in which I worked regularly throughout my youth. The survey points out that the fathers' "entrepreneurial predisposition and experiences may have been beneficial influences on their daughters' ambitions" (Vaughan et al. 1994, 9).

3. *Mother's Occupation*. According to the Vaughan et al. study, minority and female presidents tended to come from homes with employed mothers more so than did the mothers of the presidents in the total sample. My mother was a working mother—an educator. As the survey notes, "These employed mothers may have served as role models for their daughters or minority children" (Vaughan et al. 1994, 11).

In summary, observing my mother as she climbed the career ladder from elementary school teacher to secondary school teacher to district-level social studies consultant emphasized the range of opportunities available in the educational arena. Working in the entrepreneurial environment with my father stressed the fact that success depended on hard work and excellence in product and service.

Career Patterns

The pathways chosen to achieve the presidency, while allowing for some variation, do display certain typical features. The pattern of my career differed dramatically from the current norm in that my first professional experience in the community college setting was as a president. During the early 1990s, Texas was experiencing a more relaxed attitude toward movement between the two-year and four-year institutions of higher education. Several university presidents were selected from the ranks of community college administrators, and vice versa.

Apart from the lack of prior community college experience, my career pathway resembled the norm. It was interesting to note that in prior decades, there was significant movement from four-year college and university administration to the community college presidency. The Vaughan et al. study revealed that "the combined share of public school and university administrators who became community college presidents was as high as 40 percent in the early 1960s" (Vaughan et al. 1994, 16). By the late 1980s, however, the percentage of presidents coming from these sources was just over 10 percent.

The other indices explored in the Vaughan et al. survey (1994, 18–26) included:

1. *Age at First Presidency*. By the age of 50, nearly 90 percent of the surveyed community college presidents had attained their first presidential position. I became a community college president at the age of 50.

2. *Geographical Persistence*. Female and minority community college presidents were less inclined than their white, male counterparts to work in their home states (the states in which they attended high school). My presidential assignment is not in my home state. Geographical mobility played a significant role in my career, initially because of the corporate transfers of my spouse but later as a recognized element of obtaining challenging and satisfying professional assignments for myself.

3. *Educational Attainment*. Only a small percentage (16 percent) of community college presidents had associate degrees, although this trend is increasing. Having a community college education appeared to be linked to the acceptance and availability of community college education in the state where the president grew up. My home state did not have a community college system accessible to me during my youth; therefore, I had not considered pursuing an associate degree.

   Most community college presidents did have terminal degrees, with a split between the Ph.D. (47 percent) and Ed.D. (53 percent). I hold a Ph.D. in a field other than higher education, like most other community college presidents with the Ph.D. According to the Vaughan et al. study, the trend favoring noneducation Ph.D.'s may reflect emulation of universities on the part of community college search committees.

4. *Community College Teaching*. The majority of the community college presidents had faculty experience in a community college at least on a part-time basis. I had no prior experience teaching in a community college; however, I did have experience as a university-level instructor.

5. *Publications*. Less than half the community college presidents had published in the past five years, and my publication record did not differ from the norm. According to the Vaughan study, this de-emphasis on publishing is due to the heavy workloads borne by community college presidents and the minimal pressure to "publish or perish" in the community college arena.

6. *Position before First Presidency*. Chief academic officers were the source of the majority of community college presidents, with the vice president's post or the deanship cited as the familiar pattern. Following that trend, I had served as an associate vice president for academic services and planning, gaining experience on the academic reporting line. However, the data revealed that minority presidents were more likely to have served as chief student affairs officers, and that was my more immediate background, having served as a vice president for student affairs and the state's assistant commissioner for educational opportunity planning (minority recruitment and retention).

The reader will observe that although my professional background is in library science, most elements of my career pattern, particularly as a minority and female, do not differ significantly from those of the average community college president. Upward mobility in higher education is not propelled by exceptional intervention but by obtaining academic credentials and work experiences that are considered appropriate preparation for the challenging role of president.

OBSERVATIONS AND RECOMMENDATIONS

Academic librarians who desire to pursue the college presidency may find the recommendations that follow useful. It should be borne in mind that the search to fill a presidential vacancy usually produces "100 to 300 nominations, but only 5 to 15 of these are deemed to warrant serious consideration" (Kerr and Gade 1989, 15). From that handful, only one president will be chosen.

1. *Seek faculty status.* Faculty status positions librarians on the academic track that is favored in higher education as a pathway for presidential aspirants. As Vaughan et al. point out, "Of all potential routes to the community college presidency, the academic pipeline seems to be the clearest and surest" (Vaughan et al. 1994, 30).

   Librarians holding faculty rank and/or status should participate actively with their nonlibrarian peers in faculty governance, accepting committee assignments and holding organizational office when there is opportunity. With the linkage to faculty, you should be prepared to perform other activities executed by faculty, such as advising student organizations, publishing, and presenting papers in the scholarly arena, as well as performing ceremonial duties such as participation in graduation.

2. *Utilize the second master's degree to advantage beyond the library.* You should seek opportunities to teach in your second academic discipline, using the experience to build your network among nonlibrarians on the faculty and instructional administrators. Teaching will also provide insight into the operations of a college or university academic department, enhancing your sophistication in academic politics beyond the library setting.

   If the second master's degree is in a field such as business, psychology, or communications, it may open gateways to noninstructional posts in administrative services, institutional advancement, or student services. You should make certain that colleagues beyond the library are aware of your additional areas of expertise so that you will be recalled when job opportunities surface.

3. *Acquire an earned doctorate.* Job postings for senior-level administrative positions in higher education (chancellor, vice chancellor, president, vice president) often indicate that the earned doctorate is required or preferred. With the keen competition for these posts, be assured that a sufficient quantity of applicants with doctorates will enter the search process to make the selection of a candidate without the earned doctorate unlikely unless that candidate has exceptional experience for the assignment.

   The terminal degree need not be in library science. While universities tend to favor the Ph.D. in an academic discipline, community colleges are more inclined to hire presidents with the Ed. D. A number of doctoral programs specialize in preparing individuals for presidential assignments. One well-known program is the Community College Leadership Program of the University of Texas at Austin. The university also offers the Executive Leadership Institute in cooperation with the League for Innovation in the Community College.

4. *Consider "assistant to" and "assistant/associate" assignments.* These positions can offer a training ground and be the gateway to senior administrative posts. There should be agreement with the supervisor that the assignment is not a permanent one and that its challenges are expected to prepare you for more direct responsibility in the future. The assignments should also expose you to a variety of experiences, allowing you to demonstrate high-level analytical skills. You can expect the work to be demanding and the hours to be long, accommodating your supervisor's stretched schedule.

Working alongside a productive administrator and observing the positive impact of the performance by that individual's team hopefully should motivate you to pursue the next rung of administration on your career ladder. An alternative outcome is that you will learn whether or not senior administrative assignments really do meet your professional needs and redirect your energies if they do not.

5. *Encourage dean or director titles for chief administrative officer positions in academic libraries.* Titles like "head librarian" isolate librarians on the academic organizational chart, even though such titles may provide membership in administrative groups like the Deans' Council. According to Vaughan (1986, 27–30), administrative posts with the title dean or director are noted more frequently on the career ladders of those achieving the presidency. The titles dean of library services or dean of learning resources are especially valuable for clearly announcing that your position is a significant one in the academic hierarchy, a common pathway to the presidency.

Alternative position titles on the academic organizational chart utilized by some institutions are those of department chairperson or division chairperson. While these titles place the assignment on the academic track to the presidency, chairperson positions are lower in the organizational hierarchy, often reporting to a dean. To move upward into a dean's position in such an organization might require some familiarity with routines performed by instructional department or division chairpersons.

6. *Grow your job assignment to the next level.* As new tasks are added to your current job assignment, you should consider them to be an asset. These activities enable you to expand your professional repertoire of experiences and enhance your knowledge and skills base. Your reputation as an ambitious, hard worker who seeks professional challenges will become known and hopefully rewarded.

As the assignments accumulate, compare what you are doing with typical campus workloads and with the higher education norm. Be prepared to make the case for a title change and potential salary upgrade when your job tasks resemble those of a higher-ranking assignment. For example, when my assignment as associate vice president for academic services and planning assumed more student services elements, I requested an upgrade to vice president for student affairs, a newly created position, and successfully defended the proposal for the upgrade.

7. *Enhance leadership skills.* As the American Association of University Administrators (AAUA) stresses in its brochure *Preparing for the 21st Century* (n.d.), "Professional development is the responsibility of each individual." The association encourages the preparation of a professional development plan that is updated annually and reflects a commitment to lifelong learning.

Numerous conferences, workshops, institutes, and internships focus on leadership development. Sharon McDade, a Columbia University professor, describes and compares the better-known programs in her writings. The AAUA cites the Harvard Institute for Educational Management programs (IEM and MDP) and the American Council on Education (ACE) leadership development programs as particularly exemplary.

8. *Participate in assessment activities.* Service on accreditation teams, program evaluation committees, instructional discipline review task forces, and the like will expand your familiarity with how educational institutions function. Most institution-wide

assessment teams include a librarian, since the library is considered a critical element in determining the quality of the academic environment.

The intensity of the assessment experience often builds collegial bonds with team participants that extend beyond the duration of the review assignment, contributing to your professional network. Your critical analysis skills will be augmented as a result of your assessment activities, while your professional reputation is also enhanced.

9. *Attend national conferences and build an external network.* National conference participation exposes you to a broad spectrum of higher education issues and personnel. The conference speakers and workshops enrich your professional acumen. The informal discussions surrounding the meetings are a chance to exchange your ideas and build your network of professional supporters.

   Conferences sponsored by organizations such as the American Association of Community Colleges (AACC), the American Association of Higher Education (AAHE), and the American Council on Education (ACE) are among those that draw participants from staff, faculty, and administrative positions. All publish journals and newsletters about current professional issues and provide opportunities for committee participation. Often conferences have learning tracks facilitating development in specific professional areas. For example, the 1997 AACC conference had six tracks—student Development, Economic Development, Technology, Teaching and Learning, Institutional Development, and Educational Reform.

10. *Build an internal network that includes decision makers of the institution.* These decision makers can enlighten you on the campus political environment as it affects your job assignment, inform you of forthcoming professional opportunities, and introduce you to other influential college leaders. For your part, you can demonstrate to them the versatility of your skills and talents by excelling in supportive activities, such as program planning and written briefs on their special topics of interest. A significant number of presidents are internal hires identified by local decision makers as effective leaders and contributors.

    Service on committees or task forces provides a useful vehicle for meeting high-ranking administrators. Frequently, librarians are perceived stereotypically and assigned committee roles that involve recording or preserving data. When the reports of the group's activities are made, volunteer to present the information to the institutional leadership. An effective presenter often receives positive notice from college decision makers in attendance. As changes occur in the institution, your outstanding effort may identify you as an appropriate fit for an assignment for which you'd have never received consideration as an unknown.

11. *Seek mentors along the pathway to the college presidency.* While some of your mentors may be from the field of librarianship, others should be sought from non-library administrative posts. Several institutions have established mentorship programs that identify a volunteer mentor for you—sparing the protégé from having to solicit sponsorship. Other institutions, such as the Houston Community College System, have established programs, like Project Future Perfect, that encourage you to envision a leadership project and seek support from recognized institutional leaders who will mentor you through your project.

    Academic librarians often encounter library clients who might be persuaded to serve as mentors. This is one reason customer service behavior is so critical. One must be able to demonstrate to the client skills commonly perceived to be favorable attributes of college leaders, like initiative, inventive problem solving, intelligence, and effective interpersonal communication.

12. *Join community organizations and serve actively.* Presidents are expected to be highly visible community leaders. Typically, a president will belong to one or more of the following organizations: local chamber of commerce, political forums such as the League of Women Voters, social clubs, and service organizations such as Lions, Kiwanis, Rotary, and others. According to the Vaughan et al. study, 61 percent of the presidents aged 45 or younger reported membership in the Rotary (Vaughan et al. 1994, 36). Additionally, there are requests to serve on community boards, civic commissions, and public agency/private industry task forces.

Access to membership in organizations like the Rotary, Kiwanis, Lions, Toastmasters, and local chambers of commerce is fairly open, as all are seeking talented, community-oriented workers to execute programs and projects. Through participation, you will develop your communication skills and your teamwork skills, both highly prized in presidents. You should also expand the support base available to endorse your career advancement.

REFERENCES

American Association of University Administrators. N.d. *Preparing for the 21st Century: Career Development for Administrators in Higher Education.* Tuscaloosa, AL: Author.

Kerr, Clark and Marian L. Gade. 1989. *The Many Lives of Academic Presidents: Time, Place & Character.* Washington, DC: Association of Governing Boards of Universities and Colleges.

Vaughan, George B. 1986. *The Community College Presidency.* New York: Macmillan.

Vaughan, George B., Gustavo Mellander, and Beverly Blois. 1994. *The Community College Presidency: Current Status and Future Outlook.* Washington, DC: American Association of Community Colleges.

SELECTED BIBLIOGRAPHY

American Council on Education, Office of Women in Higher Education. 1994. *1993 Women Presidents' Summit. A Blueprint for Leadership: How Women College and University Presidents Can Shape the Future.* Washington, DC: Author.

Association of Governing Boards of Universities and Colleges, Commission on the Academic Presidency. 1996. *Renewing the Academic Presidency: Stronger Leadership for Tougher Times.* Washington, DC: Author.

DiCroce, Deborah M. 1995. "Women and the Community College Presidency: Challenges and Possibilities." *New Directions for Community Colleges* 89 (Spring): 79–88.

Green, Madeleine and Sharon A. McDade. 1991. *Investing in Higher Education: A Handbook of Leadership Development.* Washington, DC: American Council on Education.

Greenwood, Janet D. and Marlene Ross. 1996. "So You Want to Be a College President." *Educational Record* 77 (Spring/Summer): 24–29.

McDade, Sharon A. 1987. *Higher Education Leadership: Enhancing Skills through Professional Development Programs.* ASHE-ERIC Higher Education Report No. 5. Washington, DC: Association for the Study of Higher Education.

———. 1989. "Resource Guide." In E. Bensimon, M. Gade, and J. Kauffman, eds., *On Assuming a College or University Presidency: Lessons & Advice from the Field.* Washington, DC: American Association for Higher Education.

———. 1991. "New Pathways in Leadership and Professional Development." *New Directions for Higher Education* 76 (Winter): 87–101.

McDade, Sharon A. et al. 1994. "Programs Sponsored by Multicampus Systems, Consortia, Networks, and Associations." *New Directions for Higher Education* 87 (Fall): 41–54.

Mitchell, Patricia Turner, ed. 1993. *Cracking the Wall: Women in Higher Education Administration.* Washington, DC: College and University Personnel Association.

Ost, David H. and Darla J. Twale. 1989. "Appointments of Administrators in Higher Education: Reflections of Administrative and Organizational Structures." *Journal of NAWDAC* 52 (Summer): 23–30.

Penney, Sherry H. 1996. "Five Challenges for Academic Leaders in the 21st Century." *Educational Record* 77 (Spring/Summer): 19–23.

Presler, Wendy. 1996. "Inside the College Presidency: A Q & A with Robert H. Atwell." *Educational Record* 77 (Spring/Summer): 6–11.

Ross, Marlene et al. 1993. *The American College President.* Washington, DC: American Council on Education.

Touchton, Judith G. et al. 1993. *Women in Presidencies: A Descriptive Study of Women College & University Presidents.* Washington, DC: American Council on Education.

Chapter 16

An Academic Odyssey: Teacher, Librarian, Professor, Dean

Edward J. Jennerich

Life happens while you are making other plans, or so the cliché goes. As I've reflected on my career, this cliché has crossed my mind more than once. Growing up as the third son of two orphaned parents in Brooklyn a half century ago, I certainly could not have predicted what career, if any, lay before me.

The seeds of my relationship with librarianship were planted in my youth. As a child, I was a frequent library user both for school assignments and for story hours. The academic needs of my high school years in northern New Jersey required significant use of the high school library and the local public library. Both served my academic needs as well as satisfying the adolescent urge to ask for the keys to the family car so I could "go to the library." From my father, I received a keen interest in history, a trait for which I am eternally grateful. Even when course assignments did not require me to go to the library, I would frequently spend my study periods in the high school library reading back issues of *American Heritage* magazine.

Given my love of history, it came as no surprise that I majored in history as an undergraduate at Trenton State College. There, the serendipity of choosing a career path in librarianship was first nurtured. As a history major, I was constantly required to use the library at the behest of my mentor, Dr. Helen McCracken Carpenter, a prominent historian, educator, and author. The college and I were also fortunate in having as professor of history and library director Dr. Felix Hirsch, a prominent figure in academic librarianship. These two individuals, knowingly or otherwise, deepened my relationship with the joys of academic research, scholarship, and the world of librarianship.

I entered college in the early 1960s with the goal of studying history and earning my credentials as a high school history teacher. My career path seemed assured since occupational forecasts predicted there would not be an abundance of teachers anytime in the foreseeable future. To my surprise and consternation, at the end of my sophomore year, these same occupational forecasts announced a current surplus of teachers. Not only was the surplus in the field of history, but it also covered other fields such as English and men's physical education, where I had a modest aptitude. Given the revised employment situation, not to mention the academic requirements of the college, it was incumbent upon me to identify a minor field of study. I thought it in my best interests to choose one that would provide other avenues of employment if history positions were unavailable.

I cannot recall who suggested taking a minor in library science, but frankly this was a profession that had never occurred to me. All of my interactions with libraries had been as a patron. I was never a library aide, library monitor, or circulation assistant at any time in my high school or college career. However, the more I reflected on my own interests in research, information retrieval, interpersonal skills, and service to others, the more attractive librarianship appeared.

I began to take several courses offered by the library science department as part of its school librarian certification program, which was under the able and enthusiastic leadership of Dorothy Ferguson. The more I experienced librarianship as an academic discipline, the more I enjoyed it. I found the reference courses to be a valuable adjunct to my study of history, which began to focus primarily on the study of colonial America. What came as a surprise, however, were the other areas covered by the wide-ranging duties of a school librarian: curriculum, budgets, personnel, facilities, selection of materials, cataloging and classification, reference, and so on. The area of "administration" was a subject I found of particular interest.

As my college career drew inexorably toward its conclusion, decisions about my future direction had to be made. Encouraged by my faculty mentors in both history and library science, I began to explore the possibilities of obtaining a graduate degree. The dilemma was whether to pursue a graduate degree in history or in library science. Given the job market at the time and the germ of an idea that I might become a college librarian as opposed to a school librarian, I decided to pursue graduate work in library science. Thus, what had been born out of the necessity of choosing a minor became a career of choice.

Living in the New York City metropolitan area, I was fortunate to have several fine library schools from which to choose. I decided to go a little farther afield, and I entered graduate school at Drexel University (Drexel Institute of Technology at that time) in the fall of 1967.

In one of those interesting ironies of life, I was lured away from full-time graduate study after my first quarter by the school district where I had completed my student teaching. They were in need of a teacher for half a year. I couldn't resist the temptation to fulfill my first career goal of teaching history, but I also continued to pursue my graduate studies in librarianship on a part-time basis. As it turned out, my temporary position became permanent, and I taught in the district for three years.

At the same time, I had the good fortune to secure my first library position as evening librarian at the main campus of Fairleigh Dickinson University in Rutherford, New Jersey. My responsibilities were to serve as reference librarian and to also serve as library supervisor during the evening hours throughout the week and all day Saturday. This position provided valuable library experience and also ignited my interest in college and university librarianship.

The idea of becoming a college librarian and eventually a college library director coalesced as a result of my work at Fairleigh Dickinson University and as I continued to pursue my master of science in library science degree. Unlike many of my colleagues in library school, I had the benefit of a very strong undergraduate program in librarianship. I was able to test out of several introductory courses, thereby allowing me to pursue in greater depth my interests in reference work and to specialize in administration. While my undergraduate degree had focused primarily on developing my content knowledge of history and how to be an effective teacher, it was in the master's program in librarianship that the foundations of my administrative career were laid. My organizational skills reflected the theoretical concepts that I learned about the organization of humankind's knowledge in cataloging, classification, and reference courses. Most certainly, my knowledge of many academic disciplines was enhanced, since libraries obviously cover all areas of knowledge. Likewise, my research skills and scholarly interest were enhanced through reference courses and courses in intellectual freedom. Administratively, I began to develop an understanding of, and a facility with, personnel, budgets, and facilities as well as the importance of establishing positive relationships with external constituencies. My understanding of technology, cybernetics, and computer skills benefited from Drexel University's international reputation in engineering and computer sciences. While I was not consciously aware of it at the time, such courses would play an important part in the success I would experience as a college and university administrator.

FINDING A CAREER PATH

In many ways, preparation in librarianship prepares one to be an academic generalist, encompassing, as it does, a surprising amount of knowledge about a wide variety of academic disciplines. The study of librarianship is a generalist degree—an academic oddity in an era of narrow academic specializations. Being an "academic generalist" is also one definition of the chief academic officer of a college or university: no longer are you solely a chemist, mathematician, historian, or librarian. *You are responsible for, and are expected to be knowledgeable about, all areas of the curriculum.* Further, the chief academic officer should see that the curriculum is integrated in a meaningful way. An individual with a comprehensive view of the curriculum, as well as other appropriate faculty credentials, is an ideal candidate for the role of chief academic officer.

As I completed my master's degree, it became increasingly clear that my future lay in academe. While the possibility of becoming the director of a college or university library remained paramount, I also felt there might be equally attractive and challenging leadership positions in higher education administration, particularly as a chief academic officer or as a president. To put this emerging career track to the test, I decided to pursue a degree in higher education administration. I elected to enroll at the University of Pittsburgh because of its well-respected reputation for doctoral study in higher education administration and a strong reputation in librarianship. The late 1960s and early 1970s were very disturbing and turbulent times for anyone in higher education administration. To actively seek an academic and administrative career was cause for questioning one's sanity. In fact, while interviewing for a place in the doctoral program, I was asked why I would want to be a college or university president. Before I gave the committee a serious reply to that question, I jokingly replied: "There's a long history of insanity in my family." The committee found this retort quite entertaining. Having a sense of humor is an important trait for anyone involved in higher education administration.

Despite the turbulence of the era, these very challenges and concerns, expressed in various ways on college and university campuses, cemented my desire to pursue an academic career. I believed then, and this belief has been reinforced over the 25 years of my academic and administrative career, that the administration of colleges and universities is a distinct discipline with a disciplinary, research base of knowledge. The collegiate educational enterprise demands more than simply on-the-job training. There is unquestionably an art to academic administration, but it is equally clear there is a science to it as well.

To finance my doctoral work, I was fortunate to work as a school librarian in the Pittsburgh public schools. It provided the necessary income as well as the valuable experience required to secure my first academic position after completing the doctorate.

The doctoral course work in administration, organization, finance, fundraising, personnel, and public policy built upon many of the same areas of knowledge that were a part of my master's level work in librarianship. My knowledge of administration and the academy was broadened as well. My dissertation combined expertise in librarianship with the public policy issues involved in establishing branch campuses of colleges and universities in general and branch campus libraries in particular. Parenthetically, the analysis and recommendations of my dissertation were discussed 20 years later as the state of Washington began to implement a plan for establishing branch campuses. Testimony before the Washington State Senate led to more people's reading my dissertation 20 years after the fact than they ever did at the time it was written!

CHANGING FROM STUDENT TO PROFESSIONAL

The completion of the Ph.D. ended the degree phase of my career, although there was still much to be learned. What might appear to be an unusual educational pattern actually had a logical progression. Each stage opened new educational and career prospects. I can think of no better definition of "education" than one that opens new vistas and new areas of study and contemplation. Over my years of teaching, I've often told students that if they haven't been changed in some fundamental way by their collegiate experience, they should ask for their money back. In addition to content mastery, the collegiate experience should challenge students to question their value systems, contemplate new ideas, explore new paths for their life's work, and be exposed to the rich diversity of the human experience. The collegiate years are truly "risk-free" years in one's life when questioning, challenging, and/or reaffirming core educational and personal values is encouraged through the breadth and integration of the curriculum and through various student life activities. It's a safe bet that not many students ask for their money back.

Each stage in my educational path was a building block for the next, and the skills acquired at each stage transferred across the disciplinary boundaries of history, librarianship, and academic administration. We are all familiar with the popular literature that tell us of the number of career changes we'll experience over the course of a lifetime. Obviously, what makes such career change possible is the transferability of skills, knowledge, and theory from one field to another.

In 1974, upon the completion of the Ph.D. in higher education administration, with a cognate in library science, I was recruited by Baylor University as assistant professor of education and chair of the Department of Library Science. I began my professorial and administrative career at the ripe old age of 27. My years at Baylor University provided me with the opportunity to put into practice the combined skills learned as a student of higher education administration and library science. My charge coming into the position was relatively broad and challenging: strengthen the library science major or face the possibility of closure.

Over the succeeding nine years, enrollments tripled, the curriculum was revised, various technologies were introduced into the instructional program, additional faculty were recruited, and an undergraduate major and a graduate degree program were instituted. Due to the programmatic growth, new facilities were planned and constructed. During this period, I grew in my role as a member of the professoriate, moving in rank to associate professor with tenure. The position allowed me to pursue my administrative aspirations, develop an active research agenda, and pursue my love of teaching, receiving several teaching awards in the process. I benefited by being fully engaged as a member of the academic community through service on a variety of campus committees and other leadership positions. Similarly, I was active in state and national professional associations in library science and in academic administration.

ADVANCING TO LEADERSHIP ROLES

As a result of my successes at Baylor University, I was selected as dean and professor at the Graduate School of Library Science at Southern Connecticut State University, then the largest school of library science in the country. The role of dean was purely administrative as defined by an extraordinarily restrictive collective bargaining agreement. Nevertheless, I set about enhancing ties with the professional library community and establishing links with internal and external constituencies. The concepts learned in graduate school at both the master's and doctoral levels were invaluable. As a result of strengthening ties with our external constituencies and developing new external relationships, enrollments increased, as did financial support from grants and gifts for student scholarships and programmatic development.

Until this point in my career, my teaching and administrative duties had been primarily focused on the academic discipline of library science. I still harbored desires for broader academic responsibilities, so I was delighted to be approached about the possibility of becoming the chief academic officer at a liberal arts institution, Virginia Intermont College. I was being recruited because of the skills whose roots could be partially traced to my background in librarianship. Specifically, these skills included my broad knowledge of curricular matters, familiarity with accreditation, administrative ability, interpersonal skills, knowledge of technology, stature as an academic administrator and professor, proven experience in enrollment growth and management, and a record of building positive relationships with external constituencies. Working with internal and external constituencies, I was able to initiate long-range curricular planning, implement an integrated liberal arts curriculum, secure the college's reaccreditation, triple the number of faculty with terminal degrees, and increase enrollments.

Having accomplished what I set out to do as dean, I moved on to my present position as associate provost and dean of the Graduate School at Seattle University. I have broad responsibility for academic affairs, administrative affairs, faculty and staff contracts, liaison with state and federal legislators, all aspects of enrollment services, institutional and specialized accreditation, and other similar duties. My present position is a direct descendant of the knowledge gained as a chief academic officer at a liberal arts institution, dean of a professional school, a broad understanding of undergraduate and graduate curricular issues, and a successful record of student recruitment and retention strategies. Increased enrollments at both the graduate and undergraduate level, improved academic standards and assessment, new curricular initiatives and programmatic development, and improved communication with internal and external constituencies have resulted.

What can be learned from my experiences to date? What useful thoughts can I leave with the reader? At the most immediate level, I enjoy what I do. I believe that enjoyment is the most basic criterion for whatever work one chooses. I look forward to work each day and to the privilege of working with students, faculty, and colleagues. Why? I believe the answer is twofold: the first has to do with my love of education and working with young people, and second is a continuous desire on my own part to learn and to grow. In the first instance, I began my career with a desire to work with young people and to help them gain a greater insight into the intellectual, cultural, and political history of our country. I chose an undergraduate institution, Trenton State College, because of its well-deserved and long-enduring preeminence in combining subject mastery with teacher preparation. Over the years, my academic interests broadened from history to the entire spectrum of the liberal arts and professional education. In the second instance, I've continued to maintain my roots within the academy. I continue to learn in the true sense of lifelong learning, whether enhancing my skills at Harvard's Institute for Educational Management or learning new recreational skills in wilderness camping, painting, sailing, and coastal navigation. I continue to teach because I sincerely enjoy working with students. I've taught every grade from seventh through the doctoral level and have enjoyed each and every level. I continue to maintain a research agenda, albeit to a modest extent, given my administrative responsibilities. Each stage of my career has provided opportunities for increasing knowledge and expertise, and I have tried to take full advantage of each of these.

I've reached my present position by virtue of a nontraditional educational route of history, library science, and higher education administration combined with the traditional career path through the faculty ranks to professor and serving as department chair, dean, academic vice president, and associate provost. There is no question that some of my success can be directly traced to my training in library science. Examples from the traditional library education curriculum that are relevant to academic administration are illustrative:

Reference

Most library education programs offer courses in general reference materials as well as subject-centered reference courses. For example, it is common to have courses in humanities reference sources or scientific reference sources and so on. These courses provide a broad overview of the various disciplines. Learning the content and strengths of the hundreds of reference sources in each course provided a unique understanding of the discipline in general as well as its history and development, key individuals, and relationships within the discipline and among other disciplines. Comprehensive knowledge of curriculum has been of enormous value to me throughout my career.

The essential component of all reference work is ascertaining the information needs of each patron, a problem-solving exercise, if you will. To accomplish this task effectively requires a knowledge of the verbal and nonverbal communications skills that constitute the "reference interview": eye contact, relaxed posture, appropriate facial expressions, remembering, avoiding premature diagnosis, reflecting feelings verbally, restating or paraphrasing comments, asking open questions, providing encouragers, appropriate closure, and avoiding inappropriate opinions or suggestions. The study of the reference interview has enhanced my communication and interpersonal and problem-solving skills and has been extremely useful to me as a teacher and as an administrator. The desire to help patrons, most of whom are students, translates into a student-centered philosophy of education and higher education administration.

Professionally, the formal study of the reference interview has been a major research interest, and its integration into the curriculum of reference courses was an instructional innovation. Through the use of videotaping and role playing, students develop competence in content knowledge of reference works as well as improve their reference interview skills. Recognition of these innovations led to several campus-based teaching awards. Further research continues to lead to publications in respected journals, in keeping with the best of academic traditions. Both the teaching record and publication record were essential to my professorial role and ultimately to promotion and tenure.

Cataloging and Classification

In its simplest form, cataloging and classification are the study of how to organize the world's knowledge in a logical manner, whether Library of Congress, Dewey, or the Universal Decimal Classification. Again, we see a curricular context since the curriculum also encompasses the world's knowledge and how that knowledge is organized and taught. The fundamental concept of cataloging and classification is to organize similar subjects together on the library shelves. Even a cursory study of any of the classification tables will demonstrate the logic of proceeding from comprehensive topics to progressively more narrow ones. Assigning consistent subject headings assists the library patron in locating materials, and cross-references establish the interrelationships of knowledge and graphically demonstrate the concept that all knowledge is integrated.

In the study of cataloging and classification, if one goes beyond the mere technical requirements, a wonderful opportunity awaits, for it is here that you are presented with a marvelous overview or schematic of civilizations' knowledge. It's a curricular view, which, combined with reference, has served me very well as an academic officer.

Technology

Libraries contain information in a variety of formats, including books, audiotapes, videotapes, CD-ROMs, microforms, computer databases, Internet connections, and ephemera, to mention a few. Librarians must be able to retrieve the information and know how to use the technology that makes the retrieval possible. In providing these various library resources, the needs of the end user must be kept in mind. Here again, the focus on being student-centered cannot be overemphasized. An understanding of the instructional uses of technology has been a continual thread in my educational fabric.

An understanding of technology—its uses, its strengths, and its limitations—has increased as our world becomes more focused on technology. As part of the central university administration, I am frequently called upon to make decisions, often extremely expensive decisions, involving the seemingly endless requests for upgrades, software, databases, or networks. One of the major dilemmas facing educational institutions is how to keep abreast of the rapidly changing technological developments that support and enhance the curriculum without going broke or pricing the institution out of the market. Fortunately, given my library science background, I feel more prepared to address that dilemma than I might otherwise. The theory, complexity, and uses of technology were consistently emphasized at Drexel University with its strong focus on information science and cybernetics.

Selection of Library Materials

One of the fundamental components of education for librarianship is the selecting and acquiring of the actual materials to be included in the collection. To do so effectively, librarians must have a thorough understanding of the curriculum and the clientele. The librarian must strive to develop as comprehensive a collection as possible, representing varying points of view. Divergent views often create controversy over which views should be included or, even more onerous, that only one view should be represented. Librarians are called upon to be bulwarks against censorship and to support the values of intellectual freedom that are so vital to a vibrant, academic environment. Understanding the principles upon which the foundations of intellectual freedom rest and strongly supporting academic freedom are central to any university position, but particularly for college and university administrators, who may be called upon to explain these tenets to members of Boards of Trustees, legislators, or other constituencies.

Library Organization and Administration

The administration of libraries mirrors the administration of many other components of college and university campuses. However, few other areas within academic affairs have the advantage of someone who has had formal training in administration. Most department chairs and deans have advanced through the faculty ranks, and most doctoral programs do not provide any preparation for administrative responsibilities. In contrast, librarians benefit from course work covering budgeting, personnel, facilities, strategic planning, and other administrative topics. For example, librarians in administrative roles often supervise professionals, nonprofessionals, student workers, and, occasionally, volunteers. Supervision may involve annual performance evaluations, issues of promotion and tenure, or questions centering around collective bargaining agreements. Thus, the knowledge of personnel issues, integral to the preparation of librarians, is of particular value and importance.

The preceding examples demonstrate the transferability of skills and academic preparation from one career to another. While obviously not limitless, nevertheless, many skills learned in librarianship are transferable to a variety of career paths. In my own case, these skills were the foundation upon which my doctoral studies in higher education were built. Because of this foundation, I was able to delve more deeply into the subject matter of higher education administration and gain additional knowledge.

Libraries have historically served the educational and cultural needs of society and have been central to the concept of lifelong learning and individualized instruction. Education is a lifelong journey and not simply a four-or five-year interlude. This brief autobiographical essay is simply one person's odyssey from teacher, to librarian, to professor, to senior university administrator. How you choose to use your preparation in librarianship is limited only by your imagination, your ability to convince others that the knowledge, skills, and theories you've acquired are transferable.

I would, however, offer the following advice:

1. Don't sacrifice the knowledge to be gained in the content classes in library science to take only technology courses. Technology changes rapidly, but without the theory and content of the discipline, there is no context in which to place new developments.

2. The theory and history of the profession are important and necessary in order to adapt to an ever-changing future. The history of the book, after all, is the history of civilization.

3. Enhance your people skills. Television, the World Wide Web, and computers are solitary activities involving little personal contact with others. Employers always need people with good communications skills.

4. Don't let library science limit you to a career that is building-centered. As information retrievers, much of what librarians do can be done outside the parameters of a library building.

5. Always assume library science is a positive, unique feature of your background.

But, above all, be passionate about what you do. Without passion, tempered by reason and knowledge, one cannot hope to espouse intellectual freedom, embark into the frontiers of new technology, or inspire others to search, seek, and learn.

Chapter 17

On Becoming a Chief Information Officer in Academe: Evolving Roles of an Academic Librarian

H. E. Broadbent III

Almost 27 years after completing my first professional degree, a master of science in library science with a specialization in public library services, I found myself in the position of associate provost for information services at Dowling College, a medium-sized private, comprehensive college. How did I get there? What lessons are there in this case study that may be of use to librarians and librarianship?

I begin my narrative with this position, then return to the beginning of my career by dividing it into phases so that I can comment on the transitions and lessons learned that may be of interest. I had occupied five full-time positions, including this one. I left each position in search of change and professional growth. I want to be happy in my work, and I am happy when I am facing new challenges and creatively solving new problems.

BEING A COLLEGIATE CHIEF INFORMATION OFFICER AT MIDCAREER

According to CAUSE, a national professional organization for those who support information technology in higher education, there are about 300 chief information officers at colleges and universities in the United States. The job title chief information officer (CIO) did not exist when most of the incumbents obtained their professional credentials, and they came to this position through a variety of paths. From my own attendance at CAUSE national conferences, I observe that most CIOs come from computer science or management information systems backgrounds. Few are librarians, but from my own experience I know that librarians can be successful in this alternative career.

For myself, after four years as associate provost for information services at Dowling College, I was still discovering the many facets of this position. The scope of my position continued to evolve and included strategic planning and management for all aspects of information services, including academic and administrative computing, library, instructional media, and institutional research. For a two-and-a-half year period, I also was responsible for the office of communications and publications, which included advertising and community relations. More recently, the college's telecommunications center was added to my portfolio. In higher education today, administrative flexibility and professional agility are paramount to meeting competitive forces.

The overall challenges of a CIO are organizing the people, processes, and technology to make the organization's product or service highly successful in the marketplace—skills sharply honed in my past experiences as a librarian. Too often, the people and processes parts are left out of the management of information systems, and the results are predictably poor. This means the CIO must break down perceived barriers to change, such as "This is how we always did it," "It is not broken, so why fix it," and "It's not my job." Therefore, the purpose in placing a CIO at a high-level position in the organization is to have sufficient authority to effect change across the organization.

Defining New Leadership Roles in Academe

The position of CIO was first created at Dowling when I was hired, so the initial challenge for me was defining the job. One of my initial priorities was bringing order to a chaotic library system where the physical environment and the organizational structure had been neglected for years. My background as a college library director was excellent preparation for strengthening this key component of the college's information services organization. Confusion existed concerning the boundaries between professional and clerical/technical work. It was imperative to me that the librarians become the foundation of this new information organization. I moved quickly to position them as leaders of the Dowling College information revolution. They responded well to my support for a stronger technical infrastructure for the library and the shifting of clerical and administrative responsibilities to the support staff. The library did not have an integrated, automated system in place, and there was little confidence among the librarians that the administration would support the acquisition of such a system. With my previous experience, I knew that we could build a persuasive case.

Outside the library and on the administrative front, there was a need for implementing an integrated system of college registration, student records, financial aid, and finance. The finance system already had been scheduled for implementation before my arrival. This was an on-line distributed accounting and purchasing system, which allowed administrators and staff to create on-line purchase orders and to make on-line budget transfers. This was revolutionary compared to the former paper-based, mainframe computer system. Only when I went to the first campuswide training session did I have an inkling of the confusion that was to follow.

It was a classic case of planning for a new finance system to replicate only the functions that the old system did and nothing more. While administrators had hopes of paperless purchasing and wide-scale access to current information, the planning and implementation did not support it. The fault was not that of the administrators, for they did not know what they did not know. There had been no systematic thinking about desired outcomes of the new system in terms of management reporting and systematic controls. There had been little understanding of the capabilities of the new system or motivation to invest time in finding more efficient processes to meet these challenges. While the system vendor provided consultants to assist with implementation, their recommendations to finance-administrators had been met with disinterest. There was much for me to do.

Providing for implementation of the student modules of this system was still in the planning stages when I began at Dowling, and meetings between Dowling staff and the vendor-consultants, unfortunately, were openly hostile. There was an urgency to get the system up and running because the old system was badly out-of-date, but there was little confidence in its database quality. System upgrades had not been loaded in years due to local modifications to programming code that conflicted with new vendor releases. The main form of communication was now finger pointing.

Communicating across the Organization

New techniques for communication were urgently needed to get these projects on track. I organized an operations committee that crossed subsystem barriers and began a dialogue that enabled users to understand that the activities of one user affected all others. This understanding of a shared, relational database and the ongoing changes to it became a continuing subject of dialogue. A rolling agenda was established to address issues of ongoing implementation.

Based on my past experience, I recognized that building a cooperative partnership with vendor staff would position Dowling's controller, responsible for the finance system, and registrar, responsible for the student system, for success in ongoing system implementation activities. The concept of college ownership of the system began to develop, and we made the transition from vendor/consultants' instructing college administrators, to their teaching together, and finally to the controller and registrar's taking the leadership roles in teaching the college staff how to utilize the system. The system became ours, and the vendor's role was to help us use it better.

When the finance and student systems were stable, another revelation was the lack of planning, before my arrival, for a campus network infrastructure. The old IBM mainframe was to be retired with the old software, and the new RISK 6000 was acting as a server in the initial phase of the client–server evolution. The old bridged network began to break down as we deployed hundreds of personal computers and connected them to the network. Campuswide electronic mail, access to the Internet, and use of administrative systems caused frequent outages and campuswide frustration. It was important at this point for me to convince the college provost that these problems would only get worse if we did not develop a sound technical solution. No more bandages!

Communicating Upward in the Organization

My addressing the issue of the outdated network infrastructure was an object lesson in the need for up-to-date organizational processes in planning for new technology. First, I assured the provost that we should stem the urge to blame anyone for this "mistake." It was not a mistake: appropriate technology had been selected for the time, but now the times had changed. Then came my campaign to turn around the college treasurer's disinterest when six-digit figures were cited as the cost of creating a stronger infrastructure.

Since the old network still worked, and those who were making decisions were the least likely to be inconvenienced when the network failed, it was easy for them to think that the decision could be postponed. I knew better. As we began to work with networking consultants, it became clear to me that there was no simple solution. The consultants themselves disagreed about short-term strategies for sustaining the token ring architecture while installing a fiber-optic backbone versus moving to ethernet quickly.

Again, my past experience in understanding the administrative mind-set helped me to prepare presentations with alternative solutions and a variety of costs. It was important to take time for the college provost and treasurer to become comfortable with the terminology of networking and the uncertainty of evolving standards. Before campus service was seriously disrupted, the decision was made to install a fiber-optic backbone with routers and the first pieces of a new campus infrastructure. Perhaps, the most important breakthrough for the provost and treasurer was learning that building the network infrastructure is an ongoing process in which there is some uncertainty about future directions. This was a lesson that I had already learned from library automation projects.

Becoming a Champion of Continuous Improvement

My emphasis in the first few years was on implementing and stabilizing the finance and student systems. As a tuition-dependent institution, it was clear that administrative systems were the engine that must work every day if the institution was to thrive in a highly competitive environment. The college budget was predicated on continued growth in enrollment, and the new registration system would accommodate future growth without corresponding increases in staff. It was important that I took a leadership position, learned from library automation, that implementation is an ongoing activity. It was not acceptable to have the system operating just at baseline. We had to be aggressive in implementing new subsystems and new releases so that we could continue to make gains in productivity. I could not do this myself, but I fostered in others the belief that change and improvement would be continuous.

The challenges of ongoing implementation of administrative systems distracted me from academic computing for the first couple of years at Dowling. When I first arrived, we had constructed some new computing classrooms, which seemed to meet a need at the time. But with the growing marketplace for Microsoft Windows-based applications, there was a new wave of interest in the use of technology for teaching and learning. When a member of my technical staff retired, I hired an educator with a strong background in using technology to lead forward the instructional resources program. Her understanding of the challenges of teaching received an immediate and positive response from faculty members who wanted to improve their teaching methods.

The process for communicating with faculty regarding their teaching needs was also in need of improvement. The use of faculty in an advisory role for technology planning has evolved from political discussions of priorities for assignment of computers to individual faculty members, to a roundtable on teaching and learning where faculty share with each other their successes and failures, and we, as administrators, work with them to design appropriate learning environments.

Planning and budgeting processes also required attention. I used a consultant to address this issue because it was beyond the scope of my position to affect the budget process. The consultant recommended a multiyear technology budget with a fleet maintenance approach to hardware and network upgrades, and this has been accepted by the top administration.

Creating a Model Information-Based Organization

Step by step, I believed that Dowling College was becoming a model information organization for the twenty-first century. In creating the position of associate provost for information services, the college recognized that information and technology cross old departmental boundaries. Distributed systems and new vehicles for communication empowered administrators and staff to make informed decisions with a new sense of confidence.

So, where are they? They are on the cusp of significant change. We separated from the software vendor who also provided on-site support for academic and administrative computing. We set our sights on a more flexible, short-term consultant to make this transition and to help us to select among alternative futures. I feel that I have been successful in teaching other administrators how to plan and implement new information technologies. All had a sense that they would become masters of their own destiny and more responsible for their own system implementation.

The key words that come into play in a college's transformation into an independent, information-based organization are people, processes, and technology. The challenge is getting them all moving in the same direction at the same time and helping them feel positive about this journey together: not unlike the challenges faced by most librarians and their directors.

STARTING A LIBRARIAN'S CAREER IN PUBLIC LIBRARY SERVICE

How many of us think about the turns our careers may take when we first begin? I remember a research assignment in my very first library science master's course where the class debated whether or not librarianship was a profession. I remember my own conviction that it was a profession, and therefore one could (and should) chart a career in this important field. As we prepare for the twenty-first century, it is important to ponder the future of librarianship. Will librarianship continue to evolve and be recognized as a distinguished career in the next 10, 25, 50, or 100 years? I explore these questions not at the macrolevel, but at a personal level.

What brought me to librarianship? First, I think that it was a fascination with people in need of information. At the beginning of my career in 1970, the library was a place where people came when they needed something: a good read, a quiet place to study, a safe place to socialize, or an answer to a question. In the branches of the Free Library of Philadelphia, where I worked in my first professional position as a young adult services librarian, there was a comfortable environment for young staff members such as me and for patrons from the surrounding neighborhood. Except for book talks at the local high schools, we dealt with people on a one-to-one basis. Patrons expressed a need, and we, as librarians, responded as best we could from institutional resources—the local collection of books and periodicals or referral to the main research library.

Why did I leave this comfortable environment? What drove me to move on after only two years? First, the bureaucracy of a large institution proved to be too frustrating for my youthful enthusiasm. Why did it take months between the time that books were selected for the branch collection and when they were available on the shelf? Why did it take even longer for a catalog record to appear in the cumbersome book catalogs (and endless supplements) that served as the main access tool for branch collections? Second, I needed a sense that what I was doing made a difference in the lives of the patrons. I needed feedback that the information I provided or the book recommended for leisure reading was of some use. While we had our "regulars" at the branch library, there was not a large-enough base of continuing relationships to satisfy my professional expectations.

I would not have recognized the meaning of the word "leadership" to my professional career at the time, but I felt the urge to solve problems and to make changes. I was soon impatient in my first professional position in the large city library system, where it seemed to take forever to get nothing done. One had to ask permission to ask permission. I soon learned to ask forgiveness rather than permission, and so my evolving career began.

THE TRANSITION TO ACADEMIC LIBRARIANSHIP

Typical of my generation, educated in the late 1960s and a young professional in the early 1970s, I was searching for meaning in my professional life—a career, not just a job. After much soul-searching, my interest turned to college librarianship, and when a reference position opened in a nearby college library, I had the good fortune to be returning to academe. The appeal of this change was for long-term relationships with students and faculty and a greater sense of control over the processes creating access to information.

The sense of community turned out to be real at the Philadelphia College of Textiles and Science, where there were fewer than 2,000 students and about 100 faculty members. I was one of three librarians who had faculty rank and privileges. In the first half of the 1970s, it was a comfortable world with a well-defined curriculum in the arts and sciences and professional programs in business and textiles. With little background in business or textiles, I found that I could learn quickly as patrons articulated their needs. I also discovered, a revelation to me at the time, how highly I valued the time I spent outside the library. With such a small professional cadre in the library, I sought the intellectual and moral support of colleagues in the academic library resource-sharing consortium to which Textile belonged.

Finding Leadership Opportunities in Library Cooperation

The sense that professional colleagues outside the immediate work environment would play an important part in my professional life developed at this time. I became fascinated with the concept—new at the time—that library cooperation was an important development for the future of small college libraries, where we were feeling the knowledge explosion at the same time that institutional resources were contracting. In my desire to satisfy the information needs of my patrons at Textile, I had discovered a unique regional resource—the Union Library Catalog of Philadelphia. What began as a Works Project Administration project in the 1930s had become a huge file of master shelflist cards.

Resource sharing, largely interlibrary loan or direct lending, was receiving federal and state support through Library Services and Construction Act funds. Union lists of serials, expedited delivery systems, and early attempts of facsimile transmission characterized the period of the 1970s. All of these programs required interinstitutional meetings, the development of trust among librarians, well-articulated protocols, and, finally, formal agreements. This was just the sort of work I enjoyed. Overcoming resistance to, and fears of, resource sharing became a central professional concern because of the direct impact on service to patrons.

While resource sharing seemed to be the solution to many of our patron's needs for access to a broader range of information resources than any one institution could own, it also was difficult to accomplish. Our tools were primitive: union card files with one-year backlogs in filing, keypunched union lists of serials with limited distribution and main entry access only. Sometimes it was more efficient to know, personally, regional collection strengths and telephone to ascertain specific titles. The effort to obtain the last pieces of information needed to complete a faculty or student research project was significant, but it was beginning to define the frontiers of library service and librarianship. Professionally, it became unacceptable to turn away patrons by saying, "We don't have it."

As a reference librarian at Textile, I once again felt the frustration of gaining access to the most recent books purchased for the library. It was normal to wait until books arrived from the book jobber before sending away to the Library of Congress for card sets. Cards could arrive in weeks or months or never. In the meantime, books sat on the shelves in Technical Services when I knew that people wanted and needed them. I remember that the catalog librarian was sanguine about a backlog of up to a year's work. After all, what would she do if she caught up?

Technological Leadership as an Agent of Change

About 1975, I recall learning that several of the large libraries in the area were participating in an experiment with college libraries in Ohio to catalog using a computer. The Ohio College Library Center was working with groups of libraries to extend their experiment beyond Ohio.

From the beginning, there was some discussion of automation. It was fascinating, if somewhat ill defined. I had taken only one information science course in my master's program in library science. At the time, information science appeared to be a more systematic world than the seat-of-the-pants world of library practice being taught in library school. It also seemed theoretical and removed from the reality of daily service to those in need of information in public and academic libraries.

In my position as a faculty librarian at Textile, I was required under the faculty contract to have a second subject master's degree in order to be promoted and tenured. An unusual feature at the time was support in time away from the job in order to pursue this additional degree.

I was torn between a master's degree in business administration and one in theater, which had been my avocation while an undergraduate. It did not seem to matter to the college what area of study I pursued. If I went for the business degree, I had to take foundation undergraduate courses in accounting, marketing, and finance. While I could acknowledge the value of the content of these courses, I was too impatient at that time to take undergraduate courses. So, I decided to have fun—a master's in theater from Villanova University with half my course work in dramatic literature and half in practice (acting, directing, set design, etc.). It was everything that I wanted it to be—learning for the sake of learning and intellectually stimulating. Within two years, I had my second master's, but I was getting restless at Textile.

Another change in my life as a professional librarian was the growing amount of time I was spending outside the library. First, it was committees within the college organization; then it was local and state professional groups. Frequently, I was the only one from my library to attend. At first hesitant, I decided it was advantageous to go alone and to take the opportunity to meet new colleagues. Then, I gathered up my nerve and money to attend national meetings. I would return to my job full of new ideas. I found it thrilling to meet my local and regional colleagues at national meetings and to maintain a dialogue with these colleagues about professional challenges and opportunities.

ADVANCING TO ACADEMIC LIBRARY MANAGEMENT

As the most junior of three librarians and full of youthful enthusiasm, I felt the frustration of being full of "good" ideas but not having the power to implement them. After two years at Textile, I learned of the opportunity to be director of the library at Ursinus College, where I had been an undergraduate. I leaped at the chance to stop complaining about my frustration and to assume a leadership role. I found that having my second master's degree opened doors for me in my new assignment. Again, as a faculty librarian, my two advanced degrees allowed an appointment at the rank of assistant professor and the possibility of further promotion and tenure. Promotion to professor, however, would be reserved for those with a Ph.D.

The challenge of this new position was to apply current library practices in an environment where few policies were written, and reference services were provided by librarians who had full-time assignments in acquisitions, technical services, and so on. The establishment and staffing of a full-time reference desk, the creation of a multitiered bibliographic instruction program, and the formalization of policies were immediate challenges. The differentiated roles of professionals and support staff, the revitalization of the library committee and friends of the library, and an overt communications program followed after basic organizational issues were resolved.

Leadership in Campus Computing

Probably, the biggest opportunity for change was with the introduction of technology. Shortly before I left Textile, I had been able to persuade the director and catalog librarian that the Online Computer Library Center (OCLC) cataloging system was a fundamental change that would improve operations. Staff at Ursinus were aware of this new development, but the previous, long-term director asked them to wait to begin planning until after his retirement. My first priority as a new library director was seeking administrative support to link the college library to the OCLC network. The service was being offered by the Union Library Catalog of Pennsylvania, which later became PALINET. I was fortunate to find a young and open-minded vice president for administration who responded positively to my description of this new technological wonder—shared cataloging. Within my first year, the commitment was made. Throughout the United States, OCLC had become the most important catalyst for change in library processes and procedures.

At Ursinus, academic computing at this time was achieved through the Dartmouth (College) Time Share System. Fifteen or 20 "dumb" terminals occupied otherwise underutilized carrels on the third floor of the library. This facility was managed by a young professor in the mathematics department. Used primarily for mathematics, the system had a number of social sciences applications that were used in political science and economics courses.

Solving Practical Problems with Technology

Before arrival as library director, student programmers at Ursinus had created a periodicals list that served to extend access to these holdings beyond the librarians' cardex. While this approach worked among the librarians, its nonstandard determination of titles made it of limited use for resource sharing. In fact, within the college library resource-sharing cooperative group, it was not uncommon to share copies of lists and to search them in a round-robin fashion before the advent of union lists. At this time, it was not unusual for periodical and government document collections to be organized by titles with nonstandard approaches to determining the correct form of the title. Each library and each collection had its own rules, which made conducting research in multiple libraries confusing to students and faculty.

At the same time that we were planning for the transition to OCLC, microcomputers were becoming available for office applications. Again, I searched for a campus partner and found that the director of facilities was contemplating the acquisition of a computer for his office automation. About 1975, our choice for the desktop, after much debate, was the Commodore 64. My goal was to convert some of our untidy shoe box files and to prepare the library staff by having them become familiar with the keyboard and software applications in word processing, spreadsheets, and databases. This effort was only moderately successful. The hardware and software crashed frequently, to the discouragement of all but the most determined.

Leading the Decision to Automate the Library

Finally, in the late 1970s, the college library was reasonably well organized, using OCLC for cataloging and interlibrary loan and microcomputers for word processing, maintaining local name and address databases, and using spreadsheets for budgeting and planning. It was time to address library automation on a more systematic basis. Certainly, most large universities had automated circulation, and some had brief record card catalogs. Other smaller colleges and universities had begun to acquire first-generation integrated library systems that promised integrated acquisitions, cataloging, on-line catalog, and serials control. The price tag on this was daunting to administrators and librarians alike. Also, the cost of converting collections of 150,000 titles was seen as an obstacle. This was just the kind of challenge I liked.

In my attempt to persuade college administrators to make large capital investments in library automation, it became clear that there was little understanding on their part of the potential value of information technology in higher education. As long as the library was an established part of the institution, with only incremental requests for additional resources, present budgetary and planning processes seemed to work. When a new building was needed, again, another process was put in place. But computers and databases were mysterious to them. I can remember at least one meeting where the president said that computers were to be the ruination of libraries!

Several years of discussion with the library committee moved us to the point that the question was no longer whether or not the library was going to automate, but when. Perhaps the biggest breakthroughs came as the result of members of our Board of Trustees—lawyers, physicians, businessmen—who were seeing that automation was now a part of their own lives.

Developing Leadership Credentials

As this ongoing discussion of library automation continued, I made the decision to enter the Ph.D. program at Drexel University. I was feeling the need for additional skills and for the ultimate academic credential. The Drexel University College of Information Studies offered a program that combined information systems management, design, and evaluation with my developing interest in higher education management. The latter grew out of my involvement with campus planning at Ursinus. I had taken on the role as assistant to the president for institutional research. This allowed me to participate in a faculty/administration/board planning process and to gather, organize, and display more of the information necessary for strategic planning initiatives. It was a unique and useful assignment for me.

My course work at Drexel included core courses and seminars in the College of Information Studies and M.B.A. courses in organizational behavior and management information systems. I also was permitted to take strategic planning and higher education administration courses at the University of Pennsylvania. All of this led to a much broader understanding of organizations and the information systems that support them and allow them to be more effective.

My thesis was a case study of collection overlap among eight small, private liberal arts colleges' library collections. It proved that there was a high degree of diversity among small institutions that have similar degree programs. It suggested that elaborate efforts to coordinate monographic collection development among such institutions would be futile because existing policies and procedures already provided diversity and little overlap in collections.

Was the Ph.D. worth the personal and professional sacrifices? My answer is an unequivocal yes. I learned a broad range of analytical skills. I developed an appreciation for the many perspectives one can take on organizational management and the use of information to facilitate change. No job appeared to be too large for me. Of course, this meant that I found my position as library director at Ursinus too confining. I needed to move on. When I looked at positions at larger libraries, it looked like more of the same. I began to think that perhaps I was no longer a practicing librarian. I needed a larger forum.

MANAGEMENT OF A REGIONAL LIBRARY NETWORK

Thus began a seven-year adventure as executive director of the Pittsburgh Regional Library Center (PRLC). The thrust of this position was to help the 115-plus member libraries to better utilize their scarce resources through cooperative programs, such as OCLC, and to assist them with planning for library automation. While there was a high degree of independence in this position, there was also a Board of Trustees to provide guidance and resources. Again, this built on my library base and used the analytical and presentation skills learned in the graduate Ph.D. program. My experience with, and understanding of, the viewpoints of presidents, provosts, and deans assisted member librarians in preparing, presenting, and finally acquiring the best possible solutions for a wide variety of automation projects.

One of the major accomplishments of this midcareer position, aside from stabilizing the organization, was to undertake a capital campaign: raising over $1 million for a permanent headquarters building to replace a dilapidated rental site. I also learned that being an executive director required an additional set of skills from those required from being a librarian, and I was to learn them on the job. After seven years as executive director, I was ready to move on. I had solicited the board, staff, friends, and family to support a capital campaign. I felt I had done it all. I was feeling lonely at the top. My peer group included the other 12 OCLC-affiliated network directors. While this group was supportive, meetings were infrequent; we were scattered across the nation, and with a high degree of organizational diversity I felt we had little in common. I wanted to be part of a closer group of colleagues with whom I could communicate and grow on a daily basis.

A friend and colleague for a PRLC-member institution was not a librarian but a chief information officer. We worked together in the transformation of a member library and its integration into an information services organization. Through her, a headhunter offered me the opportunity to return to a college campus as the chief information officer, responsible for libraries, media services, academic and administrative computing, and institutional research. Given my background, it was not a difficult decision to relocate to Dowling College as associate provost for information services.

CONCLUSION

A career in librarianship is challenging and ever-changing, whether that career begins and ends in one position or travels a varied path through many different positions. Among the essential skills necessary would be broad-based communications: listening, speaking, writing, and persuasive presentation of ideas. In addition, an understanding of organizational structures and behaviors and the methods for inducing change is essential for success.

Early in my administrative experience, I learned that the most important principle for successfully communicating within an organization is understanding the audience before deciding on how to present the message. For example, if Boards of Trustees, college presidents, and faculty members do not support the developmental needs of libraries, it is not because they dislike libraries or librarians but because they do not understand the message being presented. To be successful in bringing about change, I immerse myself in their world (in their point of view) in order to understand their perspectives and needs. With my audience's perspective in mind, I formulate my presentation with a greater likelihood of success. If I do not succeed the first time, I listen carefully to their concerns and objections and then specifically address those concerns in my next presentation. Remember, giving up does not have to be an option; revising the presentation to meet the needs of the audience is the key to success.

My training in acting and my experience in public speaking have been important to me in my career and have taught me how to impart my enthusiasm for ideas to others. While working at PRLC, I took an OCLC-sponsored course on "counselor selling." This invaluable course taught me the process of selling ideas. The process focuses on the needs of the customer rather than the features of the product and remains virtually the same no matter what you are selling. When selling within your organization, you have the advantage and added responsibility of trust, based on long-term relationships. At Dowling, I continued to find it valuable to check and evaluate where I was in this process of "selling" the use of information technology for teaching and learning.

Also, of great importance in all my leadership positions has been the employment of the techniques for strategic planning learned in my Ph.D. program at Drexel and on the job at Ursinus, PRLC, and Dowling. Strategic planning has been the most important tool for bringing about change, because it provides the opportunity for others to participate in creating a successful future for their organization. While working on PRLC's strategic plan, I also implemented the process of "visioning." This involves having the planning participants describe the desired future that they see for themselves and their organization in five years, before they deal with the strategies for getting there. The excitement of visioning provides a qualitatively enhanced outcome for the strategic planning process and an additional positive tool for the participants. When the process is completed, individuals who participated in developing the shared vision also become part of its implementation and the success of their organization.

The efforts associated with continuous improvement of organizations are always challenging. Effecting change is not easy, and we are most likely to be in favor of it when it affects someone else. Resistance to change is often both an individual and group reaction and one that I constantly challenge in my role as manager. I practice a simple technique that I personally use and also share with new managers who are weary from this palpable resistance. I ask both individuals and groups to try new processes for an agreed-upon period of time, with the understanding that if things do not work out as planned, it is acceptable to revert to the previous methods of operation. This technique seems so simple but frequently is overlooked by managers. After all, what is the worst thing that could happen? It is my experience that once tested, most new processes will remain in place with some modifications. It is also helpful to understand that the procedures for bringing about improvement in small groups and large organizations are to plan, to test, and to modify. It is futile to expect the plans developed "on the drawing board" to magically bring about the expected change and improvement without on-site testing and modification. Improvement is always possible, but not without carefully implementing all preliminary steps along the way.

For librarians, it is important to focus and improve skills not only in technical areas but also in organizational development and advancement. My own career in libraries, library-related organizations, and higher education institutions; my graduate studies in several disciplines; and my personal experiences all suggest that optimism about the future and the belief that things can change for the better have been invaluable to me as my professional career evolves. So, it is my conviction that the personal, organizational, and technical skills that are fundamental to successful librarianship can be enhanced through education and on-the-job experience and can lead librarians to an ever-widening spectrum of challenging career paths.

Chapter 18

The Complex Tapestry of a Library Life

Christie Koontz

INTRODUCTION

The most interesting thing about librarians is that they are not—not usually originally librarians, that is. Library and information studies schools are filled with students choosing librarianship as a second career. This blending, mixing, or cross-training of professions, creating and building upon diverse and disparate talents and skills, provides an eclectic wealth of information proffers within the library field, each with its own complex tapestry.

I, too, experienced a previous work life before earning an M.L.S. in 1981 and a Ph.D. in 1990. Before? I was a journalist, public relations specialist, and advertising whiz. Who would have "thunk it," as they say. I currently work as research faculty in a center at Florida State University that develops applications for GIS, geographic information system software. All my life, I have worked within the information industry, of which the library is an important and usually unacknowledged member. It was an unplanned journey, by and large, based largely on my own need to participate in life and facilitate communications. May I tell you my story? Come with me now to the tiny, cane-backed chair in my father's workshop. I am the age of nine.

HOW MY TAPESTRY BEGAN

It is summer. Hot sweat drips down my nose onto paper rolled in an antique typewriter. I am typing the "Nosey News" with two fingers. It is our just-first-published neighborhood newspaper. My sister, Dottie, and I are coeditors. As I recall, I bullied her into this position, with great promises of large sums of money by summer's end. This successful coercing was a great achievement, as Dottie is my older sister. Each week we would canvass the neighborhood for news, I with pad and pen and Dottie with wallet. Donations of any amount were accepted prior to, or on the day of, publication of the "Nosey News."

Neighborhood news was captured in small, uneven, hand-drawn squares of purple mimeograph ink. My father's hand-cranked machine gave the "Nosey News" the main things it needed to be a real newspaper besides news—ink and form. The news included new dogs and deaths of dogs, new babies and birthdays, tree plantings and starts of school, and other cyclical events. By the end of the summer, our treasury was $19.92. We were publishers of a successful newspaper. My sister was pleased.

AGES 9 TO 13—AN ASPIRING INFORMATION GATHERER

From that childhood experience came inspired gathering of information for others. All my early life and adult life are devoted in one way or another to this task, personally and professionally. From the 9th to the 12th grade, I wrote a newspaper column for the high school paper. My father designed the mastheads. I, for all intents and purposes, was in my mind's eye a journalist.

Coincidentally, I entered another communications vehicle in the ninth grade. I began volunteering in the school library. I was even a member of the library club. From early childhood, my mother always took us to the library on Saturdays. I simply could not imagine a life without a library, out of school or in school, so I committed myself to ensuring the library was vital and top-notch. I developed the library habit.

Also, I read everything I could find early on, from the funny papers on Sunday to novels by age 12, even though I had not a clue what the adult characters were up to. I read in the morning before going to school by placing my foot and toes over the fold of the book to keep it open and flat. I developed the reading habit, and I was fortunate. Research indicates that if the reading or library habit is not developed as a child, it is likely never developed. (Why are juvenile book budgets so low?)

MY FIRST JOB (IS ALSO) MY FIRST LIBRARY JOB

During the spring of the ninth grade a family crisis occurred that was to redirect my life permanently, although I would not realize it until 15 years later. Standing in the kitchen of our 1940s house, by the cracked burgundy tile sink, with soft sunlight pouring over his shoulder, my father gathered us around to announce that he had lost his job. He was fired because he was too old. He was only 54.

It was the first time I saw my father cry. I was moved to get a job and help out.

I am not sure why I chose the library as a possible employer. Perhaps for me the library was "friendly." I walked the three blocks to the public library branch near my high school. I headed toward the check-out desk that I had approached with armloads of books ever since I was 7. Today, at age 15, I carried no books, only a request.

Upon hearing I wanted a job, the clerk scanned me, asking if I was 16. "You must be sixteen to work here, no exceptions," she firmly stated. I quickly nodded, yes, I was 16. Even though I was actually 15, I figured that if my father got fired because he was too old, I sure wanted to be hired because I was old enough.

Perhaps because they knew me as a user over the years, because a student assistant recently left, or because I looked desperate—or maybe I will never know for sure—I got the job. I worked there six weeks after school before I announced to my parents that I had a job. I stood by the same cracked burgundy tile counter to tell my father and mother. Looking astounded and partially as if they had failed me, they also looked confused and pleased at the same time. My father looked over my head to my mother, with an agreeing "Why not"— the deal stayed done.

FORGING LIFELONG SKILLS: DURING THE
TEENAGE YEARS

I worked at the branch library after school and on Saturdays halfway through the 12th grade. Scooting around on a wheeled stool, I read and shelved every children's picture book. I thumbed larger juvenile fiction and nonfiction books before shelving. I read and brought home books that my father and I read at the same time. The library was my ticket to the outside world, financially and fancifully. As for the purpose to which the dollar per hour was put? Mostly on my back—clothing. My father got a job within the year at the county courthouse, where he stayed way beyond retirement time, just enjoying the security of it all.

As I mentioned earlier, I also wrote for the school newspaper during those years, 9th through 12th grade. I wrote a clothes column in the 9th grade (who was wearing saddle oxfords without socks?) and mainly focused on individual student profiles in the other years. Having a job and money and a forum for your thoughts and observations matures a young person rather quickly. Both opportunities forged lifelong skills of being able to get a job, keep a job, and develop the self-confidence to communicate in print. After leaving the library job in my senior year, it would be almost 13 more years before I would think of working in a library. Yet the experience of those years was like a gem tucked deep in dark walls of a cave. One day I would mine it.

COLLEGE AND THE MINUSCULE GRADE POINT AVERAGE: THE MAKING OF AN ADULT

I went off to college, discovered dating and fun, after predominately working in high school, and promptly landed back home at the end of my sophomore year with a disappointing, minuscule grade point average. I became employed at city hall, near my father's office in the courthouse. I repaired the damaged grades at a local junior college and earned my A.A. degree. I worked in payroll. My job was to post pay raises, which turned out to be more than my pay! I hungered for something more in the communications area and was quickly hired in the city public relations office. They were probably surprised a 19-year-old could write.

RIDING MAGIC CARPET TAPESTRIES MADE OF STEEL

As I started into my junior year at a local private college, a fellow employee landed a job on a southbound Amtrak train from New York to Miami as a public relations representative. I quickly followed suit and literally jumped on the train and was employed. Within three months I left the onboard position to begin touring the country, appearing on television and radio shows supporting the public relations effort of the new company. My travels within the communications industry began to diversify and grow.

After four years with Amtrak, the mid-1970s brought a recession and government cutbacks. The public relations activities were seen as extraneous to running the train and were eliminated. I was transferred to an Oakland, California, train yard as a general supervisor. There was not much ostensibly for a communications-type to do in a train yard. So in nine months I resigned.

FROM PUBLIC RELATIONS TO ADVERTISING TO PUBLIC RELATIONS TO AN ADVERTISING DEGREE

I then sought work in San Francisco and landed a job at an ad agency as their in-house photographer. It took over 100 interviews to land a job, as well as flexibility. I stayed six months, was homesick, and consequently moved back to Florida to assist a childhood friend with her husband's gubernatorial race.

One of his campaign planks was to save Florida's historic old capitol building, circa 1845, which was about to be razed and replaced with a 27-story building. I ended up being the chairman of the successful campaign. My skills, planted in fertile ground in childhood, continued to grow. After our candidate lost in the primary, I returned to school to finish my college degree, majoring in advertising, at age 28.

THE THIRTIETH YEAR: I THINK OF WORKING IN A LIBRARY

So I majored in advertising and minored in English and sold and wrote radio advertising copy to survive. While minoring in English, I took a children's literature class from a library professor, Dr. Mary Alice Hunt (who would end up being my major professor and lifelong friend). I was enthusiastic and knew every book discussed. Memories whirled me back through time, and in each class I was atop the little stool, shelving and reading children's books. The magic of the library—all but forgotten—surrounded me. At the end of the semester, she said, ''We really need people like you, enthusiastic and a communicator in the library field, to promote and publicize libraries. I think I can help get you a scholarship.'' And she did.

During the next months, I not only continued to participate in book learning but continued to become an adult, developing and strengthening my values. For example, when I read that Florida legislators were ''stealing'' furnishings out of the old capitol, which by then was being restored, I filed a lawsuit against them! My parents were terrified something dreadful would happen to me, but the people of Florida cheered me on. While I eventually lost the lawsuit, in the interim, due to my utilizing the media to keep the issue before the public eye, many lawmakers gave their historic furniture back. I was learning that work skills can be used in the civic and volunteer arena.

Throughout my library studies, I felt a bit out of place, a communications and public relations (PR) type amid a flock of future librarians. We learned collection development, intellectual freedom, technical services, and ''yipes'' cataloging. I was so out of touch with what the cataloging teacher wanted that when the first test came back with an F, I thought it meant ''fine!'' I simply could not believe that it made that much difference how many spaces from the left the catalog description was typed. Anyway, I managed to graduate with my master's in library and information science. I immediately went to work as the assistant director of a southwestern Georgia regional library. There, the communications field came full circle for me. All aspects of communications were employed in that little regional library.

MAY THE CIRCLE OF COMMUNICATIONS BE UNBROKEN

I created a radio show and wrote a weekly newspaper column (called ''Off the Shelf''), weekly public service announcements, and posters regarding events in storefronts in the tricounty area. Serving also as a children's librarian, I became a storyteller and volunteer in classrooms and at festivals ever since, sharing literary tales—from the library—from around the world. I developed programming for this largely black American community. We wrote grants for film festivals and even wrote one to the National Endowment to televise the history of the area the library served. The documentary is still circulating in Georgia schoolrooms. It was exhilarating to utilize all my skills.

OH, NO: I, THE PR FLACK, AM GOING TO GET A PH.D.?

Around this time, I married a budding Ph.D. in economics. Within one year we were expecting my now 13-year-old daughter, Katelyn. I quit my Bainbridge position and stayed home with her for one year. Observing the value of a Ph.D., I decided to return to school and develop research skills so I could help public libraries in broader and more encompassing ways.

Another child, Thomas, now 11, was born amid my oral exams. From my advertising and public relations life was born a real desire to learn about marketing, the broader umbrella covering the two. In our field, marketing is still misunderstood and thought of as publicity, which is a minor component of it. Marketing is a planning tool that identifies who your users and potential users are and what they want and need.

So I minored in nonprofit marketing in the business school at Florida State University. This provided me with a future that offers special work and research opportunities within and outside the library field. I highly recommend cross-training whenever possible. The marketing professor, Dr. Persis Rockwood, who was my mentor, researched shopping center locations and asked me the simple question, "Had anyone studied library location?" The answer, by and large, was no.

THE TOPIC: WHERE AND HOW SHOULD LIBRARIES BE LOCATED?

So I studied 100 public library markets nationwide and developed a modeling technique to locate library facilities. A book based upon my dissertation appeared in 1997, the only one of its kind. It is a handbook for library managers—information and research (weaponry, if you will)—to facilitate the siting and location process. Who would have "thunk" it possible for me to be a book author? Perhaps the readers of the "Nosey News"?

THE QUESTION: DO PEOPLE OF DIFFERENT DEMOGRAPHICS USE THE LIBRARY DIFFERENTLY?

Interestingly and quite by accident, during my dissertation research, as I reviewed the library use and demographics of these markets, I identified 28 that were majority–minority markets. I discovered that use was different in these markets, such as higher rates of in-library use and program attendance, sometimes not counted. Yet because circulation was low, they often looked underused. I tucked that gem away, and in 1992 I applied for, and won, the top American Library Association research award, Carroll Baber Grant, to substantiate this finding. Today, in 1997, building upon my previous research, our center recently received a two-and-a-half-year, half-million-dollar federal grant to continue assessing library use in these vulnerable markets nationwide. We will develop more accurate measures of use, substantiating use so these libraries stay open and are funded at the levels they deserve.

The libraries serve people in our communities who are offered no other information access. As library professionals, we must be advocates for those who have none. We must always remind people there does not have to be a public library. There is no legal mandate. Only advocacy will keep it as a vital resource in communities across America.

DO NOT LOOK OVER YOUR SHOULDER DURING THE RACE

I think back on these choices, decisions, and crossroads, 8 years after earning my Ph.D. in 1990, and landing my current nonlibrary job two days later. If anyone had suggested to me while I was riding Amtrak's rails (with no college degree) that I would be a published and productive Ph.D. within 15 years, I probably would have fallen off the track! So it perhaps is best we do not know the future, or there will be none?

USING YOUR "LIFELONG SKILLS": PRO BONO

In the 1990s I continue to use my communications skills outside work, coupled with the impassioned principle of you-are-your-brother-and-sister's keeper that my parents saddled us with, early on. Successfully, I wrote over $1 million worth of grants for our local homeless shelter, as well as worked diligently within political circles as an advocate for homeless people. Because of this, I was nominated to run with the Olympic torch when it passed through my town on its way to the summer games in Atlanta last summer. It was a thrill and an honor. It would certainly have made front page on the "Nosey News."

Also for the past two years, I have written a column on the local paper's editorial page on various and sundry issues. The only thing missing is my father's hand-drawn masthead. He died in 1989. His hand-carved furniture surrounds me as well as my mother's hand-sewn linens and clothes. Their hands, like mine, were always busy. My mother now lives in a nearby nursing home. The little cane-backed chair that I sat in to type my first newspaper stories, from my father's garage, is now the chair my daughter sits upon to eat dinner each night—and so it goes.

EACH INDIVIDUAL TAPESTRY: "WOVEN . . . BITS OF BLUE AND GOLD"

So what is the point of my story that I asked you to listen to? Probably that each event and learning situation, whether it be by the book or by the blow—

or hardship, if you will—can be a building block. In the library profession especially, we grow and strengthen as a profession, with personnel who are individually diverse, with complex tapestries. These tapestries offer acceptance as well as complement the diversity of our multicolored users and potential users we seek. The most interesting thing about library users and future users is that they are us, and we are "them," each with our own little cane-backed chair that we pass along and grow too big for yet remain inspired by, as we continue to weave our complex tapestries.

Part VI

Bibliographic Essay

Chapter 19

Leadership in Librarianship

Rashelle S. Karp and Cindy Murdock

INTRODUCTION

As one prepares a bibliographic essay on the topic of leadership in librarianship, one is immediately struck by the revelation that "leadership" is not used as a subject heading in the major index to the literature of librarianship, *Library Literature* (Gertzog 1989). Therefore, a search for library literature about leadership must tediously pick through thousands of citations under the subject headings of "administration," "librarianship," "organizational behavior," "personnel," and specific types of administration (for example, "TQM"). In contrast, leadership *is* a subject heading in the major indexes for other professions, such as accounting and nursing.

Fortunately, searches in other primary indexes (including Proquest and ERIC) can be accomplished using leadership as a subject heading. This points out a problem that may be larger than just an access issue. Leadership as a concept in the profession of librarianship seems not to be concretely acknowledged as a legitimate entity that merits clearly identified discussion and definition.

Although individual authors and theoreticians present differing and sometimes unique perspectives on the nature of leadership, a common thread through all of the literature is the separation of leadership and management (Birdsall 1990) as different administrative forms. Management is characterized in the literature as being primarily concerned with efficiency (Bone 1981), outputs (Tees 1984), and the bottom line (Mader 1996); leadership is characterized as being vision-oriented (Taylor 1995). Similarly, managers are described as people who "fight fires" (Mackey and Mackey 1992); leaders are described as people who "turn challenging opportunities into remarkable successes" (DiMattia 1990, 22), who can plan to avoid crisis management (McClure 1980), and who manage vision rather than their jobs (Hale 1994). Other characteristics that differentiate leaders from managers include a leader's desire to lead (Kotter 1988), perceptions by others that a person is a leader (Gertzog 1992; Hersey 1984), high energy levels (Anonymous 1990; Meyer 1989), and the ability of leaders to bring their own talents to a situation rather than relying on other people's skills (Kiely 1993).

Diversity of opinion regarding leadership seems to occur most often when writers discuss the components of leadership, or "what makes a leader" (Fiedler 1967; Mitchell 1988). The essay that follows cites literature on this topic from the professions of librarianship, education, and business; the focus is on the application, rather than theory, of leadership.

CHARACTERISTICS OF LEADERS

The literature indicates that effective leadership requires direction (having a clear concept of goals to be accomplished) and force (having the vigor, dynamism, competence, and inspiration to accomplish goals) (Capps 1979). In order to achieve, it is suggested that effective leaders are facilitators (Woodrum 1989), stewards of vision (Phipps 1993), and risk takers (Terrey 1986; Heller 1989; Sweeney 1994). They are also characterized as charismatic (Sayles 1979; Willner 1984), political (Keegan 1988; White 1990), consultative (Bakewell 1993), confident (Burrow 1978), sincere (Jaycox 1996), intuitive (Totten and Keys 1994), assertive and self-aware (Albritton and Shaughnessy 1990), self-confident (Major 1993), flexible (Hill 1990) but manipulative (Tucker 1981; White 1990) and persuasive (Gardner 1989), self-disciplined (Beck and Hillmar 1990), controversial (Gertzog 1989, 1990), innovative, creative (Peters 1987; Sheldon 1991), supportive (Afolabi 1993), dynamic (Barter 1994), good at time management (Gothberg 1991), and imbued with infectious optimism (Peters and Austin 1985).

Additionally, the literature provides many suggestions regarding the ways in which effective leaders operate. Among these, it is suggested that effective leaders:

- have a talent for ambiguity (Cleveland 1985) and are able to exercise self-control (McConkey 1989)

- work hard without concern for personal gain (Baker 1995)

- empower others (Sullivan 1992; Bailey 1992) but exercise their own power wisely (Bethel 1989; Modic 1987) as they translate intent into reality (Bennis and Nanus 1985)

- excite potential funding sources (Gray 1995), motivate employees to excel (Geary 1990; Stodgill 1974; Riggs 1982), and are enthusiastic (Line 1992)

- create and communicate vision (Hanson 1988; Bennis 1989; Recardo 1995; Secor 1995), clarify values (Hitt 1988), and never lose sight of the overall library mission of continually improving services (Aluri and Reichel 1994) and the overall direction of the institution (Riggs 1993)

- have earned (Handy 1993) the loyalty (Braham 1987; Modic 1987), support (Lawson and Dorrell 1992), and trust of their staff (Bennis 1990; Sheldon 1992)

- have good communication skills and both technical and professional competence (Lester 1990; Sheldon 1991)

- engage in lifelong learning (Crosby 1990)

- are willing to share power (Maccoby 1981)

- are able to show vulnerability and provide informal leadership (Srinath 1993) while still maintaining the "psychic distance required for leadership" (McCombs 1992, 220)

- have the ability to make information-based (Euster 1989a) decisions in a timely and orderly manner (Newman, Dibartolo, and Wells 1990; Korda 1975)

- are committed to quality improvement (Senge 1990; Riggs 1993) and interdisciplinary collaboration (Gitlin, Lyons, and Kolodner 1994)

- are able to tailor their behaviors to specific situations (Blake and Mouton 1985; Schriesheim, Tolliver, and Gehling 1990) and environmental shifts (Marz and Sims 1989)

- nurture the personal development of their staffs (Townley 1989), stimulate cultural change (Anonymous 1994), deal with interpersonal conflict in nonjudgmental and non-punitive ways (Blome 1983), and value people (Creth 1988)

- are able to develop policy and plan ahead (Webber 1971)

- are able to delegate (Scanlan 1990)

- are able to direct the efforts of individuals toward a common goal (Drucker 1954)

- are team builders (Serpa 1991; Bensimon and Neumann 1993; Owen 1996)

- model desired behaviors and values (Kouzes and Posner 1987)

- are able to be concerned with both the larger picture and minutiae (Peters and Waterman 1982)

- are able to frame experience in a way that provides a basis for action (Smircich and Morgan 1982)

LEARNING TO LEAD

The literature on this topic runs the gamut from those who steadfastly maintain that while managers can be chosen, leaders cannot be made out of non-leaders (White 1987; Caulkin 1993), to those who firmly emphasize that leadership can be learned (Drucker 1996). Some even opine that to become a leader, all one has to do is have an image of oneself as a leader (DiMattia 1990). Mentoring is touted by some as an effective venue for teaching leaders to manage conflict and disagreement (Burruss-Ballard 1990) and for teaching them to articulate vision (Chatman 1992); others see mentoring as counterproductive and instead recommend that advocacy is better since it breaks down systemic barriers to equity for those not being mentored (Harris 1993). Leadership competencies that some believe can be learned include managerial competency, analytical competency, integrative competency, collaborative competency, and organizational know-how (Donnelly and Kezsbom 1994). Although it is stressed that all librarians should have leadership training (Stoffle, Renaud, and Veldof 1996), very few leadership institutes for librarians can be found in the literature, but two often mentioned are Ohio's Library Leadership 2000 Institute (Carterette 1994; Long 1995) and the Snowbird Leadership Institute (Miller 1992; Summers and Summers 1991). Among other things, these institutes focus on the types of knowledge that a leader should have, including knowledge of employees, psychology, systems, money, products and services, customers, the marketplace, the business environment, competition, enterprise, and the theory of knowledge. Skills that leaders should obtain are also covered, including skills for self-management, management of other people, management and control skills, and the ability to manage relationships outside the organization (Constable 1989; Deming 1986).

VALUE SYSTEM

It is often pointed out that a significant differentiating factor between managers and leaders is a leader's strong personal value or belief system (Cichy and Schmidgall 1996). The literature seems to agree that leaders are motivated by the societal value of their work (Sheldon 1992) and of libraries (Cino 1995). It is also pointed out that leaders have ambition to "make a difference" rather than to be the "head of something" (Wedgeworth 1989), that they strive to meet the work-related needs of others rather than their own needs (Bechtel 1993), and that they replace professional loyalty (commitment to self-serving professional interests) with institutional loyalty (loyalty to society) (McClure 1980). Leaders are also characterized as having a value system that allows them to look at how the parts of a system contribute to the parent institution's goals (Blagden 1975), "the total society of which that organization is a part" (Conger 1992, 115), and, in the case of libraries, to envision a library's unique contribution to society at large (Drucker 1976). In fact, it is even suggested that not only is a leader's value system an internal motivator, but it actually imbues the entire organization with values (Kaufman 1993) and organizational integrity (Covey and Gulledge 1992).

LEADERSHIP STYLES

The ways in which leaders behave are well described in the literature. Effective leadership is linked to administrative modeling (Maccoby 1981), various personality patterns (Euster 1989b), and universal differences in style (Moran 1992). These include the following:

- distributed leadership, in which the complexity of an organization precludes reliance on just one leader (Euster 1990), and everyone in the institution exercises "leadership-like initiative and responsibility" (Gardner 1990, xiii)

- shared leadership, during which different people in an organization fill different leadership roles at different times (Barron 1995) and in which people take responsibility for the results of their actions (Belasco and Stayer 1994)

- input-oriented (Nawe 1992) or feedback-oriented (Wright 1988) leadership, especially among women, who have been shown to be perceived as more attentive to detail than are men (Barron 1996)

- mentoring-oriented leadership, in which the leaders are effective because they mentor their colleagues (Burgin and Hansel 1990a; Hubbard 1992), encourage participation from the most timid staff members (Burgin and Hansel 1990c), actively listen to staff members (Burgin and Hansel 1990b), and create an environment where vision is shared (Iannuzzi 1992) and where the organization is transformational rather than static (Bass 1985; Riggs 1990; Tichy and Rich, 1984)

- credit-oriented leadership, in which delegated authority results in credit for a job well done going to the person who did it (Burgin and Hansel 1991a; Carr 1994°onymous 1995), and in which walk-throughs of the library result in credit going to people who do the front-line work (Burgin and Hansel 1991b; Riggs 1990)

- participative management (Broughton 1993; Lawson et al. 1993) and consensus-building leadership (Merchant 1971), in which teamwork is emphasized (Burgin and Hansel 1991c), the subordinate relationship between the director and librarians is de-emphasized (Hofstede 1983; Lubans 1988), partnership is emphasized (May and Kruger 1990), and the interdisciplinary nature of learning is more important than rules (Redfern 1980) and departmentalized patterns within the library (McAnally and Downs 1973)

- "acknowledge-create-empower" leadership (Evered and Selman 1989), in which a leader empowers people to translate vision into reality (Bennis and Nanus 1985) and avoids a "control-order-prescriptive" approach to management (Sullivan 1991)

- ensemble leadership, in which team management is replaced by a management style that puts the person "most able to hold it all together" in the leadership role (Burgin and Hansel 1992, 56)

- leadership by objectives, through which a leader helps people reach their own goals (Fields 1974) and through which a leader helps to motivate employees (Marcum 1995) and satisfy employee motives (Burns 1978)

- leadership for "learning organizations" (Worrell 1995), in which leadership focuses on making organizational changes as problems are corrected (Argyris and Schön 1978), with little or no surprise to employees (Townsend and Gebhardt 1988). This type of leadership produces an organization that becomes skilled at "modifying its behavior to reflect new knowledge and insights" (Garvin 1993, 78)

- TQM (Total Quality Management) leadership (O'Neill 1994; Carson et al. 1995; Evans 1995), in which there is an emphasis on staff participation in decision making (Butcher 1995), benchmarking to define standards for leadership (Peischl 1995), and self-evaluation management for employees (George 1995; Lubans and Gordon 1995)

CONCLUSION

It would seem that the quality of leadership is born in an individual's inherent personality and then refined by that individual's life experiences, behavioral choices, attitudinal proclivities, and core values. Thus, leadership is an elusive entity—impossible to define in abstraction but recognizable when it is modeled in reality.

Is leadership teachable? Perhaps not. It may be that leadership, like good intuition, is an acquired ability but not one that can be purposefully taught. The practice of leadership, however it is manifested, is an unrelentingly unpredictable series of steps and missteps through a constantly changing landscape of people, politics, and economies of scale. It is both enervating and energizing; it builds and destroys confidence and self-esteem, often as a result of the same decision. But regardless of its practicable form and its personal and institutional impact, in today's world, leadership is regarded as the most critical component of an effective organization (Paton and Jelking 1994) that has the ability to change (Yearout 1996). Libraries, as organizations, are not exempt from the necessity of leadership but are very much in need of it due to the demands of orchestrating the large variety of services that a library provides. Leadership in libraries begins with people who know how to take the best of yesterday and carry it into tomorrow (Kanter 1983). It is enhanced by people who are flexible, open, decisive, able to tolerate uncertainty, loyal to their institution, and caring toward human beings (Veaner 1990). Leadership is complete when a clear vision becomes the driving force for an individual's actions.

REFERENCES

Afolabi, Michael. 1993. "Challenge and Support Concepts and Their Application to Library Management." *Library Management* 14(6): 9–12.

Albritton, Rosie L. and Thomas W. Shaughnessy. 1990. *Developing Leadership Skills: A Sourcebook for Librarians.* Englewood, CO: Libraries Unlimited.

Aluri, Rao and Mary Reichel. 1994. "Performance Evaluation: A Deadly Disease?" *Journal of Academic Librarianship* 20(3) (July): 145–155.

Anonymous. 1990. "Leadership Qualities of Executive Chiefs." *Supervision* 51(11) (November): 19–20.

———. 1994. "The Importance of Leadership." *Library Management* 15(5): 30–32.

———. 1995. "Leadership Qualities." *American Printer* 216(2) (July): 14.

Argyris, Chris and Donald A. Schön. 1978. *Organizational Learning: A Theory of Action Perspective.* Reading, MA: Addison-Wesley.

Bailey, Martha J. 1992. "Leadership Characteristics of Assistant/Associate Directors." *Journal of Library Administration* 17(3): 43–54.

Baker, Shirley K. 1995. "Leading from below: Or, Risking Getting Fired." *Library Administration and Management* 9(4) (Fall): 238–240.

Bakewell, Ken. 1993. "Motivation of Library Staff." *Library Management* 14(5): 18–19.

Barron, Daniel D. 1995. "Changing our Guidelines in Changing Times (Part II)." *School Library Media Activities Monthly* 12(4) (December): 48–50.

———. 1996. "Mostly Women and Leadership." *School Library Media Activities Monthly* 12 (July): 47–49.

Barter, Richard F., Jr. 1994. "In Search of Excellence in Libraries: The Management Writings of Tom Peters and Their Implications for Library and Information Services." *Library Management* 15(8): 4–15.

Bass, B. 1985. *Leadership and Performance beyond Expectations.* New York: Free Press.

Bechtel, Joan M. 1993. "Leadership Lessons Learned from Managing and Being Managed." *Journal of Academic Librarianship* 18(6) (January): 352–357.

Beck, Arthur C. and Ellis D. Hillmar. 1990. "Overcoming Internal Barriers to Success." In Rosie L. Albritton and Thomas W. Shaughnessy, eds., *Developing Leadership Skills: A Sourcebook for Librarians.* Englewood, CO: Libraries Unlimited, pp. 49–56.

Belasco, James A. and Ralph C. Stayer. 1994. "Why Empowerment Doesn't Empower: The Bankruptcy of Current Paradigms." *Business Horizons* 37(2) (March/April): 29–41.

Bennis, Warren. 1989. *On Becoming a Leader.* Reading, MA: Addison-Wesley.

———. 1990. "The Y Competencies of Leadership." In Rosie L. Albritton and Thomas W. Shaughnessy, eds., *Developing Leadership Skills: A Sourcebook for Librarians.* Englewood, CO: Libraries Unlimited, pp. 21–27.

Bennis, Warren and Burt Nanus. 1985. *Leaders: The Strategies for Taking Charge.* New York: Harper and Row.

Bensimon, Estela Marie and Anna Neumann. 1993. *Redesigning Collegiate Leadership: Teams and Teamwork in Higher Education.* Baltimore: Johns Hopkins University Press, p. 146.

Bethel, Sheila Murray. 1989. "Qualities of Leadership." *Executive Excellence* 6(12) (December): 9–10.

Birdsall, William F. 1990. "The Library Manager as Therapist." *Journal of Academic Librarianship* (16)4 (September): 209–212.

Blagden, J. F. 1975. "Communication: A Key Library Management Problem." *Aslib Proceedings* 27 (August): 319–326.

Blake, R. R. and J. S. Mouton. 1985. *The Managerial Grid III: The Key to Leadership Excellence.* Houston, TX: Gulf.

Blome, A. C. 1983. "Conflict: Friend or Foe." *Interface* 5 (Winter): 4–5.

Bone, L. E. 1981. "Leadership Connection." *Library Journal* 106 (November 1): 2091–2093.

Braham, James. 1987. "Dying Loyalty." *Industry Week* 233(16) (June): 16–17.

Broughton, Diane. 1993. "When Being Nice Is Not Enough." *Library Management* 14(6): 21–23.

Burgin, Robert and Patty Hansel. 1990a. "Library Management: A Dialogue." *Wilson Library Bulletin* 64(5) (January): 62–63.

———. 1990b. "Library Management: A Dialogue." *Wilson Library Bulletin* 64(7) (March): 81–82+.

———. 1990c. "Tyranny of the Timid." *Wilson Library Bulletin* 64(9) (May): 77–78.

———. 1991a. "Library Management: A Dialogue." *Wilson Library Bulletin* 65(5) (January): 64–67.

————. 1991b. "Library Management: A Dialogue—Participative Management." *Wilson Library Bulletin* 65(7) (March): 77–79.

————. 1991c. "Library Management: A Dialogue." *Wilson Library Bulletin* 65(9) (May): 84–87.

————. 1992. "Library Management: A Dialogue." *Wilson Library Bulletin* 66(7) (March): 54–59.

Burns, James MacGregor. 1978. *Leadership*. New York: Harper & Row.

Burrow, Martha G. 1978. *Developing Women Managers: What Needs to Be Done?* New York: AMACOM.

Burruss-Ballard, Marsha A. 1990. "Mentoring for Leadership." In Rosie L. Albritton and Thomas W. Shaughnessy, eds., *Developing Leadership Skills: A Source Book for Librarians*. Englewood, CO: Libraries Unlimited, pp. 189–197.

Butcher, Karyle. 1995. "TQM—Will It Work in Your Library?" In *Total Quality Management in Academic Libraries: Initial Implementation Efforts. Proceedings from the International Conference on TQM and Academic Libraries*. Washington, DC, April 20–22, 1994.

Capps, R. 1979. "Challenge of Leadership and Professional Librarians." *Kentucky Library Association Bulletin* 43 (Spring): 3–7.

Carr, J. T. 1994. "Learning to Walk the Leadership Talk?" *Healthcare Executive* 9(2) (March/April): 16–17.

Carson, Paula Phillips et al. 1995. *The Library Manager's Deskbook: 102 Expert Solutions to 101 Common Dilemmas*. Chicago: ALA.

Carterette, Pat. 1994. "Library Leadership 2000: Quilting a Vision for Ohio Libraries." *Wilson Library Bulletin* 68(10) (June): 39–41, 143.

Caulkin, Simon. 1993. "The Lust for Leadership." *Management Today* (November): 38–43.

Chatman, Elfreda A. 1992. "The Role of Mentorship in Shaping Public Library Leaders." *Library Trends* 40(3) (Winter): 492–512.

Cichy, Ronald F. and Raymond S. Schmidgall. 1996. "Leadership Qualities of Financial Executives in the U.S. Lodging Industry." *Cornell Hotel & Restaurant Administration Quarterly* 37(2) (April): 56–62.

Cino, Catherine. 1995. "A Time of Change: The Need for Leadership in Librarianship." *Feliciter* 41 (September): 20–27.

Cleveland, Harlan. 1985. *The Knowledge Executive: Leadership in an Information Society*. New York: E. P. Dutton.

Conger, Jay. 1992. *Learning to Lead: The Art of Transforming Managers into Leaders*. San Francisco: Jossey-Bass, p. 115.

Constable, John. 1989. "What Makes a Good Manager?" *State Librarian* 37 (March): 4–8.

Covey, Stephen R. and Keith A. Gulledge. 1992. "Principle-Centered Leadership." *Journal for Quality & Participation* 15(4) (July/August): 70–78.

Creth, Sheila D. 1988. "Organizational Leadership: Challenges within the Library." In Anne Woodsworth and Barbara von Walilde, eds., *Leadership for Research Libraries*. Metuchen, NJ: Scarecrow Press.

Crosby, Philip B. 1990. *Leading: The Art of Becoming an Executive*. New York: McGraw-Hill.

Deming, W. Edwards. 1986. *Out of the Crisis*. Cambridge, MA: Center for Advanced Engineering Study, Massachusetts Institute of Technology.

DiMattia, Susan S. 1990. "Leadership Can Be Learned." *PNLA Q* 54 (Summer): 20–22.

Donnelly, Richard G. and Deborah S. Kezsbom. 1994. "Overcoming the Responsibility-Authority Gap: An Investigation of Effective Project Team Leadership for a New Decade." *Cost Engineering* 36(5) (May): 33–41.

Drucker, Peter. 1954. *The Practice of Management.* New York: Harper & Brothers.

———. 1976. "Managing the Public Service Institution." *College & Research Libraries* 37 (January): 4–14.

———. 1996. *The Leader of the Future: New Visions, Strategies, Practices for the Next Era.* San Francisco: Jossey-Bass.

Euster, Joanne R. 1989a. "Creativity & Leadership." *Journal of Library Administration* 10(2/3): 27–38.

———. 1989b. "The Qualities of Leadership." In A. Gertzog and J. Varlejs, eds., *Leadership in the Library/Information Profession.* Jefferson, NC: McFarland.

———. 1990. "The New Hierarchy: Where's the Boss?" *Library Journal* 115(8) (May 1): 40–44.

Evans, Anaclare F. 1995. "Total Quality Management in Higher Education and Libraries: A Selective Annotated Bibliography." In *Total Quality Management in Academic Libraries: Initial Implementation Efforts. Proceedings from the International Conference on TQM and Academic Libraries.* Washington, DC, April 20–22, 1994.

Evered, Roger D. and James C. Selman. 1989. "Coaching and the Art of Management." *Organizational Dynamics* (Autumn): 18.

Fiedler, F. 1967. *A Theory of Leadership Effectiveness.* New York: McGraw-Hill.

Fields, D. C. 1974. "Library Management by Objectives: The Humane Way." *College & Research Libraries* 35 (September): 344–349.

Gardner, John. 1990. *On Leadership.* New York: Free Press.

Gardner, J. W. 1989. "Leadership." *Library Administration and Management* 3 (Winter): 10–11.

Garvin, David A. 1993. "Building a Learning Organization." *Harvard Business Review* 71 (July–August): 787.

Geary, David L. 1990. "Are You a Leader or a Manager?" *Public Relations Journal* 46(8) (August): 16.

George, Verna E. 1995. "Performance Appraisal in an Academic Library: A Case Study." In *Total Quality Management in Academic Libraries: Initial Implementation Efforts. Proceedings from the International Conference on TQM and Academic Libraries.* Washington, DC, April 20–22, 1994.

Gertzog, A. and J. Varlejs, eds. 1989. *Leadership in the Library/Information Profession.* Jefferson, NC: McFarland.

———. 1989. "Perceptions of Leadership." In A. Gertzog and J. Varlejs, eds., *Leadership in the Library/Information Profession.* Jefferson, NC: McFarland.

———. 1990. "Library Leaders: Who and Why?" *Library Journal* 115(12) (July): 45–51.

———. 1992. "Leadership in Librarianship." *Library Trends* 40(3) (Winter): 402–430.

Gitlin, Laura, Kevin J. Lyons, and Ellen Kolodner. 1994. "A Model to Build Collaborative Research or Education Teams of Health Professionals in Gerontology." *Educational Gerontology* 20: 15–34.

Gothberg, Helen M. 1991. "Time Management in Public Libraries: A Study of Public Libraries." *Public Libraries* 30(6) (November–December): 350–357.

Gray, Carolyn M. 1995. "Systems Thinking in Information Service Delivery." *Journal of Library Administration* 20(3): 25–43.

Hale, Kaycee. "1994. 'LV' = Leadership Victory." In Miriam Drake and James M. Matarazzo, eds., *Information for Management: A Handbook*. Washington, DC: Special Library Association.

Handy, Charles. 1993. "When Companies Are Condominiums." *Director* 47(1) (August): 11.

Hanson, Charles D. 1988. "The Language of Library Leadership: Effective Communication." Paper presented at the Library Administration and Management Association President's Program at the Annual Convention of the American Library Association, New Orleans, LA, July 10.

Harris, Roma M. 1993. "The Mentoring Trap." *Library Journal* 118(17) (October 15): 37–39.

Heller, Robert. 1989. *The Decision-Makers: The Men & the Million Dollar Moves behind Today's Great Corporate Success Stories*. New York: Truman Talley/E. P. Dutton.

Hersey, Paul. 1984. *The Situational Leader*. New York: Warner.

Hill, Norman. 1990. "Self-Esteem: The Key to Effective Leadership." In Rosie L. Albritton and Thomas W. Shaughnessy, eds., *Developing Leadership Skills: A Sourcebook for Librarians*. Englewood, CO: Libraries Unlimited, pp. 57–59.

Hitt, William D. 1988. *The Leadership Manager*. Columbus, OH: Battelle.

Hofstede, Geert. 1983. "The Cultural Relativity of Organizational Practices and Theories." *Journal of International Business Studies* 14 (Fall): 75–89.

Hubbard, Gerald M. 1992. "How to Win Over the CEO on Key FM Issues." *Facilities Design and Management* 11(11) (November): 50–52.

Iannuzzi, Patricia. 1992. "Leadership Development and Organizational Maturity." *Journal of Library Administration* 17(1): 19–36.

Jaycox, Michael. 1996. "How to Get Nonbelievers to Participate in Teams." *Quality Progress* 29(3) (March): 45–49.

Kanter, Rosabeth Moss. 1983. *Change Masters*. New York: Simon & Schuster.

Kaufman, Paula T. 1993. "Leadership: Does Gender Make a Difference?" *Journal of Library Administration* 18(3–4): 109–128.

Keegan, J. 1988. *The Mask of Command*. New York: Viking.

Kiely, Thomas. 1993. "Group Wary." *CIO* 7(2) (October 15): 56–61.

Korda, Michael. 1975. *Power: How to Get It; How to Keep It*. New York: Random House.

Kotter, John. 1988. *The Leadership Factor*. Glencoe, IL: Free Press/Macmillan.

Kouzes, James and Barry Z. Posner. 1987. *The Leadership Challenge: How to Get Extraordinary Things Done in Organizations*. San Francisco: Jossey-Bass.

———. 1988. *The Leadership Challenge*. San Francisco: Jossey-Bass.

Lawson, Mollie D. et al. 1993. *Team Approach to Staffing the Reference Center: A Speculation*. Warrensburg, MO: Central Missouri State University.

Lawson, V. Lonnie and Larry Dorrell. 1992. "Library Directors: Leadership and Staff Loyalty." *Library Administration & Management* 6(4) (Fall): 187–191.

Lester, Richard I. 1990. "Leadership: Some Principles & Concepts." In Rosie L. Albritton and Thomas W. Shaughnessy, eds., *Developing Leadership Skills: A Sourcebook for Librarians.* Englewood, CO: Libraries Unlimited, pp. 17–20.

Line, Maurice B. 1992. "How to Demotivate Staff: A Brief Guide." *Library Management* 13(1): 4–7.

Long, Sarah Ann Sanders. 1995. "Growing New Leaders in Ohio [a Week-Long Leadership Institute]." *Public Libraries* 34 (January/February): 24–26.

Lubans, John, Jr. 1988. "The Manager as Counselor: How Goals Help." *Library Administration and Management* 2 (January): 28–30.

Lubans, John and Heather Gordon. 1995. "From Quick Start Teams to Home Teams: The Duke TQM Experience." In *Total Quality Management in Academic Libraries: Initial Implementation Efforts. Proceedings from the International Conference on TQM and Academic Libraries.* Washington, DC, April 20–22, 1994.

Maccoby, Michael. 1981. *The Leader: A New Face for American Management.* New York: Simon & Schuster.

Mackey, Terry and Kitty Mackey. 1992. "Think Quality! The Deming Approach Does Work in Libraries." *Library Journal* 117(9) (May 15): 57–61.

Mader, Sharon. 1996. "Instruction Librarians: Leadership in the New Organization." *RQ* 36(2) (Winter): 192–197.

Major, Jean A. 1993. "Mature Librarians and the University Faculty: Factors Contributing to Librarians' Acceptance as Colleagues." *College & Research Libraries* 54: 463–469.

Marchant, Maurice P. 1971. "Participative Management in Libraries." In Elizabeth Stone, ed., *New Directions in Staff Development: Moving from Ideas to Action.* Chicago: ALA, pp. 28–38.

Marcum, James W. 1995. "Performance Appraisal vs. Quality Management: Getting past the Paradox." In *Total Quality Management in Academic Libraries: Initial Implementation Efforts. Proceedings from the International Conference on TQM and Academic Libraries.* Washington, DC, April 20–22, 1994.

Marz, Charles C. and Henry P. Sims. 1989. *Super Leadership: Leading Others to Lead Themselves.* Englewood Cliffs, NJ: Prentice-Hall.

May, Gregory D. and Michael J. Kruger. 1990. "The Manager Within." In Rosie L. Albritton and Thomas W. Shaughnessy, eds., *Developing Leadership Skills: A Sourcebook for Librarians.* Englewood, CO: Libraries Unlimited, pp. 76–86.

McAnally, Arthur M. and Robert D. Downs. 1973. "The Changing Role of Directors of University Libraries." *College & Research Libraries* (March): 103–125.

McClure, C. R. 1980. "Library Managers: Can They Manage? Will They Lead?" *Library Journal* 105 (November 15): 2388–2391.

McCombs, Gillian M. 1992. " 'Once More Unto the Breach, Dear Friends': Shakespeare's *Henry V* as a Primer for Leaders." *Journal of Academic Librarianship* 18(4) (September): 218–220.

McConkey, Dale. 1989. "Are You an Administrator, a Manager, or a Leader?" *Business Horizons* 32(5) (September/October): 15–21.

Meyer, Michael. 1989. *The Alexander Complex: The Dreams That Drive Great Business Men.* New York: Times Books.

Miller, M. L. 1992. "Snowbird: An Experiment in Leadership." *American Library* 23 (October): 812.

Mitchell, Eugene S. 1988. "A Review of Leadership Research." Paper presented at the Library Administration and Management Association President's Program at the

Annual Convention of the American Library Association, New Orleans, LA, July 10.

Modic, Stanley J. 1987. "Is Anyone Loyal Anymore?" *Industry Week* 234(78) (September): 75–79.

Moran, Barbara B. 1992. "Gender Differences in Leadership." *Library Trends* 40 (Winter): 475–491.

Nawe, Julita. 1992. "Human Resources for Library and Information Services: Problems and Prospects." *Library Management* 13(1): 8–14.

Newman, G. Charles, Amy Dibartolo, and Margaret R. Wells. 1990. "Becoming an Effective Academic Library Manager: Preparation, Process, and Performance." *Library Administration and Management* 4(1) (Winter): 33–37.

O'Neill, Rosanna M., comp. 1994. *Total Quality Management in Libraries: A Sourcebook*. Englewood, CO: Libraries Unlimited.

Owen, Hilarie. 1996. "Building Teams on a Display of Trust." *People Management* 2(6) (March 21): 34–37.

Paton, Richard and Agnes Jelking. 1994. "No-Name Management for the '90s." *Optimum* 25(1) (Summer): 35–41.

Peischl, Thomas M. 1995. "Benchmarking: A Process for Improvement." In *Total Quality Management in Academic Libraries: Initial Implementation Efforts. Proceedings from the International Conference on TQM and Academic Libraries*. Washington, DC, April 20–22, 1994.

Peters, Thomas. 1987. *Thriving on Chaos: Handbook for a Management Revolution*. New York: Knopf.

Peters, Thomas J. and Nancy Austin. 1985. *A Passion for Excellence: The Leadership Difference*. New York: Random House.

Peters, Thomas and Robert Waterman. 1982. *In Search of Excellence*. New York: Harper & Row.

Phipps, Shelley E. 1993. "Transforming Libraries into Learning Organizations—The Challenge for Leadership." *Journal of Library Administration* 18(3–4): 19–37.

Recardo, Ronald F. 1995. "Overcoming Resistance to Change." *National Productivity Review* 14(2) (Spring): 5–12.

Redfern, Margaret. 1980. "Managing the People Part: The Changing Climate of Personnel Administration." In *Studies in Library Management*, vol. 6. Hamden, CT: Linnet Books, pp. 177–194.

Riggs, Donald. 1982. "Library Leadership: Visualizing the Future." In Edward Shaw, ed., *The Courage to Fail*. Phoenix, AZ: Oryx Press, pp. 53–65.

———. 1990. "Leadership versus Management in Technical Services." In Rosie L. Albritton and Thomas W. Shaughnessy, eds., *Developing Leadership Skills: A Source Book for Librarians*. Englewood, CO: Libraries Unlimited, pp. 226–235.

———. 1993. "Managing Quality: TQM in Libraries." *Library Administration & Management* 7(2) (Spring): 73–78.

Sayles, L. R. 1979. *Leadership: What Effective Managers Really Do . . . and How They Do It*. New York: McGraw-Hill.

Scanlan, Burt K. 1990. "Managerial Leadership in Perspective: Getting Back to Basics." In Rosie L. Albritton and Thomas W. Shaughnessy, eds., *Developing Leadership Skills: A Sourcebook for Librarians*. Englewood, CO: Libraries Unlimited, pp. 33–40.

Schriesheim, Chester A., James M. Tolliver, and Orlando C. Gehling. 1990. "Leadership

Theory: Some Implications for Managers." In Rosie L. Albritton and Thomas W. Shaughnessy, eds., *Developing Leadership Skills: A Sourcebook for Librarians*. Englewood, CO: Libraries Unlimited, pp. 9–16.

Secor, John R. 1995. "A Flavor-of-the-Month Buzzword or Step One to Designing Processes That Deliver Continuous Value to the Customer?" In *Total Quality Management in Academic Libraries: Initial Implementation Efforts. Proceedings from the International Conference on TQM and Academic Libraries*. Washington, DC, April 20–22, 1994.

Senge, Peter M. 1990. *The Fifth Discipline: The Art and Practice of the Learning Organization*. New York: Doubleday/Currency.

Serpa, Roy. 1991. "Teamwork Starts at the Top." *Chief Executive* 66 (April): 30–33.

Sheldon, Brooke E. 1991. *Leaders in Libraries: Styles and Strategies for Success*. Chicago: ALA.

———. 1992. "Library Leaders: Attributes Compared to Corporate Leaders." *Library Trends* 40(3) (Winter): 391–401.

Smircich, Linda and Gareth Morgan. 1982. "Leadership: The Management of Meaning." *The Journal of Applied Behavioral Science* 18(3): 257–273.

Srinath, Manorama. 1993. "The Organizational Climate of University Libraries." *Library Management* 14(1): 28–30.

Stodgill, R. M. 1974. *Handbook of Leadership*. New York: Free Press.

Stoffle, Carla, Robert Renaud, and Jerilyn R. Veldof. 1996. "Choosing Our Futures." *College & Research Libraries* 57: 223–224.

Sullivan, Maureen. 1991. "A New Leadership Paradigm: Empowering Library Staff and Improving Performance." In Kent Hendrichson, ed., *Creative Planning for Library Administration: Leadership for the Future*. New York: Haworth Press, pp. 73–86.

———. 1992. "The Changing Role of the Middle Manager in Research Libraries." *Library Trends* 41(2) (Fall): 269–281.

Summers, F. W. and L. S. Summers. 1991. "Library Leadership 2000 and Beyond: Snowbird Leadership Institute." *Wilson Library Bulletin* 66 (December): 38–41.

Sweeney, Richard T. 1994. "Leadership in the Post-Hierarchical Library." *Library Trends* 43(1) (Summer): 62–94.

Taylor, Merrily E. 1995. "Getting It All Together: Leadership Requirements for the Future of Information Services." *Journal of Library Administration* 20(3–4): 9–24.

Tees, Miriam H. 1984. "Is It Possible to Educate Librarians as Managers?" *Special Libraries* 75 (July): 176.

Terrey, John N. 1986. "Leadership Can Create Excellence." Paper presented at the Annual National Convention of the American Association of Community and Junior Colleges Orlando, FL, April 13–16.

Tichy, Noel and David Rich. 1984. "The Leadership Challenge: A Call for the Transformational Leader." *Sloan Management Review* (Fall): 59–73.

Totten, Herman L. and Ronald L. Keys. 1994. "The Road to Success." *Library Trends* 43(1) (Summer): 34–46.

Townley, C. T. 1989. "Nurturing Library Effectiveness: Leadership for Personnel Development." *Library Administration & Management* 3 (Winter): 16–20.

Townsend, Patrick L. and Joan E. Gebhardt. 1988. "Leadership and Quality." *Executive Excellence* 5(9) (September): 5–6.

Tucker, Robert. 1981. *Politics as Leadership*. Columbia: University of Missouri Press.

Veaner, Allen B. 1990. *Academic Librarianship in a Transformational Age: Program, Politics, and Personnel*. Boston: G. K. Hall.

Webber, N. A. 1971. "A Library Historian's Thoughts on Management." In Brian Redfern, ed., *Studies in Library Management*. London: Linnet Books & Clive Bingley, pp. 9–26.

Wedgeworth, Robert. 1989. "Nurturing Leadership: A Personal View." In A. Gertzog and J. Varlejs, eds., *Leadership in the Library/Information Profession*. Jefferson, NC: McFarland, pp. 35–41.

White, Herbert. 1987. "Oh, Where Have All the Leaders Gone?" *Library Journal* 112 (October 1): 68–69.

———. 1990. "White Papers—Managers and Leaders: Are There More Differences than Similarities?" *Library Journal* 115(11) (June 15): 51–53.

Willner, Ann Ruth. 1984. *The Spellbinders*. New Haven, CT: Yale University Press.

Woodrum, Pat, ed. 1989. "Managing Public Libraries in the 21st Century." *Journal of Library Administration* 11 (1–2): 1–51, 53–65, 67–109, 111–135, 137–171, 173–187, 189–232.

Worrell, Diane. 1995. "The Learning Organization: Management Theory for the Information Age or New Age Fad?" *Journal of Academic Librarianship* 21(5) (September): 351–357.

Wright, Diane H. 1988. "Leadership in Libraries—Feedback as Communication." Paper presented at the Library Administration and Management Association President's Program at the Annual Convention of the American Library Association, New Orleans, LA, July 10.

Yearout, Stephen L. 1996. "The Secrets of Improvement-Driven Organizations." *Quality Progress* 29(1) (January): 51–56.

Index

About the Editors and Contributors

TERRENCE F. MECH is Vice President for Information and Instructional Technologies and Director of the Library at King's College, Wilkes-Barre, Pennsylvania. He holds a doctorate in higher education (D.Ed.) from the Pennsylvania State University.

GERARD B. McCABE retired as Director of Libraries at Clarion University of Pennsylvania in January 1996. He is the editor/series adviser for the Greenwood Library Management Collection.

ELAINE P. ADAMS is Vice Chancellor for Educational Development for the Houston Community College System. She served from July 1991 through 1996 as the founding President of the system's Northeast College. Prior to these assignments, she was Assistant Commissioner for the Texas Higher Education Coordinating Board and Vice President for Student Affairs at Prairie View A&M University, where she also had been the Associate Vice President for Academic Services and Planning.

ROSIE L. ALBRITTON is Assistant Professor of Library and Information Science at Wayne State University. Her teaching and research interests include academic library management and evaluation, leadership theory and development, the impact of technology on minority populations, and the historical contributions of African Americans to librarianship. Albritton has published extensively and given numerous presentations on "transformational leadership" in university libraries and African-American "nineteenth-century social libraries."

H. E. BROADBENT III was Associate Provost for Information Services at Dowling College in New York for five years prior to his appointment in May 1997 to the newly created position of Director of Information Technology at the Free Library of Philadelphia. He was Executive Director of the Pittsburgh Regional Library Center from 1985 to 1992. Earlier career assignments included Director of the Ursinus College Library, 1975–1985, with five years as Assistant to the President for Institutional Research.

BRIAN CHAMPION has been a professional librarian for 15 years, first at the University of Alberta and most recently at Brigham Young University's Harold B. Lee Library, where he also teaches in the Political Science Department. He has also taught political science at Athabasca University and information retrieval at Grant MacEwan Community College in Edmonton, Alberta. He currently holds the position of Political Science and International Relations Librarian.

BARBARA I. DEWEY is currently Director of Information and Research Services at the University of Iowa Libraries and also held the position of Director of Administrative and Access Services at the University of Iowa. Recently, she coauthored the book *Team Power: Making Library Meetings Work* (1993) with Sheila Creth. She is the author of *Library Jobs: How to Find Them, How to Fill Them* (1987) and edited *Raising Money for Academic and Research Libraries* (1991). She has published articles and book chapters on leadership, personnel development, and planning issues.

DAVID R. DOWELL, Director of Learning Resources at Cuesta College, San Luis Obispo, California, was previously Library Director at Pasadena City College and Illinois Institute of Technology, Chicago, and was Assistant Director at Duke University. He is an active participant in ALA, ACRL, and Library Administration and Management Association (LAMA), with service on several committees of these associations.

RAVEN FONFA is Interim Coordinator for Collection Development at Leavey Library, the University of Southern California's Gateway Library, serving undergraduates.

JANET M. HURLBERT is Associate Dean of the college, with special responsibilities for faculty development, and Associate Professor and head of Instructional Services and Archives at the Snowden Library, Lycoming College, Williamsport, Pennsylvania. Previously, she was head of the Collection Management Division of the University Libraries of Virginia Commonwealth University.

EDWARD J. JENNERICH is Associate Provost and Dean of the Graduate School at Seattle University. He received his doctorate in higher education administration with a cognate in library science from the University of Pittsburgh. Jennerich also completed the Institute for Educational Management at Harvard University.

RASHELLE S. KARP is Professor of Library Science and Interim Director of Libraries at Clarion University of Pennsylvania's Rena M. Carlson Library. She teaches in the areas of collection development, indexing and abstracting, business librarianship, and library services to disabled individuals. Karp is the author of *Children and Young Adults: An Evaluative Index and Guide*, and she has written extensively in the literature about topics including academic librarianship, volunteerism, joint-use libraries, public librarianship, and school librarianship.

CHRISTIE KOONTZ is an Assistant in Research, Florida Resources and Environmental Analysis Center, Florida State University. She works primarily with geographic information systems software in applications for public library market analysis. She is the author of *Library Siting and Location Handbook* (Greenwood, 1997).

BEVERLY P. LYNCH is Professor in the Graduate School of Education & Information Studies, University of California, Los Angeles (UCLA). She was Dean of the Graduate School of Library and Information Science, UCLA, 1989–1994; University Librarian, University of Illinois at Chicago, 1977–1989; and Executive Secretary of the Association of College & Research Libraries, 1972–1976. She has published widely in the areas of academic librarianship and library organization management, her most recent book being *The Academic Library in Transition* (1995).

CINDY MURDOCK recently earned a master's degree in library science at Clarion University of Pennsylvania, and holds a B.A. in art history from Edinboro University of Pennsylvania.

GEORGE CHARLES NEWMAN is a Librarian in Information Services at Buffalo State College, New York. His prior assignments included library directorships at Buffalo State College, the University of Findlay (Ohio), and Golden West College (California). His academic interests lie in the areas of administration, leadership, organizational change, and innovation in libraries and higher education.

KENNETH J. OBEREMBT is an expatriate American who has worked in Arab world (i.e., Egyptian and Saudi Arabian) libraries for the past nine years. Currently, he manages Library Services at the King Fahd University of Petroleum and Minerals (KFUPM), Dharan, Saudi Arabia, and the KFUPM library training program. He has taught short courses and workshops in Saudi Arabia, Kuwait, and the United Arab Emirates and published on Arab world librarianship both in print and in conference papers.

DONALD E. RIGGS has been Vice President for Information Services and University Librarian at Nova Southeastern University (NSU), Fort Lauderdale, Florida, since January 1, 1997. Prior to going to NSU, he served six years as Dean of University Libraries at the University of Michigan, Ann Arbor. Riggs is the author/editor of eight books, and he has written 38 book chapters and 60 journal articles. He was founding editor of *Library Administration & Management* and is currently editor of *College & Research Libraries*.

DENNIS E. ROBISON retired in December 1997 as Dean of Integrated Learning Resources at James Madison University, Harrisonburg, Virginia. He did his undergraduate work at Florida State University and earned his master's degree in Library Science at the same university. Later, while serving at the University of South Florida, 1962–1974, he received a master's degree in Social Science Education. Prior to becoming University Librarian at his present university, 1985–1993, he served as University Librarian at the University of Richmond.

DELMUS E. WILLIAMS is the Dean of University Libraries at the University of Akron, Ohio. Prior to coming to Akron, he worked at the University of Alabama, Huntsville, Western Illinois University, and Washington and Lee University. He writes and speaks regularly on management issues relating to library management and is one of the editors of *Advances in Library Administration and Organization*.